From Existence to God

From Existence to God

A contemporary philosophical argument

Barry Miller

London and New York

First published 1992
by Routledge
11 New Fetter Lane, London EC4P 4EE

Simultaneously published in the USA and Canada
by Routledge
a division of Routledge, Chapman and Hall, Inc.
29 West 35th Street, New York, NY 10001

Typeset in 10/12pt Times by
Falcon Typographic Art Ltd, Edinburgh & London
Printed in Great Britain by
T. J. Press (Padstow) Ltd, Padstow, Cornwall

British Library Cataloguing in Publication Data
Miller, Barry
   From existence to God.
   1. God. Existence
   I. Title
   212.1

Library of Congress Cataloging in Publication Data
Miller, Barry.
   From existence to God: a contemporary philosophical argument/
   Barry Miller.
   p.   cm.
   1. God – Proof.   2. Metaphysics.   3. Logic.   I. Title.
   BT102.M55   1991
   212'.1 – dc20   91–17445

ISBN 0–415–07006–6

In tiefer Dankbarkeit gewidmet H.N.

Contents

Preface

Unlikely bed-fellows though they be, atheists and many theists do share at least one belief about God: neither party thinks that God can be proved to exist. More particularly, his existence cannot be proved by any argument having the existence of some part of the Universe as its initial premiss, i.e. the contingency argument. The reason, as we are reminded, is that the argument could succeed only if it were 'incoherent to assert that a complex physical universe exists and that God does not. There would have to be a hidden contradiction buried in such assertions.'[1] We are assured, however, that there is simply no such contradiction: 'atheism does seem to be a supposition consistent with the existence of a complex physical universe, such as our universe.'[2] Besides, as many theistic and atheistic writers never tire of repeating, arguments for the existence of God have long since been demolished by the criticisms of Hume and Kant and their latter-day disciples; and there is no reason to think that the contingency argument is any kind of philosophical Lazarus. This, then, is pretty much the received wisdom; it is also precisely what this book finds to be fundamentally flawed.

Contrary to the received wisdom, I argue that there is indeed a hidden contradiction in claiming both that, say, Fido exists and that God does not. In fact, unless God were admitted to exist, there would be an implicit contradiction in just one of those conjuncts, viz. in the apparently innocuous claim that Fido exists. For just that reason, the question 'How ever can it be that Fido does exist?' is

---

1 R. Swinburne, *The Existence of God* (Oxford: Oxford University Press, 1979), p.119.
2 ibid., p.120.

not one that we are free to ignore: it is logically inescapable. If I am right, therefore, the contingency argument receives its impetus, not from the principles of sufficient reason or intelligibility as the baneful influence of Leibniz and Clarke has led many to accept, but from the need to square the truth of Fido's existing with the companion truth that his existing could not be – logically could not be – a *brute* fact. Nor does one have to commit the fallacy of composition to show that what is true of Fido's existing is true also of the Universe's existing.

The argument that is driven initially by the inability of either Fido's existing or the Universe's existing to be a brute fact has ultimately to conclude to the existence of the God of classical philosophical theism. And, as I show in some detail, it is an argument against which strictures of the kind inspired by Hume and Kant prove to be ineffectual. Both the exposing of the apparent contradiction and the bringing of the argument to its conclusion draw upon a considerable body of metaphysics and philosophical logic, most of which is developed in chapters 2–4 and deployed in the argument that occupies chapters 5–7.

Since the book has gone through many drafts over the years, my debts are too numerous to list fully. I must, however, single out those who at some time have read the work either in whole or in part. To Christopher Williams and Peter Forrest I am particularly grateful, since each has read the manuscript *in toto*, the former doing so for an early version and the latter for the penultimate version. To these I gladly add Justin Gosling, Toomas Karmo, Alvin Plantinga, James Ross, and Richard Swinburne all of whom were generous with their comments on much earlier versions of individual chapters.

B.M.
Candlemas, 1991

Chapter 1

The central question

Although this book is avowedly about the existence of God, the central question to be addressed is not 'Does God exist? but 'How ever can it be that the Universe does exist?' This apparently eccentric procedure is designed to avert being embroiled immediately in an interminable discussion of what is meant by 'God' – is it God as conceived of by Christians, by Jews, by Muslims, by Hindus, or by some other group? It frees us, too, from the mammoth task of considering the whole gamut of arguments for the existence of God – the ontological argument, the cosmological argument, the teleological argument, the moral argument, and the argument from religious experience, all moreover in multiple versions. A merit of the present question is to exclude from consideration all theistic arguments except the one linked to the existence of the Universe, namely, the contingency argument.

A further advantage: had the notion of God been introduced at the very beginning, there would immediately have arisen a number of familiar objections against even the possibility of demonstrating his existence by any argument whatever; and we should have had to mark time while each of them was duly considered. Now, however, that the notion of God appears only late in the book, discussion of the objections can be correspondingly late, and the logical and metaphysical prologomena to the argument can begin without delay. It means, too, that when the objections do come finally to be discussed, it will not be in a vacuum, nor in relation to some merely general form of the contingency argument, but in relation to a quite particular version that will already have been presented in some detail.

Lest there be any misunderstanding, the foregoing question about the Universe should first be distinguished from a cognate one with which it is sometimes confused, namely, 'Why should anything exist at all?' The latter has been dismissed as being no question at all or as simply absurd, for 'it is not that something could provide an answer . . . but maybe nothing does, but that nothing *could*'.[1] Some eminent figures in the history of philosophy would doubtless have been surprised at so radical a suggestion, for they have taken this cognate question quite seriously, Leibniz so much so as to give it pride of place in his metaphysics. Indeed, after laying down his principle of sufficient reason, he notes immediately that 'the first question we are entitled to put will be – Why does something exist rather than nothing?'[2] While he may have been the first to use precisely that formulation, he was neither the first nor the last to have raised that same kind of question.

In the twentieth century, the question has enjoyed renewed interest, partly because of its (mistaken) association with the name of Heidegger. True enough, the conclusion of his *Was ist Metaphysik?* does present the fundamental question of metaphysics as 'Why are there beings at all and not much rather Non-being?' ('Warum ist überhaupt Seiendes und nicht vielmehr Nichts?'). And, since the question recurs both in his *Einführung in die Metaphysik* and *Vom Wesen des Grundes*, one might be forgiven for thinking to detect in it a contemporary echo of Leibniz. Natural though it might be to regard 'Non-being' as synonymous with 'nothing', Heidegger himself constantly distinguishes 'Nichts' ('Non-being') from 'nichts' ('nothing'): the former is treated not as *nihil absolutum* but as something. Hence one commentator's conclusion that 'it seems self-evident that the question for Heidegger must have a completely different sense than for Leibniz'.[3]

Contemporary interest in the Leibnizian question has not, however, stemmed solely from a misunderstanding of Heidegger. For a time Wittgenstein was fascinated by it; and, as Malcolm recounts, he sometimes had a certain experience which could best be described by saying that 'When I have it I wonder at the existence of the world. And then I am inclined to use such

---

1 T. Penelhum, 'Divine Necessity', *Mind* 69 (1960), p.182.
2 G.Leibniz, *Principles of Nature and Grace*, in R. Latta (trans.), *Leibniz: The Monadology and other Philosophical Writings* (Oxford: Oxford University Press, 1898; reprinted 1945), pp.414–15.
3 W.J. Richardson, *Heidegger: Through Phenomenology to Thought* (The Hague: Nijhoff, 1963), p.203.

phrases as "How extraordinary that anything should exist!"[4] At one time Smart too confessed to a like experience, noting that his mind seemed often 'to reel under the immense significance' of the question 'Why should anything exist at all?' – despite the fact that logic had taught him 'to look at such a question with the gravest suspicion.'[5] Neither did logic inhibit Matson who, even after decisively rejecting Leibniz's argument, felt, nevertheless, constrained to conclude by asking, 'Yet . . . why is there anything at all?'[6] Tymieniecka has claimed that 'every thorough metaphysical endeavour ultimately deals explicitly or implicitly with the question: "Why is there something rather than nothing?"'[7] Munitz has written in similar vein, 'for those who are provoked by the mystery of existence . . . . the root question is *why there should be a world at all*'.[8] Whatever the fascination aroused by such questions, however, I mention them not for their own sake, but merely to preclude their being mistaken for the question under discussion in this book.

Although the question at issue may now be clear enough, there is no assurance that it deserves to be answered. Certainly the mere framing of a question is no guarantee that it requires an answer. For example, we may be nonplussed at being asked 'Why is there grass growing in your back yard?', it never having occurred to us that there was anything unusual about so mundane a state of affairs. So, our reply may be 'Why on earth do you ask?' Responses like 'Because it just popped into my head' or 'I simply felt the urge to ask it', would simply confirm our suspicions that the query really called for no answer at all. If, on the contrary, it was reported that all yards in the area had recently been sprayed with a herbicide, we should have grounds aplenty for thinking that some explanation really was required, even if we ourselves were unable to provide it.

Applying these remarks to the question 'How ever can it be

4 N. Malcolm, *Ludwig Wittgenstein: A Memoir* (Oxford: Oxford University Press, 1958), p.70.
5 J.J.C. Smart, 'The Existence of God', in A. Flew and A. Macintyre (eds), *New Essays in Philosophical Theology* (London: SCM Press, 1955), p.46.
6 W.I. Matson, *The Existence of God* (Ithaca: Cornell University Press, 1965), p.86. Dots and italics are in the original.
7 A-T. Tymieniecka, *Why is There Something Rather than Nothing?* (Assen: Van Gorcum, 1966), p.1.
8 M. Munitz, *The Mystery of Existence* (New York: New York University Press, 1974), p.4.

that the Universe does exist?', the point is that the mere posing of it does not of itself establish the need for any explanation at all. In the absence of any demonstration that the existence of the Universe positively has to be explained, there could be no objection to the answer being merely, 'No explanation is needed. It just does exist, and that is all there is to it. That is simply a brute fact – a fact to be accepted without explanation.' Or, as Russell said in his debate with Copleston, 'I should say that the Universe is just there, and that's all. . . . I do think the notion of the world having an explanation is a mistake. I don't see why one should expect it to have one.'[9]

Grounds for posing the question have been various. Some have been constrained to do so not on any reasoned basis, nor even solely by the promptings of feelings of amazement, awe, and the like. I refer to such as H.D. Lewis, Trethowan, Pontifex, Jolivet, and Mascall (at least in his *Words and Images*), for all of whom the question is both posed and answered in what Lewis calls the 'one insight' had by 'looking "at what being stands for until it breaks into finite and infinite." It is this one leap of thought in which finite and infinite are equally present, and which cannot be broken up into steps which we negotiate one by one, that brings us to the ultimate mystery.'[10]

More recently, John Shepherd too has had recourse to an experience to show that the question of why the Universe should exist cannot be shrugged off with 'Why not?' Unlike Lewis, however, the experience is taken not as the source of some apprehension of God's existence, but merely as the starting point for an admittedly inconclusive argument for that existence. The experience in question is said to be 'an awareness of the ontological frailty of the cosmos's existence'.[11] Yet herein lies the weakness of the positions of Lewis and Shepherd alike, for it is precisely Lewis's insight or Shepherd's awareness of ontological frailty that the agnostic would question. He seeks the bread of reasoned argument, but they determinedly offer what he might regard as the stone of intuition.

In lamenting that the insight of which he speaks is sadly

9   B. Russell and F. Copleston, 'A Debate on the Existence of God', reprinted in J. Hick (ed.), *The Existence of God* (London: Macmillan, 1965), pp. 175, 177.
10 H.D. Lewis, *Our Experience of God* (London: Allen & Unwin, 1959), p.43.
11 J. Shepherd, *Experience, Inference and God* (London: Macmillan, 1975), p.62.

misrepresented when broken into a series of logical steps, Lewis is no doubt thinking of arguments like Aquinas' Third Way, and of earlier versions found in Maimonides and Avicenna.[12] He may also have been thinking of contemporaries like Etienne Gilson, Jacques Maritain, Richard Taylor, Bruce Reichenbach, and Joseph Owens, all of whom attempt to provide the question with a reasoned, rather than a merely intuitive, basis. The prime reason offered by Taylor[13] and Reichenbach[14] is precisely that of Leibniz – the principle of sufficient reason – a procedure to be noted with interest though not, as we shall see, to be imitated.

Yet there remain a great number of both theists and non-theists alike, who regard recourse to argument as perhaps more laudable, but certainly no more successful than appeal to insight. Hepburn, Hick, Flew, Crombie, Penelhum, Scriven, Mackie, and others offer various grounds for dismissing questions like 'How ever can it be that the Universe does exist?' as either gratuitous or improper, and hence requiring simply no answer. What, then, does it mean to say that it is gratuitous, or that it is improper?

Gratuitousness of the question

To treat the question as gratuitous is to say that, even if it does make some kind of sense, there are no rational grounds for posing it. Until such grounds are provided, no better answer is demanded than simply 'Why not?' In one attempt to provide a rational ground, attention is drawn to the obvious impermanence of many of the things around us: living things die, and sooner or later even inanimate things seem to degenerate. Since apparently everything can cease to exist, one might expect that eventually everything would do so. Why, then, should anything at all in the Universe have survived until now? A possible answer is that sufficient time has still not elapsed for their demise. Yet that could be known to be correct only if its underlying assumption were correct. But that assumption – that eventually there would be nothing – rests on a misconception of how the things around us 'cease to be'. They

---

12 In his *Christian Philosophy of St. Thomas Aquinas* (London: Gollancz, 1957), p.69, Etienne Gilson traces Aquinas' argument from Maimonides' *Guide for the Perplexed*, and that in turn from Avicenna's *Metaphysics*.
13 R. Taylor, *Metaphysics* (Englewood-Cliffs: Prentice Hall, 1963).
14 B. Reichenbach, *The Cosmological Argument* (Springfield: C. Thomas, 1972).

do so not by being annihilated, but by becoming something else. When Julius Caesar 'ceased to be', he left no ontological hole in the Universe: he simply became something else – a corpse. The transience of everything in the world might justify our asking why some things should exist rather than others, but not why the Universe should exist rather than nothing.

If the ceasing of things to exist is not the ground we seek, neither is it their beginning to exist. Even if the proposition 'whatever begins to exist must have some cause' were to be an entirely unobjectionable principle, it would entitle us to ask for an explanation only of those things which we know to have had a beginning. But since we cannot assume that the Universe as a whole had a beginning, we should have no reason to ask why *it* should exist. Critics of arguments for the existence of God are apt to remark that no explanation need be sought beyond the Universe, and if this were the only ground for seeking one, they could not be denied.

More generally, though, the counter to 'Why not?' has been to assert that the existence of the Universe cannot be merely a brute fact: it must be intelligible. In effect, this is simply an appeal to the principle of sufficient reason, the status of which is itself controversial. For almost a century, until Gilson[15] showed that the principle was notably absent from Aquinas, and Owens[16] showed his fellow Thomists that Humean-type criticism of its alleged self-evidence was correct, Thomists were wont to defend it by claiming its denial would entail denying the principle of non-contradiction. Subsequently, more have been convinced by Owens's argument that it is not a principle but a conclusion.

A more recent defence, however, has been to accept the principle as neither demonstrable nor necessary, but to insist on the oddity of saying 'that it is contingent. If one were to try proving it, he would sooner or later have to appeal to considerations that are less plausible than the principle itself. Indeed, it is hard to see how one could even make an argument without already assuming it.'[17] Richard Taylor has suggested that it might properly be called 'a presupposition of reason itself'.

15 E. Gilson, 'Les Principes et les Causes', *Revue Thomiste* 47 (1952), pp.38–63.
16 J. Owens, 'The Causal Proposition – Principle or Conclusion?', *The Modern Schoolman* 32 (1954–5): part I, pp.159–71; part II, pp.257–70; part III, pp.323–39.
17 R. Taylor, *Metaphysics*, p.105. A similar view takes the principle of sufficient reason to be 'a fundamental *synthetic a priori* of the mind itself, defining the very radical nature of human intelligence as dynamic drive towards

The difficulty with this position has been acknowledged even by those sympathetic to Taylor's view. Hick,[18] who is himself ready to recognize the principle as 'a fundamental principle of rationality', nevertheless denies that it can be applied to 'that ultimate state of affairs which is not related to anything yet more ultimate, by which it might itself be rendered intelligible'. The reason is simply that 'either the sum of all explanations or the final theory cannot itself require explanation'.[19] This, according to Flew, 'is not a contingent fact about one sort of system, but a logical truth about all explanations of fact',[20] the reason being that to explain something puzzling is simply to relate it to some wider context. Now, if the wider context is itself puzzling, it may be explained by being set in a wider context still, a process which can be continued until we arrive at a context than which none is wider. At that point it makes just no sense to speak of explaining the ultimate context, since *ex hypothesi* there would be no further context within which the explanation might be set. Hence, it might seem clearly to be part of the very notion of explanation that a point may be reached beyond which no explanation is possible, even in principle.

The foregoing conclusion is then applied to the claim that the Universe exists contingently. The existence of everything in the Universe is said to be explicable in principle in terms of the Universe as a whole. But, once that point is reached, why should it not be acknowledged to be the widest possible context, and hence that no explanation of that context can sensibly even be sought? If the Universe exists contingently, this just has to be accepted as a brute fact. No explanation of it can even be asked for, let alone given.

If correct, such criticism would be far more damaging than may at first appear. It would mean not merely that the principle of sufficient reason was not exceptionless, but that every application of it would be either invalid or superfluous. It would be invalid if applied to an ultimate state of affairs, and superfluous if applied to any known to be not ultimate; for if one already

intelligibility'. (W. Norris Clarke, 'How the Philosopher can give Meaning to Language about God', in E. Madden, R. Handy, and M. Farber (eds), *The Idea of God* (Springfield: C. Thomas, 1968), pp.7–8).
18 J. Hick, *Arguments for the Existence of God* (London: Macmillan, 1970), pp.47–8.
19 M. Scriven, *Primary Philosophy* (New York: McGraw-Hill, 1966), p.124.
20 A. Flew, *God and Philosophy* (London: Hutchinson, 1966), p.83.

knew *that*, there would be no point in invoking the principle. And, conversely, if one knew of no reason for asking something like 'How ever can it be that the Universe does exist?', the principle could not supply it. The question would thus remain an entirely gratuitous one.

Impropriety of the question

Some would regard the last comment as a notable understatement, since they take the question to be not a proper one at all, but merely a grammatically misleading expression. The reasons proposed for holding the question to be improper are many; most, however, would seem to fall under one or other of three headings – the nature of causal explanation, the fallacy of composition, or the fact that the question is said to elicit a nonsensical answer.

About causal explanation two points are commonly made. One is basically that proposed by Hume in the ninth chapter of his *Dialogues Concerning Natural Religion*, where he remarks, 'Did I but show you the particular causes of each individual in a collection of twenty particles, I should think it very unreasonable should you afterwards ask me what was the cause of the whole twenty'. The claim is that, since causes can, in principle, be assigned to each part of the Universe, the question of a cause for the whole Universe just does not arise.

The second point is not that the question does not arise, but that it cannot even sensibly be framed, since though 'cause' has a perfectly good meaning in situations within the Universe, it has none whatever in relation to the Universe as a whole. 'What is the cause of the Universe?' is said to make no more sense than does 'Where is the Universe?' Kant would certainly agree with this. Yet, the view is not peculiarly his: it is widely held for reasons quite independent of any distinctively Kantian ones. Hepburn voices one of them in noting that 'we are not in this case recording some observed concomitance of events, or stating a causal law according to which certain sets of events vary reciprocally. We are instead uprooting the vocabulary of cause and effect from its habitat in the language, in order to relate the known to the unknown and unknowable.'[22]

22 R. Hepburn, *Christianity and Paradox* (New York: Pegasus, 1966), p.160.

What has been said about causal explanation could also be viewed as a particular instance of the fallacy of composition, a fallacy said to be committed by anyone who asks how can it be that the Universe as a whole should exist. It is a commonplace that what can be said of items in the Universe cannot always be said of their totality – the Universe itself. Although each part of the Universe may be in a particular place, or moving with a certain velocity, it does not follow that the Universe as a whole is doing the same; it would not even make sense to say that it was. Hepburn suggests that 'the word "universe" is not a thing-word, and therefore it must not be expected to conform to the logical behaviour of thing-words'.[23] The moral is that we have no right to assume that, because 'How can it be that the Himalayas do exist?' may be a proper question, 'How can it be that the Universe does exist?' is likewise proper. As Scriven reminds us, 'some questions just do not make sense in the limit, and so it is with the present question, Why does the Universe exist? If it is pushed to the limit and answers about the function and relation of the parts of the Universe are rejected, it simply becomes an improper question.'[24]

Even if the question were neither an affront to the canons of causal explanation nor dependent on the fallacy of composition, its propriety might still be seriously suspect – precisely because of the kind of answer it is said to elicit. Smart[25] and Penelhum[26] think that any answer must be in terms of a necessary being, the very notion of which they regard as downright absurd. Penelhum concludes that the question reflects the absurdity of the answer it was designed to elicit; while Smart, less consistently, was moved merely to wonder what kind of question it could be to elicit such an answer. And Flew, although regarding that answer as but one of two possible ones, comes down on the side of Penelhum:

> this limiting question will have to be explained, either as made to measure for an answer in terms of a logically Necessary Being, or as a request to be informed of some further logically contingent fact but of the sort felt by the questioner to be somehow less brute than any law – no matter how wide its range merely 'within' the universe. . . . the first is, as we have seen, logically

23 R. Hepburn, *Christianity and Paradox*, p.169.
24 M. Scriven, *Primary Philosophy*, p.125.
25 J.J.C. Smart, 'The Existence of God', p.38.
26 T. Penelhum, 'Divine Necessity', p.182.

vicious; while the second seems to be nothing more than a bit of wishfulness chastely parading in a muddle about explanation.[27]

The plan of approach

It is one thing to frame the question 'How ever can it be that the Universe does exist?', but, as we have seen, quite another thing to show that it cannot be dismissed as either improper or gratuitous. The charge of impropriety seems to be based on the supposition that what is being asked about the Universe as a whole is something that can properly be asked only about its parts. Although I shall argue later that the charge is baseless, I shall for the moment defer to it, by changing our immediate question from one about the Universe to one about some individual in it, e.g. a dog of our acquaintance named 'Fido'. The question with which I shall begin, therefore, is simply 'How ever can it be that Fido does exist?' With such a move we gain at least temporary respite from the charge of impropriety.

The charge of gratuity, however, is not so easily evaded – not even temporarily. Hence, the more pressing task must be to examine whether there is any way of breaching what I shall call the 'brute fact defence'. Is there any way of showing it to be an offence against logic to regard Fido's existing as able to be simply a brute fact, a fact that requires simply no explanation? The strategy for answering that question will be quite simply to show that *the conditions necessary for Fido's existing are apparently impossible to satisfy*.

The conditions necessary for Fido's existing are shown, in chapters 2 and 4, to be as follows:

1.1 One legitimate way of conceiving of Fido's existing is as exemplifying two ontological categories, viz. a complete entity (Fido) and an incomplete entity (Fido's existence). (For the purposes of my argument, this does not have to be the *sole* legitimate way of conceiving of Fido's existing.)

1.2 Fido and his existence are ontologically, though not chrono-logically, prior to Fido's existing, which is to say that Fido's existing must be constructible conceptually from Fido and his existence.

However, it would be impossible to take even the first step in that conceptual construction if Fido were inconceivable except in terms of Fido's existing. Yet precisely that seems to be implied by the conclusion of chapter 3:

1.3 Fido could neither be referred to nor conceived of before he existed.

The conflict between (1.1) and (1.2) on the one hand and (1.3) on the other will leave us logically no option but to ask, 'How ever can it be that Fido does exist?', which means that the question will be neither gratuitous nor improper. Rather, it will have been forced upon us, though not, as many have maintained, to satisfy such principles as those of sufficient reason, or intelligibility, or causality, nor at the behest of some special insight, nor prompted by some special experience. On the contrary, it will have been forced on us to satisfy a principle whose credentials are impeccable – the principle of non-contradiction.

As the question is a logically inescapable one, an answer to it will just have to be sought; and the only logically acceptable answer will prove to be that Fido exists because he is caused to do so by something external to him. Obviously, that will be merely a partial answer; for if what causes him to exist is some other individual, then precisely the same kind of question must be posed and the same kind of answer given; and so on.

Much dust has been raised by the controversy over whether the phrase 'and so on' could be replaced by '*ad infinitum*'. Would there be any logical objection to saying that Fido's existence is caused by a series of causes that was infinite, rather than by one that was not infinite, but terminated by a cause that was itself uncaused? The issue, of course, is not whether there could ever be an infinite series nor even an infinite causal series, for there most certainly could. Rather, it is whether an infinite causal series would resolve the particular problem that arose from considering conditions (1.1) – (1.3). It can be answered only by determining just what, if any, are the conditions to be met by a causal series that would have necessarily to be terminated under pain of not being a causal series at all were it left unterminated. If my subsequent analysis of that problem is correct, there are certain well-defined conditions to be met by any such series, although they prove not to be those attributed to the *per se* subordinated causation espoused by Thomists. They do, however, turn out to be met by the kind of causation required to cause Fido to exist; and hence I conclude that Fido cannot exist unless, ultimately, he is caused to do so by something the existence of which is not caused – an uncaused cause.

Thus far there has been no mention of that entity – the Universe – about which some have said our existential question could properly not even be framed. Having skirted those objections by restricting the discussion to the quite uncontroversial figure of Fido, it will be possible to avoid them no longer; for it will be entirely proper to enquire why the uncaused cause of Fido should not be the Universe. The answer will be found in the earlier discussion of necessarily terminating causal series. There it will have been shown that whatever terminates the series, and hence is uncaused, must be such that there is no real distinction between it and its existence, a point which at this stage I merely note without explaining, since no brief account of it is possible. The result, however, will be to show that, far from being the uncaused cause, the Universe is itself caused by it. Thus, after having detoured by way of the question 'How ever can it be that Fido does exist?', we shall finally be able to answer our original question of how ever can it be that the Universe does exist.

The conclusion I draw is that the Universe exists only because it is caused to do so by something which is itself uncaused. I shall then argue that this uncaused cause is not only unique, but differs quite radically from any of its effects. While its effects are individuals (and whatever a universe of individuals requires), the uncaused cause itself will prove not to be an individual, except in an analogical sense of that term, and still less is it a property or relation. The individuals that are its effects have existence as a real property; the uncaused cause, though it does exist, is not distinct from its existence but is what is called Subsistent Existence, the notion of which will be defended at some length. Moreover, even if the effects of the uncaused cause should never in fact cease to exist, it would in principle be always possible that they should; whereas the uncaused cause itself could never cease to exist, nor have begun to exist, and for that reason it is said to exist necessarily. Responding to repeated charges that the notion of necessary existence is an incoherent one, chapter 8 will be devoted to explaining and defending its use.

Since the being so described bears the key marks of the God of classical theism, it will emerge therefore that the answer to 'How ever is it that the Universe exists?' is not merely that it is caused to do so by an uncaused cause, but that it is caused to do so by God. Hence, what began as an enquiry into the existence of the Universe will conclude by being a new form of the contingency argument for the existence of God. In chapter 9, therefore, it is fitting that the argument be tested against the many long-standing objections that have been raised against the possibility of ever proving that God exists.

Chapter 2

Sense structure and ontology

Non-theists, and indeed many theists also, would agree that, taken by itself, the truth of 'Fido exists' commits us to the existence of Fido and no other entity but him. Naturally, our commitment could easily be extended, simply by considering 'Fido exists' not in isolation, but in conjunction with other truths. Non-theists, for instance, would readily admit that the conjunction of 'Fido exists' with certain laws of nature would commit us to the existence of a great deal more than Fido, e.g. the existence of his dam and sire, of air and water, etc. While not demurring about that, certain theists would want to include more than the laws of nature, and to conjoin 'Fido exists' with such other propositions as the principles of sufficient reason, of intelligibility, or of causation. From that conjunction they would then proceed to infer the existence of a cause of the Universe.

The difference between the two parties is a familiar one, upon which I have no wish to arbitrate here, and which I mention merely to exclude it completely from the immediate discussion. What I do wish to challenge, however, is not their differences but the one point on which they both happen to agree, namely, that the truth of 'Fido exists' commits us by itself to the existence of no entity other than Fido. Indeed, the underlying theme of this book is that such a view can be sustained only by ignoring the ontological implications of 'Fido exists', viz., which ontological categories are exemplified in Fido's existing, how their exemplifications are related to the whole, and how they are related to each other. In this chapter, however, I shall be drawing out the ontological implications not of 'Fido exists' but of the atomic proposition 'Fido is black'. I do so because I have yet to establish that 'Fido exists' is an atomic proposition,[1] whereas 'Fido is black' may safely be taken to be atomic. Later, when chapter 4 has established that 'Fido exists' is not a quantified proposition (e.g. '$(\exists x)(x=\text{Fido})$') but is no less atomic than 'Fido is black', the conclusions drawn in regard to 'Fido is black' will readily be applicable to 'Fido exists'.

I begin by adopting the Fregean position that the ontological categories exemplified in Fido's being black are to be assigned in accordance with the linguistic categories of the expressions in the proposition made true by it: 'Fido is black'. On this view Fido is an individual because a name stands for it, and existence is a property because a predicate stands for it.[2] There may, however, be initial resistance to this view and a preference for its converse, namely, the suggestion that the linguistic expressions in 'Fido is black' are to be assigned their categories in accordance with the ontological categories exemplified in Fido's existing. On this view 'Fido' would be a proper name because it stands for an individual, and '___ is black' would be a predicate because it stands for a property.

Well, let us indulge the latter view for a moment to see where it would lead us. If it were correct, we should be supposing that someone could be quite clear about the ontological categories exemplified in Fido's being black (e.g. object and property), but quite unclear as to which of them 'Fido' stood for and which '___ is black' stood for. Anyone who was unclear about that, however, would be quite unclear about how 'Fido' and '___ is black' functioned in our language. And whoever was unclear about such a fundamental feature of our language would have to be equally unclear about what kinds of things those two expressions stood for. But if one were unclear about what kinds of things 'Fido' and '___ is black' stood for, it would be impossible to say, even in principle, which was which among the ontological categories exemplified in Fido's being black. Since that flies in the face of our initial supposition, it is a supposition that must be abandoned. Consequently, it is essential that the logical category to which an expression belongs be determined not by what the expression

1 For the notion of an atomic proposition see the short glossary of terms on pp.17–19.
2 Using linguistic categories *alone*, however, it is impossible to determine whether Fido is concrete or abstract, and whether existence is a real property or not. For such purposes linguistic criteria must be supplemented by non-linguistic ones.

stands for, but solely by the way in which it is employed in the language.[3] Only by determining the way it is employed in language is it possible to determine the correlative ontological category of what the expression stands for.

In view of what I have just said, the answers to these questions will be determined by answers to the correlative semantic questions concerning 'Fido is black'. What, then, are the linguistic categories exemplified in 'Fido is black'? Well, that depends on how the proposition is analysed for, as illustrated in the following schemata, more than one logically independent way has been proposed for doing so, e.g.

2.1 $F(a)$
2.2 $F(a, b)$
2.3 $F(a, \beta)$

According to (2.1), 'Fido is black' is conceived of as having two logical parts – 'Fido' and '____ is black' – related to each other as argument to linguistic function.[4] According to (2.2), the logical parts would be three – arguments 'Fido' and 'black', and linguistic function '..... is ____'. 'Fido' and 'black' would be expressions of the same type. Analysis (2.3) is like (2.2) in having three logical parts – arguments 'Fido' and 'black' and linguistic function '..... is ____'. Unlike (2.2), however, the two arguments would be of different logical types, as indicated by a Roman letter in the one case and a Greek letter in the other. Whether there be one argument or two, and, if two, whether they be of the same or different logical types is of no consequence so far as the correctness of the analyses is concerned: so far as concerns the purposes of this book I have no difficulty in allowing that all three analyses may be equally correct. My own preference, however, is for (2.1) which is Fregean, and which I shall now be employing.

Taking as our starting point that 'Fido is black' can be analysed into 'Fido' and the predicate in 'Fido is black', I shall now attempt to spell out how those two parts are related both to each other and to the proposition to which they belong. Finally, I shall be concerned also with the ontological implications of these findings.

---

3 Cf. M. Dummett, *Frege: Philosophy of Language* (London: Duckworth, 2nd edn 1981), pp.55–8.
4 The notion of a linguistic function will be explained in section II of this chapter.

Hence the following chapter division.

Section I will consider how an atomic proposition as a whole is related to its logical parts, e.g. how the sense of 'Fido is black' is related to that of 'Fido' and the predicate. The question to be settled is whether the parts are logically prior to the whole, or vice versa.

Section II will consider how one logical part of an atomic proposition is related to the other, e.g. how the senses of 'Fido' and of the predicate in 'Fido is black' are inter-related. The question is whether the sense of the predicate is a sense in its own right, or whether it is merely a feature of the sense of 'Fido is black'.

Section III considers the ontological implications of true atomic propositions, e.g. 'Fido is black'.

Before embarking on these tasks, however, it will help reduce the possibility of misunderstanding if I explain immediately some of the terminology to be used in this and succeeding chapters.

Propositions   Following Geach, I shall be using 'proposition' to mean 'a sentence serving to express a complete thought, to say what is or is not so'.[5] Two points are to be noted about a proposition, thus understood:

2.4 Propositions may differ in either of two ways. They may differ in regard to what they express, namely, a Fregean thought (sense). They may differ also in regard to how they express it, namely, the language they use to express the sense or thought. 'Fido is black' and 'Tom is lonely' differ in regard to what is expressed; 'Fido is black' and 'Fido ist schwarz' express the same sense, but differ in the language they use to do so.

2.5 Not every occurrence of a proposition need be an assertion. For example, neither 'Fido is black' nor 'He will not show up in the dark' is being asserted in 'If Fido is black, he will not show up in the dark'.

Atomic propositions   Atomic propositions are propositions composed of merely a singular term and a simple predicate.

Propositional parts   I distinguish at least three kinds of propositional

5 P.T. Geach, 'Names and Identity' in S. Guttenplan (ed.), *Mind and Language* (Oxford: Oxford University Press, 1975), p.139.

parts, viz. verbal, grammatical, and logical. Verbal parts are simply the discrete words that occur in a proposition, e.g. 'Fido', 'is', and 'black'. Grammatical parts are such words, groups of words, or inflections as perform distinct grammatical roles, e.g. 'the dog' as subject, 'bit' as verb, and 'the cat' as object in 'The dog bit the cat'. I shall speak no more of verbal and grammatical parts, but hereinafter shall be concerned solely with logical parts, the number of which is determined by the number of logical roles to be distinguished in a proposition. For example, in 'If anyone hits Fido, he is foolhardy', there are certain words or groups of words that need to be recognized if a truth-value is to be ascribed to the proposition. Such would be the proper name 'Fido', the phrases 'hits Fido' and 'is foolhardy', the propositional operator 'if _____ then .....', and the combination 'anyone _____ he .....' which can be represented formally as a second-level predicate. For reasons which will appear later, I do not say that all such *expressions* are the logical parts of 'If anyone hits Fido, he is foolhardy'. I do say it of 'Fido'; but, for the rest I say simply that they are merely verbal parts which indicate, signal, or flag the presence of logical parts. The meaning of this claim, and the reasons for it, are given later in this chapter.

Predicates   In general, a predicate is whatever can be said of something. Predicates may be of various levels, depending on whether the 'something' of which they may be said are objects, first-level properties, second-level properties, etc.[6] If said of an object, a predicate is of first-level; if said of a first-level property, the predicate is of second-level; if said of a second-level property, the predicate is of third-level; and so on.

Because a predicate is not merely a sense, but a sense-bearing expression, a difference between predicates may stem either from what they express (their sense) or from how they express it (the language used). Hence, 'Fido is black' and 'Fido ist schwarz' contain different predicates, because, although each expresses the same sense, they employ different language to do so.

Predicate sense   As indicated above, predicate sense is what a predicate says, as distinct from the language in which it is said. Thus, the sense of a first-level predicate is whatever a proposition

---

6 Properties are what a predicate stands for, or what are attributable to something by a predicate. The level of a property is the same as the level of its correlative predicate.

says about the individual named in it, e.g. what 'Fido is black' says about Fido. Of course, the predicate in 'Fido ist schwarz' expresses precisely the same sense.

Predicate expression   The language in which a predicate says what it says. It is the expression (inscription or sound) used to express predicate sense. About it I mention three points.

2.6 Different expressions may express the same sense, e.g. the predicate expression in 'Fido ist schwarz' expresses the same sense as the predicate expression in 'Fido is black'.

2.7 The one expression may be used to express different senses, as in 'Something is a board (plank)' and 'Something is a board (committee)'.

2.8 As I shall be arguing later in the chapter, even instances of the one predicate expression are non-interchangeable and unquotable. A case in point would be instances of the one predicate expression exemplified in each of 'Rover is black' and 'Fido is black'.

I THE WHOLE/PART RELATION IN ATOMIC PROPOSITIONS

As mentioned earlier, this section is to consider the relation between an atomic proposition and its logical parts. More specifically, the question is whether a grasp of the sense of the proposition presupposes a grasp of the sense of its parts, or vice versa. Is the sense of 'Fido is black' grasped through grasping the senses of 'Fido' and of the predicate, or conversely? Drawing upon arguments from Dummett, I shall be supporting the former alternative, namely, that 'Fido is black' is grasped in virtue of a (logically) prior grasp of the senses of 'Fido' and of the predicate in that proposition.

Central to our concern is Dummett's distinction between two quite different ways of analysing propositions, for one of which he reserves the term 'analysis', and the other, the term 'decomposition'.[7] The parts into which analysis divides a proposition differ in one significant respect from those resulting from decomposition. Analysis distinguishes those parts in a proposition that need to be

---

7 M. Dummett, *The Interpretation of Frege's Philosophy* (London: Duckworth, 1981), pp.271–7.

recognized in order to determine its truth-conditions and sense. On the other hand, the parts resulting from decomposition are *not* necessary for determining the proposition's truth-conditions and sense; rather, a grasp of those parts presupposes a grasp of the proposition.

To illustrate the difference between the logical parts resulting from analysis on the one hand and decomposition on the other, consider the proposition 'If anyone hits Fido, he is foolhardy'. Since the aim of *analysis* is to distinguish only such parts as need to be grasped in order to determine the proposition's truth-conditions, the first step is to recognize that those conditions can be determined only by grasping the senses of the second-level predicate 'For anyone, he ____ he .....' and of the first-level predicable 'if ____ hits Fido, ____ is foolhardy'. That leads immediately to the second step, namely, to recognize that the sense and extension of the first-level predicable is in turn determined by the sense and extension of *its* parts: the predicables '____ hits Fido' and '____ is foolhardy'. As is evident, therefore, that analysis is the converse of what Dummett has called the 'constructional history' of a proposition, and which in the present example would go thus:

2.9 From the arbitrary propositions 'Tom hits Fido' and 'Bill is foolhardy' remove the names 'Tom' and 'Bill' to form the predicables '____ hits Fido' and '____ is foolhardy'.

2.10 Insert the same name (e.g. 'Peter') in each of the gaps to form the two propositions 'Peter hits Fido' and 'Peter is foolhardy'.

2.11 Operate upon those propositions with the operator 'if ____, ...' to form 'If Peter hits Fido, Peter is foolhardy'.

2.12 Remove 'Peter' from the proposition to form the predicable 'If ____ hits Fido, ____ is foolhardy'.

2.13 Conjoin this predicable with the second-level predicate 'For anyone, he ____ he .....' to form 'For anyone, if he hits Fido, he is foolhardy'.

The parts arrived at by analysis, or conversely, the parts which feature in the proposition's constructional history as illustrated in (2.9)–(2.13) are what Dummett calls 'constituents'.

It should now be noted that there is one predicate in 'If anyone hits Fido, he is foolhardy' that was not even hinted at in the preceding paragraph. This is the predicate formed by extracting the name 'Fido' from the proposition to obtain 'if anyone hits ____, he is foolhardy'. It was ignored earlier precisely because it had just no part to play in determining the proposition's truth-conditions. There are other purposes, however, for which it does have a role to play, e.g. for the drawing of such inferences as:

Anyone who hits dogs is foolhardy.
Fido is a dog.
Therefore, anyone who hits Fido is foolhardy.

This inference is possible only because the predicate 'if anyone hits ____, he is foolhardy' is present in both the first premiss and the conclusion.

'Decomposition' is the term that Dummett reserves for the process by which such predicates as 'if anyone hits ____, he is foolhardy' are formed; and the parts so formed are called 'components'. Because components are formed by extracting from a proposition one or more occurrences of a proper name (or, in some cases, predicables), they presuppose a logically prior grasp of the sense of the proposition from which the extraction is made. Constituents, on the contrary, presuppose no prior grasp of the sense of the proposition constituted by them; rather, a grasp of the sense of the proposition presupposes a grasp of its constituents.

Expressed in terms of the constituent/component distinction, the question for the present section is whether the logical parts in 'Fido is black' are constituents or components of it. Now, if the first-level predicate '____ is black' were like the first-level predicate 'if anyone hits ____, he is foolhardy', then the sense of 'Fido is black' would have to be grasped prior to a grasp of '____ is black'. In the case of 'Fido is black' (and unlike the case of 'If anyone hits Fido, he is foolhardy'), however, there is clearly no other predicate in virtue of which it could be grasped. Consequently, *if* it were to be grasped prior to '____ is black', the proposition 'Fido is black' would have to be grasped as an *unstructured* whole.

Well, could 'Fido is black' be grasped as an unstructured whole? If Davidson is right, our capacity for the correct use of unsurveyably many propositions is explicable only if those sentences are regarded as derived from a base that itself is not

unsurveyable. Yet that would be impossible if atomic propositions were to be grasped as unstructured wholes rather than as
articulated into the senses of their logical parts. If grasped as
unstructured, not only could no new propositions be formed by
combining part of one atomic proposition with part of another,
but even complex propositions would be restricted to compounds
from atomic propositions. Nor could a base be acquired simply by
a process of decomposing propositions grasped as unstructured;
for decomposition would require some part (name or predicable)
to be recognizable, so as to be extracted from the proposition that
was allegedly grasped as unstructured. Yet, for a proposition to be
grasped as an unstructured whole is precisely for it to be grasped in
such a way that *neither* a name nor any other sub-propositional part
is recognizable in it. Since no such part *is* recognizable, and since
extraction presupposes that some part is recognizable there is just
no way of extracting any part from a proposition that was grasped
as unstructured. What all this means is that 'Fido is black' cannot
be grasped as unstructured. On the contrary, it can be grasped only
as articulated into the senses of its logical parts, 'Fido' and '___ is
black'. Thus, those parts are not components but are constituents:
it is only in virtue of their senses being grasped that the sense
of 'Fido is black' can itself be grasped.[8] So much, then, for the
relation between an atomic proposition and its logical parts.

II THE PART/PART RELATION IN ATOMIC PROPOSITIONS

Turning now to the question of how the parts of an atomic
proposition are related to each other, we ask what kind of
relation must hold between a name and a predicate if they are
to form an atomic proposition? It is clear that the unity of a
proposition differs vastly from that of a mere list, or even the mere
juxtaposition, of expressions. Perhaps not quite so obvious, though
equally true, is that it differs from the model of a jigsaw puzzle, a
model which has sometimes been thought to accord with Frege's
views on propositional unity during his *Grundgesetze* period. In
jigsaw puzzles one begins with a heap of variously coloured and

---

8 Dummet offers a further argument for this conclusion in *The Interpretation
of Frege's Philosophy*, pp.308–10.

shaped pieces of board, selects a piece from the heap, and then searches for the piece or pieces which will fit onto the first piece so as to form part of a larger pattern. Starting from a disorganized mass of pieces, a picture may be formed with each piece holding the position that it was made to occupy. If the relation between the logical, as distinct from merely verbal, parts of a proposition were to be regarded in similar fashion, then those parts too would *fit* together rather like the parts of a jigsaw puzzle. The jigsaw analogy, however, would be appropriate only if all of an atomic proposition's logical parts were discrete, as parts of a jigsaw are discrete. I shall now be arguing that the relation between the parts of an atomic proposition is not one between two discrete parts for, although one part is discrete the other is not: it is not detachable from the proposition in which it occurs. Of course, every *verbal* part (i.e. word) in the proposition is discrete. Not so, however, with every *logical* part: some are, some are not. This is so, no matter whether we adopt a Fregean analysis or one or other of the Leśniewskian-type analyses mentioned earlier.

A Predicates are undetachable expressions

I shall argue that the name and predicate in an atomic proposition are related to each other as complete expression to incomplete expression. The terms 'complete' and 'incomplete' derive from Frege whose main use for them was in regard to entities: objects were complete entities whereas functions were incomplete. The notion of incompleteness or unsaturatedness is a difficult one, however, so much so that Frege confessed to being unable to define it, and concluded that he must confine himself 'to hinting at what I have in mind by means of a metaphorical expression; and here I rely on my reader's agreeing to meet me half way'.[9] In regard to the incompleteness of predicates, however, I think we can do more than 'hint' at its meaning.

We might begin by comparing the notion of an incomplete entity like a function with that of, say, an incomplete house. A house without a roof might be called an incomplete house, but could

---

9 G. Frege, 'What is a Function' in P.T. Geach and M. Black, *Philosophical Writings of Gottlob Frege* (Oxford: Blackwell, 1960), p.115. In 'Concept and Object' (p.55) he makes the same point: '"Complete" and "unsaturated" are of course only figures of speech; but all that I wish or am able to do here is to give hints'.

exist in its own right and quite irrespective of whether the roof was ever added to it. A function, however, could not exist in its own right: it could exist only to the extent that there were arguments to complete it and values that were the completed function. Although both arguments and values could exist independently of any function, no function could exist independently of them. Another difference between the roofless house and a function is that the roofless portion of the house forms a distinguishable part of the finished house, whereas a function is indistinguishable in any of its values. Thus, although the number 8 is the value of the cube function for the argument 2, neither the cube function nor 2 are distinguishable parts of 8.

Despite having been spoken of as functions (linguistic functions[10]), predicates differ significantly from functions proper, even though having something in common both with them and with concepts. What they have in common is simply that all are instances of *mapping*, as illustrated in the following examples:

Function proper	1	2	3	4	.	.	.
	1	8	27	64	.	.	.

Fregean concept	Rover	Spot	Fido	.	.	.
	T–V of 'Rover is black'	T–V of 'Spot is black'	T–V of 'Fido is black'	.	.	.

Linguistic function	'Rover'	'Spot'	'Fido'	.	.	.
	'Rover is black'	'Spot is black'	'Fido is black'	.	.	.

Functions proper map from and into the *same* domain; more specifically, they map objects (e.g. numbers) on to objects. In this respect they differ both from Fregean concepts and from linguistic functions. There is yet another respect in which they

10 G.E.M. Anscombe and P.T. Geach, *Three Philosophers* (Oxford: Blackwell, 1969), pp.143–4.

differ from linguistic functions. Unlike the *values* of the foregoing cube function which contain neither arguments nor function, the values of the linguistic function contain both arguments (names) and 'function' (predicate). Because of these two differences, the term 'function' is not used univocally of predicates, but only analogously. Consequently, the mere fact that functions proper are related to *their* arguments as incomplete to complete does not allow us to infer that linguistic functions are related to their arguments as incomplete to complete. It may indeed be true that they are so related; but, if so, it will be for some reason other than whatever analogy they may have with functions proper. It is that reason that we must now seek.

First to be noted is that, if a predicate is an incomplete expression, it is not simply in virtue of its being part of a proposition; otherwise each logical part of every proposition would be an incomplete expression. Clearly, that is not the case; for a proposition may be part of a complex proposition, and a name may also be part of a proposition, though neither propositions nor names are incomplete expressions. What, then, does it mean to say that a predicate is incomplete? As I shall argue, it means that a predicate is an *unquotable*, undetachable expression. Unlike a function proper, the incompleteness of a predicate is not to be understood as its being unable to be distinguished in its values; rather, although readily distinguishable in its values (propositions), a predicate is, none the less, not detachable from them. Such is the incompleteness of a predicate that it cannot even be written down except in writing down the proposition in which it occurs.

Geach has long argued for this position. His central point is that, to recognize a predicate that is common to two propositions, it is not enough to recognize merely the *words* they have in common. Rather, one has also to recognize the *pattern* they have in common. Based on this insight, an argument might be constructed thus:

2.14 No predicate can be recognized in a proposition unless it be recognized as a pattern in that proposition.

2.15 But, a pattern cannot be detached from that in which it is a pattern.

2.16 Therefore, no predicate can be detached from the proposition in which it occurs.

In regard to premiss (2.14), the inadequacy of recognizing mere expressions and the correlative need to recognize a pattern is evident in the Polish proposition 'Maria zabiła Jana' ('Mary kills John'), which contains the same word ('zabiła') as does 'Joanna zabiła Jana'. The inflection of the verb 'zabił' is determined by the feminine gender of 'Maria' and 'Joanna', and would be absent if 'Maria' were replaced by a name of masculine gender, e.g. 'Janek'. Even on a superficial view the predicate expression and subject expression are so interwoven that they cannot be disengaged from each other. Consequently, it is not even plausible to suggest that their common predicate could be disengaged from the propositions containing it. Even more striking than Geach's examples are some in which subject and predicate are still more closely interwoven, e.g. in the propositions 'Maria uśmiechnęła sie' and 'Jan uśmiechnala sie' ('Maria (Jan) smiled'), in which the difference in gender between the subject expression 'Maria' and 'Jan' is marked not merely by the presence or absence of 'a' at the *end* of the verb, but by the presence of 'a' and 'ę', respectively, more *internal* to the verb.

The point that predicates are not constituted by words alone can be made more perspicuously still, by showing that they need not be constituted by words at all, but simply by a pattern . For instance, a very limited kind of language might have its names written in lower case, and its predicates indicated by varying the height of one or more letters that compose the names, e.g.:

	Possible language	*English translation*
Name:	christopher	Christopher
Propositions formed with the name:	Christopher	Christopher is black
	cHristopher	Christopher is wise
	chRisTopher	Christopher is angry

In such cases there would be no *words*, nor even any inflection, attached to the name to indicate the presence of a predicate. On the contrary, the predicate would be indicated solely by the pattern of letter heights in the inscription of the name.[11]

We might therefore agree with Geach that, if we think of his (and the other) examples, 'surely the temptation vanishes

---

11 Of course, the names would need to be reasonably long, if we were to obtain even a modest range of predicates. Moreover, if Frank Ramsey were right in thinking that names and predicates are interchangeable, then names might be indicated by the patterns of letter heights in the inscription of a predicate. The argument of this book, however, is quite neutral as to whether Ramsey is right or wrong, since it assumes only that the Fregean analysis is at least one legitimate analysis of atomic propositions.

o regard the predicate . . . as a simple sign with its slots for proper names quite external to it'. The predication is not effected by the bare word 'zabił', nor even by 'zabiła'. Rather, it s effected by the functional expression 'ξ zabił(a) ζ', which, as he notes, is shorthand for the following:

> The name ξ in the nominative case, and the name ζ in the accusative case, are combined with a token word 'zabił', inflected to agree in gender with the name ξ.[12]

At this point it might be objected that, even if there are some languages in which a predicate cannot be recognized without recognizing some pattern in a proposition, there are others in which that is patently not the case. Surely the predicate common to 'Fido is black' and 'Rover is black' is nothing but the expression 'is black'. Surely, there is no need to understand the predicate as conforming to a certain instruction, e.g.

> The name ξ is placed adjacent to, and to the left of, the token phrase 'is black'.

The answer is, 'most surely there is such a need'. Admittedly the instruction is both so simple and, to us, so obvious that we may be inclined to discount it as entirely trivial. It may seem that, even without any such instruction, we could perfectly well combine the expressions 'Fido' and 'is black' to form the proposition 'Fido is black'. That suggestion is not without a grain of truth; for we can make sense even of English that has been severely butchered, and we might well understand a foreigner who reversed the normal word order by uttering 'Is black Fido'. However, the intelligibility of butchered English has its limits; and there are many possible patterns that might exceed those limits. A few written examples are given below.

2.17   is black

                    o
                    d
                    i
                    F
2.18   is black

                            Fido

12 P.T. Geach, 'Names and Identity', p.148

2.19   is black   Fido

We may be tempted to regard (2.17), (2.18), and (2.19) as
'unnatural' as compared with the 'naturalness' of our present
way of writing English. Yet, no one way of writing it is any
more natural than the others. And that should alert us to the
fact that, in different circumstances, our present way of writing
it might have seemed every bit as contrived as (2.17) seems to
us now. Lifelong familiarity with the present pattern exhibited in
'Fido is black' should therefore not mislead us into dismissing it
as trivial. Hence, the difference between 'Maria zabiła Jana' and
'Fido is black' is not that there is some pattern to the former,
but none to the latter. Rather, there is a pattern to both: it is
simply that the pattern happens to appear to us as more striking
in the former and notably less so in the latter. So, our earlier
conclusion remains intact: predicates cannot be detached from the
propositions in which they occur. Although in some languages the
expressions used in forming *predicates* can be detached, there are
no languages in which the predicates themselves can be detached
or placed within quotation marks.

The position for which I have been arguing can now be set out
in more detail.

2.20 The predication relation – that is, the relation of predicate
to name – is essentially that of a pattern added to (or
superimposed upon) the name to result in a proposition.

2.21 Although an atomic proposition is something more than a
name, the 'something more' need in principle involve no
words additional to the name. Even though in practice it will
indeed involve more words than a name, those additional
words are not themselves the predicate.

2.22 What, then, is the role of the additional words in (A)–(C) and
in the Polish examples? Their role is simply to differentiate
what is predicated, e.g. to differentiate between *what* is
predicated in 'Fido is black' and in 'Fido is lonely'. As we
saw, the same task could be performed solely by variations in
patterns (e.g. the heights of the letters in 'fido') without any
additional words. An obvious disadvantage of that method is
that differences of patterns (and, hence, predicates) would
be severely limited. Far better, therefore, to retain the
one basic pattern for all predications, and to achieve the
required differences by means of words, thus providing the

possibility of virtually unlimited numbers of predicates. The same predicate *pattern* is to be found in both 'Rover is black' and 'Rover is lonely'. The difference in *what* is predicated in each case is indicated by the difference in the words used to form that pattern.

2.23 Although the pattern may be described in words, that description has no place in the proposition, and is not to be mistaken for the predicate.

2.24 Since what is essential to predication is the pattern that marks a proposition, and since patterns are undetachable from what they are patterns of, no predicate can be *detached* from the proposition in which it occurs. Even in such propositions as 'Fido is black' the pattern remains undetachable. By removing the words 'is black' we do not *detach* the pattern; we simply destroy it.

2.25 Since the predicate is a pattern that characterizes a proposition, we may also follow Geach by speaking of it as a *feature* of a proposition.

2.26 The foregoing conclusion suffices to discredit the view that predicates are quotable expressions detachable from the propositions in which they occur. On such a view, they might have been regarded as being marked by slots into which names could be plugged to form a proposition. In that case, 'Fido is black' would have been formed by plugging 'Fido' into the slot in '___ is black'. A predicate would thus have been a proposition in waiting, or a proposition manqué, so to speak.

t is apparent that the union between the logical parts of a proposition is quite unlike that between the parts of a jigsaw puzzle or between a socket and a plug. It is, indeed, a very much more binding union, so binding as to be indissoluble. It is indissoluble because one of the parts is not a linguistic entity in its own right, but is entirely parasitic upon the proposition in which t occurred. Precisely for this reason it deserves to be called an *incomplete* expression. It is incomplete not in the relatively weak sense in which a wall might be called an incomplete house or a chapter might be called an incomplete story, namely, an isolated fragment of a whole. Rather, it is incomplete in the strongest possible sense, namely, that it cannot occur even as an isolated fragment. If it does not occur in a proposition, it does not occur

at all. That means, consequently, that the predicate can be neither
'is black' nor '____ is black'; for obviously each of them is what the
predicate is not, namely, a quotable expression. On the contrary,
the role of 'is black' is merely to *indicate* or *signal* the presence
of a common predicate in 'Fido is black' and 'Spot is black'.
The predicate itself, however, is not quotable: it is not even a
proposition manqué such as 'is black' might have been thought
to be. It is, as Geach says, simply a feature of, or pattern in, a
proposition.

Predicate sense

It might now be asked whether what has been concluded about
predicates is equally true of predicate sense. For instance, it
might be objected that, while the earlier conclusions apply at the
syntactical level, it has yet to be shown that they are applicable to
the semantic level as well. Just because the predicate *expression*
in 'Fido is black' is a feature of the whole expression, why should
a similar relation be claimed between the *senses* of those two
expressions?

The objection ignores the fact that at no stage were we operating
solely on the level of syntax; for at no stage were we concerned
solely with expressions (inscriptions) whether predicate expressions, propositional expressions, or name expressions. On the
contrary, neither 'Fido is black' nor 'Fido' was taken to be
solely an expression. The former was taken to be an expression
having-both-a-sense-and-a-truth-value (i.e. a proposition), and
the latter was taken to be an expression-having-both-a-sense-
and-a-semantic-value, and hence as a name rather than a mere
inscription. Neither was the predicate mistaken for a pattern in
mere expression, but was shown to be a pattern in a proposition,
i.e. a pattern in a *sense-bearing* expression. That being so, the
argument was conducted at a level that embraced syntax and
semantics alike: the relation in question held not between mere
expressions but between sense-bearing expressions.

Perhaps, however, the objection might be pressed by urging
that, even if our conclusions did concern predicates and propositions (and not just predicate expressions and propositional
expressions), that still would not entitle us to conclude that the
senses of a predicate were features of the sense of a proposition.
To that I would reply with the following argument:

Our thoughts would be incomprehensible even to ourselves, if their sense structures were impossible to grasp, at least in principle.

But we have no access to our thoughts independently of the linguistic expressions in which they are expressed; and *a fortiori* we have no means of grasping the sense structure of the thoughts except by way of the logical (as distinct from grammatical) structure of those linguistic expressions (propositions). Consequently the sense structure of those propositions just *is* the logical structure of the thoughts they express; and if it were not, it could never be grasped at all.

Therefore our thoughts would be incomprehensible even to ourselves, if their sense structure were not the same as the logical structure of the propositions used to express them.[13]

But our thoughts are not incomprehensible to ourselves.

Therefore, their sense structure is the same as the logical structure of the propositions used to express them.

Therefore, since the predicate expression in a proposition is a feature of that proposition, the sense of that predicate will be a feature of the sense of the proposition.

n conclusion, then, the thesis of the predicate's being a feature of a proposition, and undetachable from it, might be illustrated by the non-linguistic analogue of a vase formed from a lump of clay. The resulting vase would conform to a pattern that could have been described in advance. Although that description is of course no part of the vase, the shape to which the description applies not only is part of the vase, but an undetachable part as well. The analogy with the predicate is fairly clear, though, like all analogies, it should not be pressed too far. The lump of clay may be likened to the name 'Fido', and the vase to the proposition 'Fido is black'. The shape of the vase may be likened to the predicate in the proposition, and the expression '____ is black' (or the description 'A name is placed to the left of, and adjacent to, the token expression "is black"') may be likened to the description of the pattern that is embodied in the vase. The predicate is no less a feature of the proposition than is the shape of the vase; and it is no more quotable or detachable from the proposition than is the shape detachable from the vase.

3 Naturally, there are as many legitimate sense structures as there are legitimate logical structures of the propositions used to express them.

B Predicate instances

The existence of predicate instances

One consequence of the incompleteness or unquotability of predicates is that, even though we may well continue using descriptions like 'the predicate in "Fido is black"' in referential position, we should at least be so aware of the logical impropriety of doing so as to eschew its misleading ontological implications. The only referent appropriate to a description in that position is an object i.e. a complete entity. Hence any use of 'the predicate' in that position would be appropriate only if it referred to a complete entity, albeit a linguistic one, e.g. a *quotable* expression like 'is black'. In saying, for example, 'The predicate in "Fido is black" is the same as the one in "Rover is black"', we would leave ourselves open to the question, 'And just which one is that?' Yet, any such question is as unanswerable as 'Which philosopher was that?' would be, if asked in response to 'Socrates was a philosopher'.

What, then, are we to say about the use of a description like 'the predicate in "Fido is black"'? The first thing to say about it is that it is no less misleading ontologically than the TV advertisement 'Brand X puts whiteness back in your sheets'. It is misleading because, just as the use of 'whiteness' might suggest that whiteness is an (abstract) object, so the foregoing use of 'predicate' might suggest that a predicate too was an object, albeit a linguistic object, a quotable expression. The second thing is that, just as the TV advertisement can be reframed to avoid any suggestion of whiteness being an object, so the use of 'predicate' can be reframed to avoid any suggestion of a predicate being a complete (i.e. quotable) expression. In the former case, the result would be 'Brand X makes your sheets white again'. In the latter case it would be,

2.27 Fido is what is said of Rover in 'Rover is black'[14]

or

2.28 What is said of Fido in 'Fido is black' is what is said of Rover in 'Rover is black'.

14 Both occurrences of 'is' are of course predicative; neither one is the 'is' of identity.

There are two points to note about (2.27) and (2.28). One is that the expression 'what is said about Fido in "Fido is black"' is always substitutable both *salva veritate* and *salva congruitate* for 'is black'. For precisely that reason it is not to be construed as occurring in referential position; and, for that reason, it could offer no ground for the kind of improper questions mentioned above. The other point is that, even in (2.28), neither the expression 'what is said of Fido in "Fido is black"' nor the expression 'what is said of Rover in "Rover is black"' occurs in referential position; for the 'is' which links them functions neither as a copula nor as the 'is' of identity. Rather, it indicates the presence of a second-level predicate '___ is.....', from which (2.28) is formed by filling the slots with first-level predicables.

As can be seen, the possibly misleading way of speaking is avoided only at the price of verbosity and inelegance. Naturally, we are quite free to choose the more concise and elegant, but possibly misleading, use if we wish. However, we are no more free to embrace its misleading ontological implications than we are to embrace those of using 'whiteness' in 'Brand X puts whiteness back in your sheets'.

The points I have been making are one consequence of accepting the undetachability of predicates. Another consequence is that the predicate-expression-in-'Fido is black' and the predicate-expression-in-'Spot is black' are *not interchangeable*. Why? Because interchangeability would presuppose that the expression occurring in one proposition could be isolated from that proposition and used in a different proposition by being attached to another name. But, predicates are quite undetachable from propositions; and so they could never be interchanged. In any case, they are merely features of propositions; and it clearly makes no more sense to speak of interchanging or transferring features than it does to speak of eating thoughts or drinking wishes.

Two points have now emerged:

2.29 In one respect, the predicate in 'Fido is black' is the same as that in 'Spot is black'; for what is said about Fido is precisely what is said about Spot.

2.30 In another respect, the two incomplete expressions are *not* the same; for the one can occur nowhere but in 'Fido is black', whereas the latter can occur nowhere but in 'Spot is black'.

Although we may be able to make do with the term 'predicate' to capture the first point, we need some other term to capture the second. For that purpose, I shall introduce the term 'predicate instance'. 'Fido is black' and 'Spot is black' contain predicate instances which are alike both in saying exactly the same of Fido as of Spot and in so doing by using language tokens of the same type. None the less, the instances undoubtedly do differ, for one can occur nowhere but in 'Fido is black' whereas the other can occur nowhere but in 'Spot is black'. To deny any difference on the grounds that predicate instances could not differ except in regard to sense would be to invoke a semantic version of the Identity of Indiscernibles, and one which is no less misconceived than is the correlative ontological claim that there can be no difference between two individuals except in regard to properties (whether relational or non-relational).

I should stress that the notion of predicate instance does not purport to be at all explanatory: it does not pretend to make the unity of a proposition any clearer than it already is. It is simply a corollary of recognizing the predicate expression as incomplete in the sense already explained. The notion of a predicate instance would be problematic only if predicate expressions were regarded as complete, i.e. capable of occurring in their own right.[15]

III ATOMIC PROPOSITIONS AND ONTOLOGY

I began this chapter by specifying both its goal and the means by which that goal would be attained. The goal was to determine the ontological categories exemplified in Fido's being black and the inter-relations between these exemplifications. The means of doing so was by following Frege's view that the ontological categories exemplified in the things we talk about reflect the linguistic categories of the expressions we use to talk about them. The first and major step, therefore, was to determine the linguistic categories of the expressions in 'Fido is black' together with their inter-relations. From that it would be a comparatively simple step

15 Additional objections to predicate instances are discussed in the Appendix to this chapter.

to determine the correlative ontological categories of what those expressions stood for and the inter-relations between them. The major step has now been completed with the following semantic conclusions.

2.31 In the sense of 'Fido is black' are to be distinguished the senses of 'Fido' and of the predicate in 'Fido is black'. The two senses are *constituents* of 'Fido is black', i.e. they are logically prior to the sense of the proposition as a whole.

2.32 'Fido' has complete sense.

2.33 The sense of the predicate is incomplete. It is simply a feature of, or pattern in, the sense of 'Fido is black'.

The correlative ontological conclusions, then, are the following, upon the first and third of which I shall elaborate subsequently.

2.34 In Fido's being black are to be distinguished two ontological categories exemplified by Fido and his blackness. Fido and his blackness are *constituents* of Fido's existing, i.e. they are ontologically prior to Fido's being black.

2.35 Fido is a complete entity.

2.36 Fido's blackness is an incomplete entity, a property instance. It is simply a feature of, or pattern in, Fido's being black.

The constituents of Fido's being black

My use of the term 'constituent' in an ontological context requires some explanation. The terms 'component' and 'constituent' were introduced earlier in the chapter, though at the semantic level rather than the ontological level, i.e. in regard to the sense of 'Fido is black' rather than in regard to Fido's being black. Roughly, constituents were those parts without which a proposition could not be built up; components were those parts into which a proposition could be broken down or decomposed, but which were not required in the logical construction of the proposition. As I mentioned, the terms stem from Dummett who uses 'constituent' to refer to those logical parts of a proposition that have to be recognized in determining its truth-conditions, i.e. they are the logical parts that must be employed in delineating what he calls the 'constructional history' of a proposition. Components, on the contrary, are parts that do not have to be recognized either in determining a proposition's truth-conditions or in delineating its constructional history, though they may have to be recognized for purposes of inference.

I am now extending the use of 'constituent' and 'component' from the semantic context of propositions and their parts to the context of ontological wholes and their parts.[16] Parallelling the semantic distinction, the ontological distinction is roughly that between parts from which an ontological whole can be *built up*, and parts into which it can be *broken down* or decomposed, but which are not required in its construction. In an extended sense of the terms, the former may be called 'constituents' and the latter 'components'. The building up and decomposition of which I have been speaking are of course only conceptual, not physical. To be a little more precise about the use of the terms, I shall mean by *constituents* of an ontological whole, any of its parts which would need to be recognized under pain of not knowing what the whole was in itself (rather than knowing it simply in its relation to something else). Thus, Fido and his blackness would be constituents of Fido's being black, if it were impossible to know what Fido's being black was in itself without recognizing the presence in it of Fido and his blackness. Likewise, I shall mean by *components* of an ontological whole, any of its parts that would *not* need to be recognized in order to know what the whole was in itself.[17] In drawing these distinctions I am not assuming that all ontological wholes have ontological parts of any kind, nor am I assuming that those containing constituents must also have components.

So far as Fido and his blackness are concerned, both have either to be components or both constituents: it is impossible that one be a component and the other a constituent. The reason is simply that, according to the Fregean-type analysis, Fido and his blackness are

16 By ontological parts I shall not mean spatio-temporal parts, but categorial ones. Candidates for such parts would be substance, properties, relations, haecceities, the bare particulars of Bergmann, the tropes of D.C. Williams, the individuating operator of Castañeda, and so on. While mentioning these as candidates for being ontological parts, there are very few of them that I would endorse as being *successful* candidates.

17 As an example of constituents and components, consider the case of Delta, an ontological whole having parts a, b, c, d. To know what Delta is in itself one might have to recognize it as made up of a, b, c, d. If so, they would be constituents of Delta. However, one might not need to recognize it as containing $(a,c), (a,d), (b,d), (a,b,d)$, and so on. Consequently, these would be components of Delta.

the *only* parts in Fido's being black.[18] Consequently, if one of them had to be recognized in order to know what Fido's being black was, the remaining part would, *ipso facto*, have also to be recognized for that same purpose.[19] Well, if Fido and his blackness have both to be components or both constituents, which are they? To determine whether they are components, let us assume not only that Fido exists but also that he is barking, and that 'Alpha' denotes Fido's being black and 'Beta' denotes Fido's being barking. Let us now suppose that Fido and his blackness were components of Alpha. Since Alpha has no parts except Fido and his blackness, and they are both being taken to be components, there would obviously be no other parts available to be constituents in Alpha. But if there were no constituents in Alpha, there could be no components either. Why? Simply because a component is any complex part that remains when a constituent is taken to be extracted from the whole. If the whole had no constituents, none could be extracted from it, not even conceptually. So, in that case, there could be no components.

Were Alpha to have no constituents, it could be known in the first instance only as an unarticulated whole, as ontologically simple.[20] But, if known in the first instance as ontologically simple, it could *subsequently* no more be known to be ontologically complex than a spatial point could be known to be spatially complex. Hence, to say that neither Fido nor his blackness were constituents of Alpha would be to say that it was an unarticulated whole, and thus that it had no parts at all. The supposition that Fido and his blackness *are* components of Fido's being black has therefore led to the self-refuting conclusion that Fido's being black has *no* components.

18 As I have said earlier, I do not claim that the Fregean-type analysis is the *only* legitimate one. For the purposes of my argument it suffices that it be at least *a* legitimate analysis.

19 Naturally, this contrasts with the semantic example of 'Anyone who hits Fido is foolhardy', in which 'Fido' could be a constituent without 'Anyone who hits ___ is foolhardy' being one also. That was possible only because there were logical units more basic than 'Anyone who hits ___ is foolhardy', and *they* were constituents. In the case of Fido's existing, however, there are no ontological units more basic than Fido and his existence; and so it is impossible that the presence of one be recognized in the whole without the other also being recognized as present.

20 This has a semantic analogue; for if 'Fido' had not been a constituent in 'Anyone who hits Fido is foolhardy' it could have had no such component as 'Anyone who hits ___ is foolhardy'. More generally, any proposition without a constituent part would have to be grasped in the first instance without being grasped as having any parts at all: it would have to be grasped as an articulated whole, i.e. as logically simple.

If that were not refutation enough, it would mean also that Alpha and Beta could not be known to have any common element. But Fido is known to be common to Alpha and Beta. Once again, therefore, Fido and his blackness cannot be components of Alpha; both are constituents thereof.[21]

Fido's blackness is both a property instance and an incomplete entity

According to my earlier explanation of the term, a first-level property (whether real or not) is whatever is attributed to an individual by a predicate. Hence, Fido's blackness is a property. Moreover, because the expression that attributes it to Fido is both a predicate instance and an incomplete expression, Fido's blackness is not a universal property but a property instance and an incomplete entity.[22] Just as the predicate instance in 'Fido is black' cannot occur except in that proposition, so too the property instance which is Fido's blackness cannot occur except in Fido's being black: it can have no independent existence.

IV CONCLUSION

Those who claim that proper names have no sense[23] might be inclined to question ontological conclusions derived from premisses which presuppose the contrary view. At this point therefore I should note that the conclusions in question could equally have been reached from premisses that rely on no such presupposition. Individuals could have been shown to be self-individuating (and, hence, *complete* entities) by arguing that the contrary view – whether in the form proposed by Russell, or Goodman, or Castañeda, or D.C. Williams – has the untenable consequence that

21 Although Alpha has no components, it ought not be thought that *no* ontological whole could have component parts.
22 There is nothing tautologous about saying that a property instance is an incomplete entity, for G.F. Stout, D.C. Williams, and K. Campbell have all been prepared to allow that property instances are *not* individuated by anything else and *are* capable of existence quite independently of anything to which they might happen to belong. Property instances of that kind have been called 'tropes' by Williams and Campbell. The view that predicate instances are individuated *ab alio* and are incapable of independent existence is mostly, though not unanimously, thought to be Aristotle's. It seems also to have been held by Aquinas.
23 E.g. Mill, Kripke, and Putnam.

individuals are instantiable.[24] As for the properties had by individuals, they could have been shown to be individuated by those individuals (and, hence, to be *incomplete* entities) by exposing the ineradicable difficulties of theories, like Trope Theory, which allow property instances to be individuated in their own right (and, hence, to be complete entities).[25] And, finally, Fido and his blackness could have been shown to be constituents of Fido's being black by arguing that, otherwise, it would have been impossible to distinguish between Fido and his blackness. Thus, the conclusions drawn in this chapter could all have been reached by a different route. For two reasons I have not taken that route. One is that it would have required a treatise on individuals and individuation; the other is that, for roughly the same reasons as those proposed by Dummett, I think the referential view of proper names is wrong and that they do have a sense.

Before concluding, I should point out that 'Fido is black' has been used in this chapter as an arbitrary atomic proposition: it has done duty for any true atomic proposition. If, therefore, 'Fido exists' were later shown to be no less an atomic proposition than is 'Fido is black', the present chapter may be taken to have established the categorial structure of Fido's existing no less than of Fido's being black. That is to say, Fido's existing could be taken to consist of Fido and his existence, which would be related to Fido's existing as constituents thereof and to each other as complete entity to incomplete entity. Being constituents means that they would be ontologically prior to Fido's existing, and hence that the latter should be conceptually constructible from them. That condition could readily be met if Fido's conceivability were not dependent on his existing or having existed. It is far from obvious that it could be met if, as I shall argue in the next chapter, the converse is true. It is from that conflict that our central problem will emerge.

24 Cf. my 'Individuals and Individuality', *Grazer Philosophische Studien* 37 (1990), pp.75–91.
25 ibid.

UNIVERSITY OF BRISTOL

Department of Philosophy

9 Woodland Road
Bristol
BS8 1TB

Chapter 3

The inconceivability of future individuals

Although I have chosen to investigate what is meant by Fido's existing, I could equally have chosen to do so for Spot, Rover, George Bush, or Joan Sutherland: Fido simply does duty for any concrete individual. Since it is only individuals that are concrete that I want now to discuss, it might be helpful to distinguish them from those that are not the subject of this chapter, viz. abstract individuals. Speaking generally, individuals are to be contrasted with universals, the mark of a universal being its instantiability (though not necessarily its being actually instantiated), and the mark of an individual being the ability to instantiate universals together with the inability to be itself instantiated in anything. Individuals, however, may be concrete or abstract. They are concrete if they can either effect a real change or be subject to a real change or both; otherwise they are abstract. Abstract individuals, like sets, are a sub-group of abstract entities, and can neither begin to exist nor cease to exist, but exist necessarily.[1] Since they exist necessarily, there is never a time when they could not be both referred to and conceived of.[2] Whether such entities as sets are *actually* referred to and conceived of at any time would depend on there being at that time an entity capable of doing the referring and conceiving. As for concrete individuals, even if their existing should in fact neither have a beginning nor an end, it is at least *possible* that they have begun to exist and that they will cease to exist. Unlike abstract individuals, they exist contingently

1 Strictly speaking this is true only of such abstract entities as are not constituted from concrete entities, e.g. sets of concrete entities.
2 Whatever else may be said of the status of *fictional* individuals, there is at least one particular respect in which they are like abstract entities, viz. there is never a time when they could not be conceived of.

rather than necessarily. That being the case, one might well ask whether their difference from necessary abstract entities extends to their being at any time inconceivable or 'non-referrable to'. More particularly, could a concrete individual have been either referred to or conceived of before it existed? That is to be determined in this chapter.

It is sometimes thought, and even thought to be self-evident, that Socrates, for example, could not have come to exist unless prior to his existing it was *possible* that *he* exist. Of course, since this is a *de re* claim, it could be true only if there were some *re*s to which the potentiality or capacity for existence could be ascribed. It would make no sense to ascribe a potentiality or capacity to Socrates, if there were no Socrates in any world to be a subject of the ascription. So, if the *de re* claim is to be true, there must be some sense in which we can say that *there is* a Socrates. Since Socrates is not actual, the 'is' would obviously have to be understood in a sense other than 'is actual'. Hence, there would have to be a Socrates, though not one that *is* actual, but only one which *could* be actual. Something having the potentiality to be actualized might thus be said to be a *possible* Socrates.

However much our robust sense of reality may be affronted by a proposal of this kind, it is one which has enjoyed some currency, being described disapprovingly by Quine as 'the view that concrete individuals are of two kinds: those that are actualized and those which are possible but not actualized. Cerberus is of the latter kind, according to this view; so that there *is* such a thing as Cerberus, and the proper content of the vulgar denial of Cerberus is more correctly expressed in the fashion "Cerberus is not actualized".'[3]

A much modified version of this view has been proposed by Plantinga. Although he allows that 'Hamlet and Lear do not in fact exist; but clearly they could have',[4] he denies that there is now any possible Hamlet or Lear to which the possibility of existing might be ascribed. What does now exist are two individual essences (haecceities), each of which could become

3 W.V. Quine, *Methods of Logic* (London: Routledge & Kegan Paul, 3rd edn, 1974), p.214.
4 A. Plantinga, *The Nature of Necessity* (Oxford: Oxford University Press, 1974), p.153. This claim was made before his proposed distinction between existing and being actual. Had it been made later, the phrase 'do not in fact exist' would have been replaced by 'are not in fact actual'.

actual by being exemplified in Hamlet and Lear respectively. Until now, and maybe forevermore, these haecceities remain unexemplified. Thus, while neither Hamlet nor Lear can now be referred to, their haecceities can be both referred to and conceived of. Moreover, because the haecceities are now conceivable, there is a real sense in which the individuals that would exemplify them are also conceivable even now. This is a view which I shall discuss at length later in the chapter.

Views like the foregoing seem to presuppose that the sole difference between existing individuals and future individuals is that the former *are* actual, whereas the latter merely *could* be actual. If the distinction between existing and being actual were accepted, a future individual, or at least its individual essence (e.g. Socrateity), might be said to exist without being actual. Moreover, that same individual or its essence, which now merely exists, *could* be actualized or incarnated in real life. Thus, on what might seem to be an eminently reasonable view, the real-life Socrates would have been no less conceivable before he came to exist than after he did so.

This conclusion is precisely what I shall be denying. Instead, I shall be arguing that prior to its existing no concrete individual could be conceived of by anyone or in any way. As a corollary, there can be no singular proposition about any concrete individual before it exists; the only propositions about future individuals are general ones, albeit as particular as one may wish to make them. Lest these claims be misunderstood, however, I should explain immediately what they do *not* deny. They do not deny that even now descriptions are conceivable which fit no individual that has ever existed, but which may turn out to fit some individual that has yet to exist. Nor do they deny that quite detailed predictions may be formulated which no existing individual could fulfil, but which may indeed be fulfilled by an individual that has yet to exist. It may be tempting, and even natural, to construe these admissions as tantamount to accepting the conceivability of future individuals. I shall be arguing that the temptation is to be dismissed, and that 'Tom satisfies description D' does not warrant the conclusion 'Tom was conceived of in description D', nor does 'Tom fulfils prediction P' warrant the conclusion 'Tom was conceived of in prediction P'. Even if an individual could have been exhaustively *described* before it existed, that is not to say that it could have been *conceived of* at that time.

Hence, the present claim is *not* that no description could ever be uniquely satisfied by a future individual, for of course it is possible, albeit highly improbable, that I now describe my niece to be born in two years, the last current model Mercedes to come off the assembly line in three years from now, and the island to emerge from the Atlantic ocean in fifty years, and describe them no less successfully than a niece born last year, a Mercedes now in the showroom, or the island of St Helena. Nor is it being denied that propositions employing the description may be *made true* by some future individual. What is being denied, is simply that such propositions are *about* any future individual. Precisely what is being conceived of in such descriptions and predictions, and how it differs from conceiving of Tom are questions to be answered, however, only after the foreshadowed conclusions have been vindicated.

I SOCRATES COULD NOT BE *REFERRED* TO BEFORE EXISTING

This claim is not to be confused with the trivial one that what *never* exists can never be referred to. It is the rather more substantial claim that no *past or present* individual could have been referred to *before* it began to exist. The argument turns on the simple truth that, once a proposition like '"Socrates" refers to Socrates' was true at a given time *a*, nothing *thereafter* could prevent its having been true at that time. This, I should note, is sharply to be distinguished from the claim that '"Socrates" refers to Socrates' could not be true at one time but false at a later time. Although I think that it too is true, it plays no part whatever in the following argument.

3.1 Had '"Socrates" refers to Socrates' ever been true at any time *a* before Socrates existed, it could *thereafter* never fail to have been true at time *a*.

3.2 But, until Socrates did come to exist it was always possible that he not come to exist, and hence that '"Socrates" refers to Socrates' should never have been true at time *a*.

3.3 Therefore, it is not the case that '"Socrates" refers to Socrates' could have been true at any time *a* before Socrates existed.

In arguing for (3.1) and (3.2), it will be helpful to employ the following symbols:

Let *p* be the proposition '"Socrates" refers to Socrates'.
Let *a* be any time *before* Socrates came to exist.
Let *b* be any time *after* *a* but *before* Socrates came to exist.
Let 'T*ap*' be '*p* is true at time *a*'.
Let M be the operator 'it is possible that'.

Argument for premiss (3.1):

3.4 Suppose that '"Socrates" refers to Socrates' had in fact been true at time *a* before he came to exist in 470 BC, i.e. T*ap*.

3.5 But, if that had been the case, it would at time *b* have been no longer possible to prevent '"Socrates" refers to Socrates' from having been true at time *a*, i.e. if T*ap* then T*b*~M~T*ap*.

3.6 Therefore, at time *b* it would have been no longer possible to prevent '"Socrates" refers to Socrates' from having been true at time *a*, i.e. T*b*~M~T*ap*.

3.7 But (3.6) entails that at time *b* it would not have been true that '"Socrates" refers to Socrates' possibly be prevented from having been true at *a*, i.e. ~T*b*M~T*ap*.

3.8 Therefore, at time *b* it would not have been true that '"Socrates" refers to Socrates' possibly be prevented from having been true at *a*, i.e.~T*b*M~T*ap*.

Argument for premiss (3.2):

3.9 It is possible that the conditions at time *b* could have been such as to have prevented Socrates from ever coming to exist.

3.10 But, had Socrates never come to exist, he could never have been referred to.

3.11 Therefore, at time *b* it would have been possible that 'Socrates' never have referred to Socrates.

3.12 But, had 'Socrates' *never* referred to Socrates, '"Socrates" refers to Socrates' would not have been true at time *a*.

3.13 Therefore, at time *b* it would have been true that '"Socrates" refers to Socrates' possibly be prevented from having been true at *a*, i.e. T*b*M~T*ap*, which contradicts (3.8).

In examining the argument's premisses, it needs to be remembered that the necessity employed in the argument is not logical, but is the kind which Prior confessed to borrowing from Ferdinand of Cordova,[5] namely, the notion of a 'truth that can no longer be prevented' because the time for preventing it is now past.[6] Consequently, I am decidedly not saying it would have been *logically* impossible at *b* that '"Socrates" refers to Socrates' not have been true at *a*. I am saying simply that at *b* it was no longer possible to *prevent* '"Socrates" refers to Socrates' from having been true at *a*, since it had in fact been true at *a*.

As for the source of the contradiction between (3.8) and (3.13), it is obvious that (3.8) is true if (3.5) is true, and that (3.13) is true if (3.9) is true. If both (3.5) and (3.9) are true, the contradiction will stem from the falsity of (3.4), viz. in supposing that '"Socrates" refers to Socrates' could have been true even before Socrates existed. Premisses (3.5) and (3.9) will therefore bear closer attention .

Premiss (3.5)

If '"Socrates" refers to Socrates' had in fact been true at time *a*, it would at time *b* have been no longer possible to prevent '"Socrates" refers to Socrates' from having been true at time *a*, i.e. if T*ap* then T*b*~M~T*ap*.

This premiss claims merely that, *if* the proposition had been true at *a*, nothing *subsequent* to *a* could *then* have brought it about that the proposition had *not* been true at *a*. This is simply the unexceptionable claim that the proposition could not have been both true and not true at the same time, at *a*. Hence, premiss (3.5) does not claim that, *if* '"Socrates" refers to Socrates' had been true at time *a*, it had *necessarily* to have been true at *a*. On the contrary, it allows that it might well not have been true at *a*, though such a possibility would have obtained only in the period *prior* to *a*. It is only subsequent to that time that there ceased to be any such possibility: had it been a settled fact that '"Socrates" refers to Socrates' was indeed true at time *a*, nothing occurring subsequent to *a* could prevent its having been true at *a*. As Prior

5 A.N. Prior, *Papers on Time and Tense* (Oxford: Oxford University Press, 1968), p.76.
6 This notion is to be found also in Aristotle, Aquinas, and other mediaevals. Sarah Waterlow has dubbed it 'relativized temporalized' necessity or *RT*-necessity. Cf. Sarah Waterlow, *Passage and Possibility: A Study in Aristotle's Modal Concepts* (Oxford: Oxford University Press, 1982).

expressed it, 'the passage of time may eliminate "possibilities" in the sense of alternative outcomes of actual states of affairs, and cause that to be no longer alterable which once might have been otherwise'.[7]

Lest there be any suggestion of fatalistic implications in this premiss consider that, according to fatalism, it is a logical or conceptual truth

3.14 that, if some particular state of affairs does *now* obtain or *has* obtained, then there was never any possibility either of its not now obtaining or of its not having obtained, and

3.15 if some particular state of affairs *will* obtain, there is no possibility that it will not obtain.

Now, premiss (3.5) does not imply (3.14), since it does not claim that there would *never* have been any alternative to 'Socrates' referring to Socrates at time *a*. Rather, it claims merely that *subsequent* to that state of affairs obtaining at time *a*, there was *then* no possibility of its not having obtained at time *a*. Nor is (3.15) implied, for premiss (3.5) is concerned solely with what *has* obtained and has no implications at all for what has not yet obtained but *will* obtain. For both these reasons, therefore, the premiss offers no support to fatalism.

Premiss (3.9)

It is possible that conditions at time *b* could have been such as to have prevented Socrates from ever coming to exist.

This premiss would doubtless be strongly resisted by anyone of determinist bent. Such a one might insist that, before an individual existed, predictions could be made not simply about *some* individual or other, but about that very individual which does now exist. That is to say, such predictions could be singular rather than merely general. Indeed it might be argued that, even in 472 BC Socrates could have been referred to in terms of a then existing parcel of matter from which he could not be prevented from coming to exist in 470 BC.

Against this suggestion it must be said that Socrates' birth would have been unpreventable in 472 BC only under the following conditions, neither of which can be met:

7 A.N. Prior, *Papers on Time and Tense*, p.77.

3.16 If the Universe were inherently deterministic in character.
3.17 If it were impossible that Socrates should have developed
     from energy or matter which, *subsequent to the prediction*,
     appeared in the Universe from no prior source of energy or
     matter, e.g. if continuous or even discontinuous creation hap-
     pened to occur in the Universe subsequent to the prediction.

As for (3.16), the determinist view of nature would seem to be
doubly confounded – on the one hand in the area of quantum
mechanics and on the other in the area of thermodynamics.
Indeed, quantum mechanics threatens it in two ways. One is
the ineradicably *statistical* character of the quantum mechanical
laws; the other is the *non-causal* character of those laws. Their
statistical character alone makes it impossible to be specific about
just what would follow upon any quantum mechanical event. Nor
could this lack of specificity be dismissed as simply a defect
afflicting our *knowledge* but not at all reflected in the nature
of things. On the contrary, the 'no hidden variable' argument[8]
has shown that the statistical character of the laws manifests
an indeterminacy inherent in the Universe and not eradicable
even in principle by the supposition of hidden variables. Hence,
even if the laws had been causal, their causality would have
been merely *probabilistic*; and even that suffices to undermine
determinism. In fact, however, the laws are not causal at all,
for it follows from the Bell Inequality[9] that quantum mechanics
contains law-governed statistical correlations that bear *no causal*
relation whatever to any earlier correlation. Not only are the later
events not determinate effects of the earlier ones, they are not even
probabilistic effects. So, that is one more reason for rejecting a
deterministic universe.

   In itself, the non-causal character of the laws should occasion no
surprise, since we are already familiar with laws of just that kind
e.g., the Conservation Laws. Forrest calls them *negative* laws.[10]

---

8 S. Kochen and E.P. Specker, 'The Problem of Hidden Variables in Quantum
  Mechanics', *Journal of Mathematics and Mechanics* 17 (1967), pp.59–87;
  G. Hellman, 'Einstein and Bell: Strengthening the Case of Microphysical
  Randomness', *Synthese* 53 (1982), pp.461–504.
9 J.S. Bell, 'On the Einstein Podolsky Rosen Paradox', *Physics* (1964),
  pp.196–200.
10 P. Forrest, *Quantum Metaphysics* (Oxford: Oxford University Press, 1988),
  p.97.

As distinct from *positive* laws, which tell us what does or is likely to cause what, the negative laws tell us nothing of the sort. On the contrary, they tell us merely the *constraints* that are placed on a system, the limited possibilities available within a system. Although different from either the causal or the historical models of explanation they are genuinely explanatory none the less, their explanatory role being to show that fewer possibilities are available than we may have thought.

As I said, there is nothing remarkable about negative laws *in se*. Nor would it be at all remarkable in the present instance for *some* of the laws in quantum mechanics to be negative ones. What does render it quite remarkable is that *all* of them are negative laws: not one of them is causal.[11] *Without causality, however, there can be no determinism*. None the less, there is nothing philosophically outrageous about this absence of causality, for

> we have no justification for insisting that the laws of nature be positive. Perhaps we have a metaphysical intuition that every change has a cause. But to convert that into an a priori argument for positive laws would require an extra premiss, namely that the physical sciences will serve to specify what causes what. And to assume that extra premiss a priori is to play Science Says.[12]

Thermodynamics presents itself as no less inimical to determinism than does quantum mechanics, and notably in regard to the behaviour of a system when forced into a far-from-equilibrium condition that threatens its structure. Under those conditions it approaches a critical moment – a bifurcation point – at which point the Nobel Laureate Prigogine has concluded that it is *inherently* impossible to predict the next state of the system: its future course is simply a matter of chance. Once the new course is embarked upon, determinism takes over again until the next bifurcation point is reached. Moreover, the role of chance is not restricted simply to *what* happens at the bifurcation point, but extends also to the question of just *when* that point will occur: that, too, is unpredictable even in principle.[13] So much, then, for condition (3.16). Of the findings of thermodynamics and those

11 ibid., p.144.
12 ibid., pp.144–5.
13 I. Prigogine and I. Stengers, *Order out of Chaos: Man's New Dialogue with Nature* (New York: Bantam, 1984).

of quantum mechanics, *either one* would have sufficed to show that the Universe was not inherently determinist. As it happens, both do so.

As for condition (3.17), the creation of matter or energy would be untenable on intrinsic grounds only if every change were to require a cause. As we have just seen, however, even at the macro level not all laws are causal, and at the level of quantum mechanics no law is causal. Consequently, not every change requires a cause; and that means that the coming to be of energy or matter from no prior source within the Universe remains intrinsically possible – not only logically possible but physically possible as well. Indeed, it is a respectable notion in science, having already been employed in cosmological theory by Hoyle and abandoned by him, not because of any problem inherent in the notion, but simply because the evidence seemed to favour a different hypothesis to account for the state of the Universe.

Not only can the possible creation of matter not be precluded on intrinsic grounds, it cannot be precluded on extrinsic grounds either since no state of affairs could preclude the creation of matter unless that event were dependent on already existing matter. There could be no such dependence, however, for the creation of matter is *ex hypothesi* the coming to be of matter or energy from *no* prior matter or energy. For these reasons, therefore, it is not impossible that Socrates should have developed from energy or matter which appeared from no prior matter or energy and which could not have been referred to at the time of the prediction, since at that time it would neither have existed nor have been able to be predicted. Thus, condition (3.17) is no more satisfied than is condition (3.16); and that is further reason for denying that Socrates could have been referred to before he existed.

I might express the conclusion of this section by adapting a comment from Ryle, and saying that the prediction of the birth of a son to the man and woman who came later to generate Socrates could, in principle, be as specific as you please. But one thing the forecaster could not do – logically and not merely epistemologically could not do. In his prediction he could not use with their normal force the term 'Socrates' or the pronoun 'he'.[14] At no time before Socrates existed could 'Socrates' have referred

14 G. Ryle, *Dilemmas* (Cambridge: Cambridge University Press, 1954), p.27.

to him:[15] as Prior once intimated, not even God could have done that.[16]

II SOCRATES WAS *INCONCEIVABLE* BEFORE EXISTING

The argument is simply as follows:

3.18 No concrete individual could have been referred to before it existed.

3.19 If no concrete individual could have been referred to before it existed, it could not have been conceived of before it existed.

3.20 Therefore, no concrete individual could have been conceived of before it existed.

The argument for the second premiss is entirely straightforward. For an individual to be conceivable, it must be possible to say at least something about it: that of which literally nothing could even in principle be said, and about which literally no proposition could even in principle be formed, would be inconceivable. But nothing could be said, nor any proposition be formed, about anything to which no reference was possible; and that is precisely the case with any concrete individual before it existed. So, no concrete individual could be conceived of before it existed.

As is shown in the Appendix to this chapter, the argument survives a battery of objections against both its premisses, some of the more persistent being illustrated by the following responses:

'But surely I can even now conceive of the 10,000th Mercedes to be produced after today.'

'But surely Socrates' mother would have conceived of Socrates a year before his birth, had she described him accurately enough.'

'But surely "the Smiths' first child" designates the baby to be born to the Smiths in a year from now.'

Against rejoinders of this kind the main point to be made will be simply that, although the descriptions in question are applicable to just one individual (i.e. are *uniquely* applicable), they nevertheless can offer no clues at all as to *which* one that individual may be. While predetermining that *precisely one* instance can satisfy them,

15 Various objections to this conclusion are discussed in the Appendix to this chapter.
16 A. Prior, 'Identifiable Individuals' in his *Papers on Time and Tense*.

they are quite incapable of predetermining the *precise one* it will be. In one world it might be one individual, in a different world it might be another; any such individual (though assuredly only one) would satisfy them.

Let me repeat that the thesis that concrete individuals could not be *conceived of* before they existed is decidedly not to be confused with the one that individuals could not be *described* before they existed. Rather, it does not even deny the possibility of the description being exhaustive in the sense of embracing, *per impossibile*, each one of the properties and relations that an individual might have when it did exist. It does deny, however, that conceiving of any such *description* entails conceiving of the *individual* so described. It thereby denies the Identity of Indiscernibles, and affirms that in principle the difference between individuals may indeed be indiscernible.[17] That is to say, it allows for cases in which not even God could specify a property, or a relation, or an item from any other ontological category which an individual (say, X) would have but all others would lack. He would be committed to saying that 'X=X and is not identical with W,Y,Z, etc.', without, however, being able to specify what the difference between them was. It is indeed essential to an individual that it be different from others; it is not essential to an individual that it be possible, even in principle, to specify in what the difference consists.

III THE CHALLENGE OF PLANTINGA'S HAECCEITISM

According to the foregoing arguments, the impossibility of conceiving of Socrates before he existed rests on the impossibility of referring to him before he existed. Obviously, the argument would be defeasible if the possibility of referring to Socrates were not a *necessary* condition of his being conceived of. If, for example, there were a necessary entity that was an essence of Socrates and of him alone, then the essence would be no less conceivable than any property is, and Socrates would be conceivable in terms of *it*. Moreover, being a necessary entity, it would have existed and have been conceivable before ever Socrates existed. Hence, Socrates too would have been conceivable before he existed. Now, as I mentioned earlier in the chapter, Plantinga thinks that there are indeed such necessary entities. They are what he calls

17 I use the term 'indiscernible' not in the narrow sense of 'unobservable' but in the broader sense of 'unspecifiable'.

'unexemplified haecceities', and it will be instructive to consider whether Socrates really could have been conceived of in terms of any such haecceity.

Plantinga's notion of an haecceity is somewhat idiosyncratic, being shared neither by Scotus nor by contemporaries like R.M. Adams.[18] As Plantinga understands it, an haecceity is an individual essence, which in his terminology means that it is both a necessary property of the individual in question and also one that no other individual could possess. As with any unexemplified property, an haecceity is said to exist and be conceivable before ever being exemplified in any individual. On this view, therefore, an individual essence of Socrates would both exist and be conceivable before being exemplified in Socrates. And if that individual essence could be conceived of before Socrates existed, then that would be reason enough for saying that Socrates himself was conceivable before he existed.

Naturally, all of this assumes that there really could be such properties as unexemplified haecceities, an assumption that has now to be tested. Plantinga's explanation of an haecceity is in terms of another property, called 'thisness'.

A thisness is the property, for some object x (some actually existing object x) of being that very object x.[19]

The thisness of Socrates is the property of *being Socrates*, and that property clearly would not have existed had Socrates not existed. According to Plantinga, however, there is a closely related property which *would* have existed even if Socrates had not, namely, whatever property it is that stands in the *is the thisness of* relation to Socrates. Had Socrates not existed, whatever it is that now stands in that relation to Socrates 'would have been an unexemplified essence that had essentially the property of being a thisness if exemplified'.[20] It 'could have existed even if Socrates hadn't. Under those conditions it would have been an unexemplified haecceity rather than a thisness; but it would have been none the worse for that.'[21] Moreover, it would have been

18 Cf. his 'Primitive Thisness and Primitive Identity', *Journal of Philosophy* 76 (1979), pp.5–26, and 'Actualism and Thisness', *Synthese* 49 (1981), pp.3–43.
19 In J.E. Tomberlin and P. Van Inwagen (eds), *Alvin Plantinga* (Dordrecht: Reidel, 1985), p.335.
20 ibid.
21 ibid., p.337.

conceivable; and, through conceiving of *it*, we could properly be said to conceive of Socrates even before he existed.

Since Plantinga agrees that Socrates could not have been *referred* to before he existed, the basis for his conceivability at that time could not have been a conception of haecceity A as 'the haecceity that could be exemplified in nothing but Socrates'; for, if Socrates could not then have been referred to at all, *a fortiori* he could not then have been referred to by a name. Even though he could not have been referred to, however, he would still have been conceivable before he existed provided that,

3.21 he were then conceivable under the rubric of 'the individual that will exemplify haecceity A', and

3.22 haecceity A were exemplifiable in no individual but the one in which it came later to be exemplified.

Now, it might seem that A was indeed exemplifiable in no individual but the one in which it came to be exemplified, for precisely that might seem to be the clear outcome of the following argument:

A is a thisness, if exemplified.

Therefore, as exemplified in Socrates, A would be the thisness of Socrates, i.e. it would be that in virtue of which Socrates is Socrates.

But that in virtue of which Socrates is Socrates could not be that in virtue of which Plato is Plato, or Aristotle is Aristotle, etc.

Therefore, A could not have been exemplified in Plato, Aristotle, etc.

Therefore, A could have been exemplified in nothing but Socrates, i.e. in nothing but the individual in which it came to be exemplified.

The question now to be asked is whether haecceity A really could be the kind of entity required for this sort of argument to succeed; and the immediate task is to determine what conditions A would have to satisfy to ensure that the argument did succeed.

Necessary conditions to be satisfied by haecceity A

The first condition is a negative one, namely, that A could not be a universal property, not even one that was so restricted as to be exemplifiable only exactly once. Although being the first person on the moon is a universal property that is exemplifiable exactly once, that does not entail its having been exemplifiable in no individual but the one in which it was exemplified – in Neil rather than in Margaret, Mary, or Tom. It was irrelevant which individual came to exemplify it, provided only that the individual was the first person on the Moon. In regard to this kind of property, therefore, one could not argue as has been argued in regard to haecceity A, that it could have been exemplified in nothing but the individual in which it came to be exemplified.

Since A could not be a universal property, presumably it would be singular. In that case, we need to know whether it is singular *in se* or *ab alio*. That is to say, is it singular in itself or singular in virtue of the individual in which it is exemplified, as are property instances of the kind sometimes thought to be favoured by Aristotle and Aquinas? On this latter view, even if there were no difference in degree between Socrates' instance of wisdom and Plato's instance, the wisdom of Socrates would nevertheless be distinguished from the wisdom of Plato simply in virtue of being Socrates' rather than Plato's: the instances would be particularized by the individual in which they were exemplified. For haecceities, however, the fact that they are supposed to individuate an individual (rather than vice versa) precludes their being singular properties of the Aristotelian kind, i.e. singular *ab alio*. They could thus only be singular *in se*, and at least in that particular respect would be like the tropes proposed by D.C. Williams[22] or the singular properties suggested by G.F. Stout.[23]

Since A's being singular *in se* is a necessary condition for the soundness of the foregoing argument and since two other necessary conditions are already evident in that argument, there are at least three conditions A must satisfy:

3.23   that it be a property which is singular *in se*.
3.24   that it be exemplifiable only in Socrates.
3.25   that it be that in virtue of which Socrates is Socrates and not any other individual.

22 D.C. Williams, 'On the Elements of Being I & II', *The Review of Metaphysics* 7 (1953-4), pp.13–18 and 171–92. Cf. also K. Campbell, *Abstract Particulars* (Oxford: Blackwell, 1990); K. Campbell, 'The Metaphysic of Abstract Particulars', *Midwest Studies in Philosophy* 6 (1981), pp.477–88.
23 G.F. Stout, *Studies in Philosophy and Psychology* (London: Macmillan, 1930), p.386

The difficulty is to reconcile (3.23) with (3.24) and (3.25) for, as I shall now explain, there are serious problems about the ability of a property that is singular *in se* to satisfy either of the other two conditions. In regard to (3.24), the problem is to know what Plantinga means by 'exemplification'. For example, Trope Theory and Aristotelian theory, both of which do recognize singular properties (though of different kinds), rightly distinguish two relations had by property instances: one is the relation between the instance and the *universal* which it exemplifies, and the other is the relation between the instance and the *individual* in which the exemplification occurs. Thus, the universal property of wisdom (W) could be exemplified *by* an instance w_1, and this exemplifying instance would occur *in* the individual O to which it belonged. That is to say, w_1 would be the terminus of two relations, one being with W and the other with O: it would exemplify W, but would be exemplified *in* O.[24]

Naturally, there is no room for such a distinction in theories like Russell's, Goodman's, and Castañeda's; for, by not recognizing singular properties, they *ipso facto* preclude any relation between singular ones and universal ones. However, Plantinga's omission of the distinction cannot be explained on that score, since he does recognize at least one singular property (haecceities). The first thing we need to know about his use of 'exemplification', therefore, is whether it is being employed in either of the foregoing two senses or, perhaps, in some other sense. We might surmise that

---

24 In Aristotle a distinction is drawn between 'being said of something as subject' and 'being in something as subject'. Cf. J.L. Ackrill, *Aristotle's Categories and De Interpretatione* (Oxford: Oxford University Press, 1974), p.74; R.E. Allen, 'Individual Properties in Aristotle's Categories', *Phronesis* 14 (1969), pp.31–9; G.E.M. Anscombe and P.T. Geach, *Three Philosophers* (Oxford: Blackwell, 1969), pp.8–10, 17; H. Granger, 'A Defense of the Traditional Position concerning Aristotle's Non-substantial Particulars', *Canadian Journal of Philosophy* 10 (1980), pp.593–606. Ackrill's interpretation is contested by G.E.L. Owens, 'Inherence', *Phronesis* 10 (1965), pp.97–105; M. Frede, *Essays in Ancient Philosophy* (Oxford: Oxford University Press, 1987), chapter 4. R. Dancy, in 'On some of Aristotle's First Thoughts about Substances', *Philosophical Review* 84 (1975), p.354, is 'inclined to adopt Owens's view'.

In the case of trope theory, an ordinary individual (O) is explained by Williams as being a *concurrence sum* of tropes, e.g. $a_1+b_1+c_1+ \ldots w_1$, where w_1 is a wisdom trope. The universal property Wisdom (W) is the set of all wisdom tropes, e.g. $\{w_1, w_2, w_3, \ldots w_n\}$. To say that w_1 is exemplified *in* O would be to say that it is part of the concurrence sum that is O. To say that W is exemplified by w_1 would be to say that w_1 is a member of the set that is W. Cf. D.C. Williams, 'On the Elements of Being, Part I', *Review of Metaphysics* 7 (1953–4), pp.1–18.

he is using it in the sense of 'exemplification *in*'; but, even if that were correct, we should still need to know what he means by 'in'. In Trope Theory it means 'being a member of a bundle of tropes', that bundle having the structure of a concurrence sum. Even those bundle theories which employ only universal properties are no less explicit about the meaning of 'exemplification *in*', which indeed is the sole sense of 'exemplification' that they employ. What it means for Plantinga, however, remains obscure.

While ever the account of an haecceity's exemplification remains so unclear and programmatic it would be a leap in the dark, or at least in the gloom, to accept that haecceities really could be exemplified in anything at all. But that is by no means the main problem; for, even with the inadequate account of it that we do have, there are two further difficulties, the first of which is the conflict between (3.26) and (3.27) below.

3.26 On the one hand, if A were exemplifiable solely in the individual in which it would be exemplified, A *would* have to be *co*-exemplifiable solely with whatever kinds of universal qualitative properties (say, F,G,H) were appropriate to the individual (viz. Socrates) that we now know to be human.

3.27 On the other hand, haecceity A would *not* have to be co-exemplifiable solely with F, G, H rather than with any other group of properties; for the exemplification of F,G,H neither entails nor is entailed by the exemplification of haecceity A.

Although (3.26) is straightforward enough, (3.27) requires some explanation. It has to be noted that the exemplification of haecceity A could have been entailed by the joint exemplification of F, G, H only if those three properties were like A in being able to occur conjointly in no individual other than the one in which they did occur. But that cannot be accepted by Plantinga, since it would presuppose the truth of the Identity of Indiscernibles which he rightly rejects. What, then, of the reverse entailment: could the exemplification of A (which is a non-qualitative property) entail the exemplification of F, G, H which are qualitative properties? There are two cases to be considered, depending on whether A is to be taken simply as a *this* rather than as a *this such-and-such*.

Now, to say that A was simply a *this* would be to say two things:

3.28 There is no property which A has *essentially*.
3.29 It is not essential to A that it have any properties at all, not even non-essential ones.

The reason for (3.29) is that its denial would be a denial of (3.28) also, since it would mean that it *was* essential to A that it have some non-essential property, viz. the property of having at least one non-essential property. Hence, if A were simply a *this*, there could be no general property Q such that *necessarily* whatever had A had Q; otherwise, A would have one essential property, viz. the property of *being, if exemplified, co-exemplified with* Q. That is to say, there are no general properties F, G, H such that the exemplification of an A that was a *this* would entail the exemplification of F, G, H. Nor, as was noted earlier, does the reverse entailment hold.

It now remains to be asked whether either of these entailments would hold if A were not a *this* but were a *this such-and-such*. Certainly, co-exemplification of F, G, H would still not entail the exemplification of A. In regard to the reverse entailment, however, the answer is not immediately clear. Admittedly, the existence of a this such-and-such can entail the existence of *some* qualities, e.g. the existence of this (instance of) blue would entail the existence of this (instance of) extension, and the existence of this giraffe would entail the existence of whatever properties were appropriate to a giraffe. What we need to know, however, is whether A could be a this such-and-such, the existence of which would entail the existence of properties appropriate to a human being. Obviously, that would be trivially the case if the this such-and-such were this man, e.g. Socrates. But, even apart from its triviality, that is just no help since this man is a concrete entity whereas A is supposed to be abstract.

This *humanity* might be a possible candidate, for humanity is certainly abstract. 'This humanity', however, might be construed in two ways, similar to two ways of understanding 'this blue', which might mean either 'this shade of blue' or 'this instance of blue', the former being abstract and the latter concrete. Similarly, 'this humanity' might mean 'this kind of humanity (e.g. a particular *race*)' or 'this instance of humanity (i.e. a particular *individual*)'. The latter is concrete, and hence could not be an haecceity. While the former is abstract, it too could not be an haecceity because, if it individuated anything, it would individuate races, not concrete individuals. The conclusion to be drawn is that, although there are some cases in which a *this such-and-such* would entail the exemplification of properties peculiar to a man, in none of them could the *this such-and-such* be an haecceity. So, having noted earlier that the exemplification of F, G, H could not entail the exemplification of A, it has now emerged that the reverse entailment would not hold either, not even if A were a *this such-and-such*.

Since exemplification of A neither entails nor is entailed by exemplification of F, G, H, there is apparently no restriction on the qualitative properties with which A could be co-exemplified. Irrespective of whether A were merely a *this* or a *this such-and-such*, the disconcerting consequence is that Socrates (i.e. the entity exemplifying A) could well have been a poached egg, as Armstrong[25] once conceded in regard to his 'thin' particulars, and as is no less true in regard to an haecceity. Hence, if 'Socrates' were the name of any individual that exemplified A, then 'Socrates' could have referred to a man, a rhinoceros, or a poached egg. And if we follow Frege in accepting that a proper name must have an associated criterion of identity, we should then have to say that the man, the rhinoceros, and the poached egg were three different individuals. And that is to say that A could have been exemplified not simply in the individual in which it was exemplified but in at least two other individuals, thereby breaching condition (3.25).

As I said, there is a second objection to A's satisfying condition (3.25). Let us suppose haecceities H_1 and H_2 to have been exemplified in individuals O_1 and O_2. One role of H_1 is to differentiate O_1 from O_2 and from all other individuals; mutatis mutandis, the same can be said for the role of H_2. However, since H_1 differs from H_2, we are now entitled to ask just what it is that differentiates *them*. Being themselves non-qualitative, their ultimate differentiator could obviously not be a qualitative one unless the Identity of Indiscernibles were true, which it isn't. So, what could their non-qualitative differentiator be? Since haecceities are non-qualitative differentiators, it might seem natural to appeal to haecceities of haecceities (second-level haecceities) as providing the required difference. This, of course, would lead to the need for third-level haecceities to differentiate the second-level ones,

25 In public discussion at a session of the Australasian Association of Philosophy, Sydney, 1990.

and so on *ad infinitum*. A more attractive alternative would be to block off the infinite regress by treating haecceities as primitive, meaning thereby that they would differ from each other not in virtue of anything else (e.g. a second-level haecceity) but simply in virtue of their being the kinds of entity that they are.

The problem with allowing haecceities to be self-differentiating is that it is tantamount to admitting that they are entirely superfluous. Their *raison d'être* was to differentiate one individual from another. If, however, in order to account for the difference between individuals, it were acceptable to say that haecceities are themselves self-differentiating, it should be equally acceptable to say that individuals are themselves self-differentiating, thus eliminating the need for any haecceities at all. Individuals would be primitive, differing from each other not in virtue of any haecceities but simply in virtue of their being individuals. The previous objection to the possibility of A's satisfying (3.25) queried A's ability to perform its putative role. The present objection to (3.25) is even more basic, since it queries not simply whether A can fulfil a certain role, but whether there is any role for it to fulfil.

It might be thought that the foregoing objection proves too much. Since thisnesses are exemplified haecceities, then by rendering haecceities superfluous, the objection would surely render thisnesses superfluous also. But, since thisnesses are not superfluous, the objection must fail. To detect the fallacy in this proposal it should be recalled that recognition of thisnesses is a consequence of denying the Identity of Indiscernibles by arguing that there is more to an individual than suchnesses.[26] From that conclusion, however, it does not follow that the 'something more' (thisness) can be provided only by some non-qualitative property (haecceity). On the contrary, it could equally well be provided by the individual itself, with it being both non-qualitative (albeit endowed with qualities) and self-differentiating.[27] Since either alternative is compatible with recognition of thisnesses, there is no logical compulsion to opt for haecceities, and thus no compulsion either to understand the property of *being Socrates* as A-standing-in-the-*is-the-thisness-of*-relation-to-Socrates. Indeed, if the objections to condition (3.25) are valid, that is precisely how it cannot be

---

26 Cf. R.M. Adams, 'Primitive Thisness and Primitive Identity', *Journal of Philosophy* 76 (1979), pp.5–26.
27 Having been held by Aristotle, the view that individuals are non-qualitative (though not bare) and self-differentiating is by no means novel.

understood. That, however, is certainly not to reject the notion of thisness; it is merely to reject its being understood in terms of A's being primitive, rather than in terms of Socrates' being primitive. If it is Socrates (rather than A) which is primitive, his thisness is simply the property of being Socrates (or of being identical with Socrates). To take individuals as self-differentiating is therefore not to reject the notion of thisness but only to recognize haecceities as the ontological excess that they are.

To sum up: at first sight it might have seemed plausible to suggest that Plantingian haecceities undermine my earlier argument by offering a means of the conceiving of individuals even when they could not yet be referred to. Indeed, the suggestion would have been entirely correct – had only an haecceity been exemplifiable in nothing but the individual in which it was exemplified. However, haecceity A could have been so exemplified only if the aforementioned condition (3.23) had been reconcilable with (3.24) and/or (3.25). An open verdict had to be returned in regard to (3.24). As to (3.25), however, it proved to be irreconcilable with (3.23), once it became clear not only that there was no role to be fulfilled by haecceities but that, even if there were a role, haecceities would be unable to fulfil it. Consequently, Plantingian haecceities certainly could not be entities that are exemplifiable in nothing but the individual in which they come to be exemplified. For just that reason they offer no means for the conceiving of individuals before they existed, and hence pose no threat to our original conclusion that no individual could be conceived of before it existed.

IV THE CHALLENGE OF UNIVERSALISM

Universalism challenges our original conclusion no less than does haecceitism, though on different grounds. It is the view that sentences like 'He believes that that butterfly is sick' would express intrinsically or essentially the same thought quite irrespective of whether 'that butterfly' referred to butterflies a, or b, or c or even if, as in the case of an hallucination, it referred to no real butterfly at all.[28] The first three cases would be distinguished purely by there being an external relation between the one thought and either a,

28 Cf. S. Blackburn, *Spreading the Word* (Oxford: Oxford University Press, 1984); S. Blackburn, 'Invited Introduction: Finding Psychology', *Philosophical Quarterly* 36 (1986), pp.111–22; S. Blackburn, 'Thoughts and Things', *Proceedings of the Aristotelian Society*, supp. vol. 53 (1979), pp.23–41, also P. Carruthers, 'Russellian Thoughts', *Mind* 96 (1987), p.28, n.15.

b, or *c* respectively – a *right* relation (RR), as Blackburn calls it. The thought in the hallucination case would be distinguished, of course, simply by the lack of any RR at all. On the universalist view, it would be the one thought which could occur in all possible worlds, and in that sense might be called 'universal'.[29] The identity of such a thought would obviously be independent of the object, if any, to which it might have an RR, and for just that reason it is also called 'identity-independent' or 'existence-independent'.

According to universalism, the content of a singular thought is unaffected by whether there exists or does not exist any individual to which it has a 'right relation': in both cases its content would be the same. Since the same thought could exist irrespective of there being any individual to which it had a 'right relation', the conclusion must be that the notion of an individual being employed before an individual existed would be no different from that employed after the individual existed. If that were true, our earlier conclusion would have to be abandoned.

To present and to refute the arguments for universalism would require an impossibly long digression. I shall therefore do little more than list both some of the main considerations supposedly favouring it and my reasons for finding them rather less than compelling. The considerations offered for universalism seem to be of four kinds:

3.30 From sameness of actions may be inferred sameness of thoughts governing those actions. But the actions directed towards an existing individual may be the same as one directed towards no individual at all. *Ergo*, universalism.[30]

3.31 From sameness of experiences (e.g. in doppelgänger cases) may be inferred sameness of thoughts generated by those experiences. But different objects can be responsible for the same experiences. *Ergo*, universalism.[31]

---

29 Blackburn (*Spreading the Word*) seems to think that the thought would be universal also in the sense of being general rather than singular, though this view is not shared by Carruthers who insists that 'demonstrative thoughts are genuinely singular, in that their content is not equivalent . . . to the content of any descriptive thought'. (Cf. P. Carruthers, 'Russellian Thoughts', p.28, n.15.)

30 Cf. H. Noonan, 'Russellian Thoughts and Methodological Solipsism', in J. Butterfield (ed.), *Language, Mind and Logic* (Cambridge: Cambridge University Press, 1986), pp.69–70; P. Carruthers, 'Russellian Thoughts', p.21.

31 S. Blackburn, *Spreading the Word*, chapter 9.

3.32 An object encountered on different occasions may not be recognized as the same object, even though it may have undergone no changes whatever from one occasion to the other. *Ergo*, universalism.[32]

3.33 Co-referential singular terms cannot be substituted *salva veritate* within that-clauses. *Ergo*, universalism.[33]

Consideration (3.30) would succeed only if the actions in question had necessarily to be governed by singular thoughts, whereas the fact is that they could equally be governed by general thoughts. So, the conclusion drawn from (3.30) is a *non sequitur*. Considerations (3.31), (3.32), and (3.33) all suffer from a failure to distinguish individuation from discernible differentiation, and labour under the misconception that to apprehend an individual *qua* individual is to apprehend it as *discernibly* different from every other individual. It is not. Rather, it suffices simply that the individual be apprehended as non-instantiable. Non-instantiability, however, entails only that an individual will be different from every other individual, but not that it will be *discernibly* different, i.e. not that it will be possible even in principle to specify just what the difference is. Consequently, there is no reason to expect that experiences of doppelgängers should generate the same thoughts, nor that an individual should be recognized as the same when encountered on two occasions between which it remained unchanged, nor that an individual presented under one mode of presentation should be *recognizably* the same when presented under a different mode.

Although much more could be said both in exposition and criticism of universalism, it must suffice to have mentioned both how it would purport to challenge our earlier conclusion that Fido would be inconceivable before he existed, and to have given at least some indication of why this challenge is no more successful than that of haecceitism.

V CONCLUSION

One consequence of Fido's being inconceivable before he existed is that he cannot be conceived of except as existing or as having existed, i.e. as completing or as having completed his existence

32 S. Blackburn, 'Invited Introduction: Finding Psychology', p.119.
33 S. Blackburn, *Spreading the Word*, chapter 9.

To conceive of his existence, however, is to conceive of an instance of existence that could occur only in Fido's existing; and that is to say that Fido's existence could be conceived of only in terms of Fido's existing. Now, that in turn means that even Fido could be conceived of only in terms of his existing, and that is directly at odds with his status as a *constituent* of his existing. So, already there are signs that the conclusion of the present chapter may be difficult to reconcile with those of chapter 2. There would be such a difficulty, however, only if the kind of conclusions inferred in chapter 2 from the truth of 'Fido is black' could be inferred also from the truth of 'Fido exists'. And whether that is possible depends on whether 'Fido exists' is like 'Fido is black' in being an atomic proposition, i.e. whether the predicate in 'Fido exists' is a first-level one. That is the question to be discussed in the next chapter.

Chapter 4

Existence is a *real* property

In this chapter I shall be be challenging and rejecting two familiar views, one being that '___ exists' is not a first-level predicate, and the other being that existence is not even a first-level property of any kind let alone a real one rather than a Cambridge one. Before embarking on these themes, however, I shall be rebutting the widely-held views that to admit existence as a property of individuals is to be led inevitably into rank absurdity, whilst to admit '___ exists' as a first-level predicate is to become enmeshed in an insoluble paradox generated by negative existential propositions.

Prominent among those convinced of the absurdity of regarding existence as a property of individuals, Hume mistakenly maintained that the idea of existence 'when conjoined with the idea of any object makes no addition to it'.[1] Charitably interpreted, however, he might be taken to be saying that if existence were a property of things, it would be one that made absolutely no difference to them. Just that point has been made more colourfully by David Londey in inviting us to 'reflect on the absurdity of a sheep-farmer who daily inspected his flock with the aim of sorting the existing sheep from the non-existent ones – searching for the stigmata of existence'.[2] As to the paradox generated by negative existential propositions, it is said to arise in this way. If '___ exists' is a predicate, then its negation should be a predicate also. But if '___ does (do) not exist' is a predicate, then in 'Dragons do not exist' it is predicated of dragons. But it can be predicated of dragons only if they exist. And similarly for all negative existential propositions – paradoxically, if it is to be

1 D. Hume, *A Treatise of Human Nature*, book I, part II, section VI.
2 D.G. Londey, 'Existence', *Philosophia Arhusiensis* 1 (1970), p.3.

predicated at all, '____ does (do) not exist' can be predicated only of what *does* exist.

Many would say that such difficulties are entirely to be expected so long as we are so obtuse as to treat '____ exists' in singular existential propositions as a first-level predicate, when it is nothing of the sort. If only we were to accept it as a second-level predicate, we should remove perhaps the strongest ground for regarding existence as a property of individuals. Thus, in one move we should avoid putative paradox and absurdity alike. Moreover, singular existential propositions would be treated in the same way as general ones, and thus there would be no need for multiple senses of '____ exists'. Indeed, '____ exists' itself would be made redundant, being replaced by the more general apparatus of quantifiers and identity, as Russell, Quine, and Hintikka each in their various ways have tried to do. And, finally, there would be no need to recognize, as did the early Russell, entities that subsist in addition to those which exist. Thus, the theory would seem not only to solve the problem, but to do so with an economy that is part of its appeal.

Despite this superficial appeal, the theory has to be rejected for it 'solves' problems only by introducing some of its own, as is explained in the Appendix to this chapter. I shall be arguing both that '____ exists' can be predicated of individuals (section I) and that existence is a real property of individuals rather than a merely Cambridge one (section III). I shall be arguing too (in section II) that the alleged absurdities and paradoxes are generated not by either of these conclusions, but by the mistaken assumption that, '____ exists' could not stand for a real property without '____ does not exist' doing so as well.

I '____ EXISTS' AS A FIRST-LEVEL PREDICATE

The argument for this view goes as follows;

> What can be predicated of a kind differs absolutely from what can be predicated of an individual.
> But '____ exists' is predicated both of individuals and of kinds.
> Therefore, '____ exists' has two senses, one as predicated of individuals, the other as predicated of kinds.

Although there are two ways in which a predicate might be conceived of as being applicable to both kinds and individuals, it is not difficult to show that neither is tenable. One way would be for a second-level predicate to be said of both individuals and kinds, the other for a first-level predicate to be said of them. In regard to the first alternative, we must be clear as to precisely what kind of expression can be said of what the first-level predicate refers to (e.g. a kind, or Fregean concept). If we consider the proposition '$(\exists x)(x$ is $F)$', the first level predicable is '___ is F.' The second-level predicate attached to it is, however, not simply '$(\exists x)$', but '$(\exists x)(x$___$)$'. If we now ask whether the second-level predicate could equally well be attached not only to a first-level predicable but to a proper name, it is clear that it could not. The bound variable, which filled the gap in '___ is F', has nowhere to go when '___ is F' is replaced by a proper name. The expression that results from such a combination is therefore not even a closed sentence. Nor does anything better come of the second alternative mentioned above. If '___ is F' and '___ is G' are two first-level predicables, then the result of combining them would be '(___ is G) is F' or '(___ is F) is G'. Once again, neither combination would be even a closed sentence, as the gap would be filled by neither a bound variable nor by a proper name. Thus, it follows that no predicate, whether of first-level or second-level, can be said *both* of individuals and of kinds. And that establishes the major premiss.

The minor premiss can be proved in two ways – either by contrasting singular existential propositions with one kind of general existential proposition, or by contrasting two kinds of general existential proposition. As an example of a singular proposition in which '___ exists' is predicated of an individual, one might be tempted to suggest 'Socrates exists', were it not for oft-voiced protests of its not being 'usable outside philosophy'.[3] Rather than resist that claim, therefore, the example I propose is one that unquestionably *is* usable outside philosophy, viz. 'Socrates no longer exists'.[4] This the protesters would attempt to dismiss on another score, claiming that if '___ exists' were a first-level predicate then 'Socrates no longer exists' would generate precisely

3 C.J.F. Williams, *What is Existence?* (Oxford: Oxford University Press, 1981), p.79.
4 It might be objected that this means simply 'Socrates is no longer alive'. However, if 'exists' were synonymous with 'is alive', we should be entitled to say 'The original St Paul's is no longer alive'.

those paradoxes and absurdities mentioned above. As we shall see, their claim cannot be sustained, since it assumes that if existence is a real property then so too must *non*-existence be a real property, an assumption against which I shall argue at length in section II, and so shall not anticipate the argument here.

That, however, is not the only objection to 'Socrates no longer exists' as an example of a first-level use of '____ exists; for it is claimed that 'There is such a person as Socrates who no longer has the property of existing' is absurd, no less absurd, so it is said, than 'There is such a substance as phlogiston which lacks the (timeless) property of existing'. The latter is indeed absurd, for it is saying that there both exists and does not exist such a substance as phlogiston. However, the parallel with the proposition about Socrates is merely superficial; for whereas the former employs only the second-level sense of '____ exists', the latter employs both first- and second-level senses. Hence, it cannot be accused of claiming, absurdly, that there both exists and does not exist such a person as Socrates. It is saying, rather, that there is such a person as Socrates, and that that person does not exist (any longer); and, so, it is using 'is' in the second-level sense in the first clause, but 'exist' in the first-level sense in the second clause.

Not only is 'There is such a person as Socrates, who no longer has the property of existing' not absurd in the sense of being self-contradictory, it is not even absurd in the sense of being paradoxical. It is true that, if 'Socrates no longer exists' predicates '____ does not exist' of Socrates, we seem bound to allow that a property (viz. non-existence) can be acquired when there is no subject to acquire it; and that has all the appearance of paradox. For the appearance to have any substance, however, non-existence would have to be a *real* property. It need not be paradoxical at all if non-existence is only a Cambridge property like that of something's rising in price, or becoming famous; and if anything is a Cambridge property, it would have to be non-existence. So, the objection lapses.

Turning now to the second-level uses of '____ exists', they are both numerous and non-controversial. 'Men exist' is a case in point, for it may often be rendered as '$(\exists x)(x$ is a man)', thus showing it not to be about any individual but, rather, about the property *being a man*; for it says that being a man is instantiated at least once. Hence, 'Socrates no longer exists' and 'Men exist' provide the evidence necessary for our minor premiss that '____

exists' is predicable both of individuals and of kinds; for the only way of eliminating the difference between them is to reparse 'Socrates' as a predicable, a move which is discredited in part 1 of the Appendix to this chapter.

There is, however, a second way of proving the minor premiss, and this even without recourse to any *singular* existential propositions. It can be done by showing that not even all general existential propositions are about kinds, but that some are about individuals. As an example of the two kinds of general existential proposition, consider the occurrences of 'elephants exist' below;

4.1 'Elephants exist, but mermaids do not.'
4.2 'Elephants exist, but dinosaurs do not.'

In (4.1), '____ exists' is being said of the property of being an elephant, not about individual elephants, whereas in (4.2) it is being said of individual elephants, not about the property of being an elephant.

The foregoing claim can readily be substantiated. Since, in (4.1), 'Elephants exist' is being contrasted with 'Mermaids do not', the sense in which 'elephants' is being used will be the same as that in which 'mermaids' is being used. Now, 'Mermaids do not exist' makes sense only if it means that all predications of the form '*x* is a mermaid' are false. And it cannot mean that any proper name which turns '*x* is a mermaid' into a true statement will turn '*x* does not exist' into a true one, the simple reason being that there are no non-fictional proper names available for substitution in '*x* is a mermaid'. Hence, 'mermaids' is being used to refer to the property of being a mermaid, not to individual mermaids. Thus, 'elephants' in the accompanying clause must refer to the property of being an elephant. One might try to escape that conclusion by suggesting that a fictional name might well be substituted for '*x*', as of course it might. That, however, would do nothing to alter our conclusion since fictional individuals are not concrete individuals any more than rocking horses are horses. So, there are no grounds for saying that non-fictional proper names can be substituted in '*x* is a mermaid', and so no grounds for saying that 'mermaids do not exist' can be equally about kinds or about concrete individuals.

In (4.2), on the contrary, neither do 'elephants' refer to the property of being an elephant nor 'dinosaurs' to the property of being a dinosaur. If they did, the proposition would not only be false, but the 'but' would be quite misleading since there would be no point of contrast between the first and second clauses. The only way to retain that contrast is for 'elephants' and 'dinosaurs' to refer to individuals. So, in (4.2), 'Elephants exist' is a general existential proposition that is about individuals, as contrasted with the same clause in (4.1) which is not about individual elephants but merely about the property of being an elephant.

Thus the minor premiss – that '____ exists' is predicable of both kinds and of individuals – has been vindicated a second time. From it and the major it follows that '____ exists' has two senses, one as predicable of individuals, the other as predicable of kinds, and which have been called by Geach the *actuality* and *there-is* senses respectively.[5] Hence the fallacy in 'Existence is not a predicate', a dictum which would allow the 'there-is' sense, while precluding the actuality sense. It is of course the actuality sense in which we are interested, and about it there are two further things we need to know. One is whether the property correlative to it (viz. existence) is irreducible to other properties, a question which is answered in the affirmative in part 2 of the Appendix to this chapter. The other is whether it is a real, rather than a merely Cambridge property, and that will be addressed in section III of this chapter, i.e. after discussing what underlies such persistent opposition to '____ exists' being a first-level predicate.

II BASIC FLAW IN DENIAL OF FIRST-LEVEL VIEW

Looking afresh at the paradoxes and absurdities allegedly generated by accepting '____ exists' as a first-level predicate, we might note that they stem not from allowing existence to be a property, but from allowing non-existence to be one. Only by thinking that non-existence was some kind of real property would any sheep-farmer be led to the absurdity of inspecting his flock 'with the aim of sorting the existing sheep from the *non*-existent ones'. Only if non-existence were a real property would it seem paradoxical that '____ does not exist' could be true of Socrates only after there was any Socrates for it to be true of. Only if non-existence were a real property could 'Socrates no longer exists' imply that Socrates had suffered some posthumous loss.

5 P.T. Geach, 'What Actually Exists', *Proceedings of the Aristotelian Society*, supp. vol. 43 (1968), pp.7–16, especially pp.7–8.

Considered thus, therefore, it might seem strange that the blame
has been laid on treating existence as a real property of individuals,
when it should surely have been laid on treating non-existence
as one. Why deny that existence is a real property, when it was
necessary only to deny that non-existence was one?

Perhaps the answer lies in the mistaken belief that the two
denials are inseparable, and so there could be no denying non-
existence to be a real property of individuals without denying
existence to be one also. After all, if properties are what predicates
stand for, how could it be said that '____ exists' stood for a real
property, but that '____ does not exist' did not? If we accept
existence as a real property, are we not bound also to accept
non-existence as one? Clearly, these suggestions rest on two
assumptions that need now to be tested:

4.3 that 'Socrates does not exist' contains a negative existential
    predicate.
4.4 that a negative existential predicate stands for a real prop-
    erty.

In regard to (4.3), although '____ does not exist' is a grammatical
predicate in 'Socrates does not exist', it does not follow that it
must also be a logical one. We need to recognize the possibility of
construing the proposition as having the logical form of 'It is not
the case that (Socrates exists)'. In that case, what is predicated
(though not asserted) of Socrates would be simply '____ exists'
(and not '____ does not exist'); and what would be asserted is
that it is not the case that Socrates exists. On such an analysis
of singular negative existential propositions, '____ does not exist'
need not be recognized as a predicate, and nor therefore need
non-existence be recognized as a property of any kind, whether
real or Cambridge.

The distinction being invoked above is one between internal or
predicate negation on the one hand and external or propositional
negation on the other. The difference between them has sometimes
been thought to be that 'Socrates (does not exist)' says something
about an individual (Socrates), whereas 'It is not the case that
(Socrates exists)' says something about a proposition, namely, that
the proposition 'Socrates exists' is false.[6] In neither case, however,
is anything said about a proposition. On the contrary, in both cases

6 C.J.F. Williams, *What is Existence?*, p.124.

something is said about an individual, namely, Socrates; the cases differ only in what they say about him. The former says that non-existence is had by Socrates; the latter denies that existence is had by Socrates.[7]

The distinction between internal and external negation in this context has sometimes been dismissed as 'a distinction without a difference'. Consider, however, the example '*a* is not moral' which may mean either of two things. It may mean that *a* has the 'property' of being non-moral; alternatively, it may simply be denying that *a* has the 'property' of being moral. Internal negation ('*a* (is not moral)') is being used in the first case, but external negation ('It is not the case that (*a* is moral)') in the second. If, therefore, the distinction between internal and external negation were one without a difference, those two renderings should mean the same. Yet, that is just what they do not mean; for the first is to be taken as '*a* is immoral', but the second as the quite different '*a* is either immoral or amoral'. The distinction seems therefore to be a substantive one.

If the distinction is a substantive one, it is not a matter of indifference whether 'Socrates does not exist' is rendered as '(Socrates) does not exist' or as 'It is not the case that (Socrates exists)'. Because it is the former but not the latter that gives rise to problems, the latter is clearly to be chosen. In that case, 'Socrates does not exist' would not contain '____ does not exist' as a logical predicate; and so we could recognize existence as a real property without the embarrassment of having to recognize non-existence as well. One might have thought that even those who admit only the rendering in terms of external negation (and deny any difference here between it and internal negation) would be able to accept this conclusion.

There is, none the less, a further objection that might be raised for, even if '____ does not exist' has no logical role in 'Socrates does not exist', it must surely be admitted that 'It is not the case that ____ exists' does have such a role, and that it is indeed a negative predicate. Since it is a negative predicate, and since properties are what predicates stand for, does not this mean that, wriggle as we might, we are unavoidably committed to the occurrence

---

7 Of course, if it is denied that existence is had by Socrates, it will *follow* that the proposition 'Socrates exists' is false. That, however, no more entitles us to say that the implicans is *about* the implicandum than conversely.

of some negative existential property? If so, the escape from the absurdities and paradoxes will have proved to have been entirely illusory.

It can of course hardly be denied that by removing the name 'Socrates' from 'It is not the case that (Socrates exists)' we obtain the negative predicate 'It is not the case that ____ exists'. However, it should now be clear that the property for which it stands cannot be a real one. Why? Because the predicate has no more part in the constructional history of 'It is not the case that (Socrates exists)' than had the predicate 'If anyone hits ____, he is foolhardy' in the constructional history of 'If anyone hits Fido, he is foolhardy' discussed in chapter 2. Consequently, if 'it is not the case that ____ exists' were to stand for any property of non-existence, that property could not be a real one, but only a Cambridge one. Now, paradox could not arise simply from non-existence being a property, but only from its being either a real one, or being among such Cambridge ones (if any) whose acquisition is conditional upon their subject of attribution existing at that time. Being a Cambridge property that requires no such pre-condition, non-existence belongs to neither class; and hence its attribution to a deceased Socrates generates no paradox whatever. So much for considering 'Socrates does not exist' as being negated externally.

The paradox can be shown not to arise even if the negation in 'Socrates does not exist' were to be *internal* rather than external. Of course, it is true that a predicate can be obtained by removing 'Socrates' from the proposition, though this time it will not be 'it is not the case that ____ exists,' but simply '____ does not exist.' The question is whether that predicate stands for a real rather than a Cambridge property; and the first thing is to decide whether it forms part of the sentence's constructional history, which is as follows.

4.5 Remove the proper name from an arbitrary sentence, 'Caesar exists', to obtain the predicable '____ exists.'

4.6 Negate this predicable to form '____ does not exist.'

4.7 Insert 'Socrates' in the gap in '____ does not exist' to form '(Socrates)(does not exist)'.

Since '____ does not exist' *does* form part of this constructional history, we as yet have no licence to preclude the property for which it stands from being a real one.

To settle that question we need some criterion for deciding

when individual *a* could lack some real property *F* only by having another real property non-*F* correlative to the one it lacks. Well, let us consider this not in regard to existence but in regard to the property red. The question is whether the absence of redness from something which could be red must bespeak the presence of a real property correlative to red. Certainly, if *a* were a piece of wood then it could lack redness only if it had some colour or colours other than red – be it brown, cream, fawn, or whatever – none of which could be dismissed as mere Cambridge properties. That does not settle the question, however, since the result would be very different if *a* were not a piece of wood but a piece of glass. Now, although glass is like wood in being something that *could* be red, it is also unlike wood in that its failure to be red does not mean that it is any colour at all: it may be quite colourless. To say that it is non-red, therefore, is not to say that it has any *correlative* property, or at least not any that is real. It might of course be said to have the property of being non-coloured; but, then, so too might a pain or a flash of insight, though their being non-coloured could hardly be claimed as a real, rather than a Cambridge property. Reflecting on this example, it is not difficult to see that lack of a real property *F* bespeaks the presence of a correlative *real* property non-*F* only if *F* and non-*F* are differentiae of the one generic property. Thus, if red and non-red were related as differentiae of the property of being coloured, red could be lacking in an *a* that was coloured only if *a* had some colour other than red.

The relevance to the discussion of non-existence is fairly clear. If lack of existence in *a* (which had existed) were to bespeak the presence in *a* of non-existence as a real rather than as a Cambridge property, existence and non-existence should be related to some real property just as red and non-red would have had to be related to the real property of being coloured. For convenience, let us call this generic property '*E*'. Then, just as red and non-red would have had to be understood as *coloured* red and *coloured* other than red, so existence and non-existence would have to be understood as being *E* in an existential way and being *E* in a non-existential way. Thus, whether *a* existed or did not exist, it would have some form of being: it would be *E*. But that is false. Hence, even if 'Socrates does not exist' were to contain the predicate '____ does not exist', the property stood for by that predicate would be no more than a Cambridge one. Consequently, no paradox could arise from 'Socrates does not exist'. This has already been demonstrated for the case where the negation was taken to be external to the proposition; it has now been demonstrated for internal negation as well.

To sum up what I have been saying so far in this section. I have been arguing that there is no truth in the longstanding belief which denies that 'Socrates no longer exists' contains '____ exists' as a first-level predicate. It has done so on the grounds that, if '____ exists' really were a first-level predicate, there could be no denying that 'Socrates no longer exists' contains a negative existential predicate, viz. either '____ does not exist' or 'it is no longer the case that ____ exists'. In either case, so it is claimed, there would be no escaping the paradoxes and absurdities of existence. Such a view employs three main premises, the first two of which are quite explicit, but the third merely implicit.

4.8 that predicates are formed by removing a proper name from a proposition,

4.9 that predicates stand for properties,

4.10 that any negative existential property would have to be either a *real* one, or, if a Cambridge property, it must be one whose acquisition is conditional upon its subject of attribution existing at that time.

I accept (4.8); and I accept (4.9) as well. What I do not accept is the unspoken assumption expressed by (4.10). As I have shown, (4.10) is not true of the property stood for by the predicate 'it is not the case that ____ exists'. The same point holds even when the negation is taken to be internal, and the predicate is '____ does not exist'. There, too, the relevant property is a Cambridge one. Thus, *no matter whether the distinction between internal and external negation in this context is accepted or rejected*, the result is the same. In neither case are we committed to Socrates acquiring any property, real or Cambridge, whose acquisition is conditional upon Socrates existing at that time. In neither case, therefore, does 'Socrates does not exist' generate the paradoxes or absurdities which would make it impossible to count '____ exists' as a first-level predicate and existence as a real property of individuals. There is indeed no such impossibility.

In arguing for the foregoing conclusion, I have been responding to the challenge to produce a sentence which can be recognized as usable outside philosophy and which is formed by wrapping '____ exists' round a genuine proper name. If I have argued correctly, such propositions as 'Socrates no longer exists', 'Socrates came to exist', and 'Socrates ceased to exist' are among the various quite straightforward examples that fit the bill. For one thing, their use of '____ exists' as a first-level predicate has been shown to have none of the unacceptable consequences alleged by Williams and many others. For another thing, they certainly are 'usable outside philosophy'.

III EXISTENCE IS A REAL PROPERTY

Thus far I have argued that none of the various attempts to avoid acknowledging existence as a real property of individuals has been successful. I have argued also not only that the paradoxes and absurdities of existence stem from treating non-existence as a real, rather than a Cambridge property of things, but that even though non-existence is only a Cambridge property it does not follow that existence, too, is a Cambridge property. The aim has been the negative one of removing various objections to accepting existence as a real property of individuals. Yet, no matter how successful that negative process might be, its outcome could not be the positive one of establishing that existence was indeed a real property. It is for that conclusion that I shall now attempt to argue.

A real property is one whose presence or absence makes a real difference to the individual which has it. Consequently, if existence were a real property of Socrates, its possession would have to make a real difference to him. The question is: does existence make any real difference to Socrates? It is not enough to say that Socrates' existence is a real property simply because it 'makes him actual', for that assumes *being actual* to be a real property, which is every bit as debatable as the claim that existence is a real property. To avoid begging the question in this way, let us therefore refrain from comparisons between Socrates as having existence (i.e. as being actual) and Socrates as having ceased to exist (i.e. as no longer being actual). Let us, rather, restrict ourselves exclusively to comparing like with like. That is to say, let us restrict ourselves to comparing two times, at *neither* of which does Socrates exist, viz. before he began to exist and after he has ceased to exist. Such a comparison should show whether the having of existence left any real effect on Socrates.

The effect has been undeniable; for it was impossible either to refer to him or to conceive of him before his conception, whereas it became possible to do both once he began to exist. Still more importantly, it even *remained* possible to do both even after he had died. This effect is, moreover, a real one. It is not like the difference between not being actually referred to and being actually referred to, which difference would be a merely Cambridge one, since something may be no more affected by being referred to than by not being referred to. On the contrary, to be *able* to be referred to does bespeak something real in Socrates. Yet, it cannot be identified with the difference between being actual and not being actual, for even when Socrates is *no more* he can still be referred to, whereas he could not be referred to when he was *not yet*.

Socrates' being referable to is both a real effect in Socrates and a consequence of his existing or having existed. However, if his existence were no more than a Cambridge property, it could have had no real effect on him. That is to say, had his existence made no *real* difference to him, he should have been able both to be referred to and to be conceived of before he existed no less than after he did so. So, Socrates' existence is a real property of him.

Critics might suggest that this conclusion simply cannot be right, for surely it would be open to precisely the same kinds of objections as Averroes raised against Avicenna's alleged claim that existence is an accident. Against this I merely note that, unlike this interpretation of Avicenna, although my claim to existence's being a real property of Socrates does entail both that it is a referent of the first-level predicate '____ exists' and that it makes a real difference to Socrates, one thing it does not entail is that existence is an *accident* of Socrates. Although it is undoubtedly *accidental* to Socrates, that does not allow us to conclude that it is also an accident of him. The reason is simply that, were it an accident it would be ontologically *posterior* to Socrates whereas it is in fact *prior* to him. To say that it is accidental to Socrates is to say that there is no contradiction in denying existence of him. To say that it is ontologically prior to Socrates (albeit chronologically concurrent with him) is to say that, although existence is completed by Socrates in the sense of being individuated by him, it is not completed by him in the sense of his being somehow 'already there' to be actualized by it. To think otherwise would be to conceive of Socrates as having *in se* the potential or capacity to be actualized by existence. It would mean that, even before

Socrates did in fact exist, there was already the *possibility* that *he* exist. But, as argued in the last chapter, at that time there could never have been any such possibility: until he did exist there was not even the possibility that *he* exist. There was literally *nothing* of which it could be said, '*It* is what was actualized when Socrates came to exist'.[8]

IV CONCLUSION

The profusion of points and opinions discussed in this chapter may have belied the essential simplicity of its strategy. The rationale for denying that '____ exists' is not only a first-level predicate but also one irreducible to any other first-level predicates stemmed from the paradoxes and absurdities that such a position was alleged to engender. Starting from the premiss that what can be predicated of an individual differs absolutely from what can be predicated of a kind, I argued *for* the distinction between first- and second-level uses of '____ exists' and, in the Appendix to this chapter, have defended that distinction against the spate of alternative proposals, ranging from the plausible to the contrived, some for treating '____ exists' as a second-level predicate and some for reducing it to various kinds of *non*-existential first-level predicates, whether formal or otherwise. As for the alleged absurdities and paradoxes, they were readily resolved by exposing the falsity of their assumption that if existence were a real first-level property, then *non*-existence ought likewise to be a real property.

Since '____ exists' is predicable of concrete individuals, existence is a first-level property. But that is not all; Fido's existence is not only a first-level property but a real one, for his having existence has made a real difference to him. Although a genuine property, it is not an Aristotelian accident of Fido, even though it is most certainly accidental to him. In a paper on existence not only this point but the relation of Fido's existence to Fido could have been developed at quite some length. For the purposes of the argument in the following chapter, however, such a development would be only a needless distraction. For those purposes all that need be recognized about existence is that it is a real property of Fido,

8 This, I take it, is at least part of what Aquinas meant in saying that existence (*esse*) was 'the actuality of all actualities and the perfection of all perfections' (*De Potentia*, VII, 2 ad 9um).

though not an Aristotelian accident: it is 'accidental and prior' to Fido.[9]

More importantly, having determined that '____ exists' can be predicated of Fido, this chapter has thereby established that 'Fido exists' is no less an atomic proposition than is 'Fido is black'. Consequently, we are finally entitled to draw from the truth of 'Fido exists' the same kind of conclusions as were drawn from the truth of 'Fido is black'. As was noted in chapter 3, however, there are indications that those conclusions conflict with Fido's being inconceivable before he existed. The nature and resolution of that conflict will now be pursued in chapter 5.

9 The phrase is from J. Owens, the doctrine it expresses is from Aquinas. Cf. Aquinas, *Quodlibetales*, 12, q.5, a.1; J. Owens, 'The Accidental and Essential Character of Being in the Doctrine of St.Thomas Aquinas', *Mediaeval Studies* 20 (1958), pp.1–40, reprinted in J.R. Catan (ed.), *St Thomas Aquinas on the Existence of God* (Albany: State University of New York Press, 1980), pp.52–91; J. Wippel, 'Essence and Existence', in N. Kretzmann, A. Kenny, and J. Pinborg (eds), *The Cambridge History of Later Medieval History* (Cambridge: Cambridge University Press, 1982), especially pp.394–5.

Chapter 5

Why existence? The *penultimate* answer

In this chapter we come finally to address directly the central task of the book, which is to determine not only whether the question 'How ever can it be that Fido (or any existing individual) does exist?' must be asked, but also how it must be answered. As remarked earlier, there could be no grounds for asking such a question if Fido's existing were taken to be simply a brute fact; for a brute fact is by definition one for which any explanation is simply unnecessary. It would be quite perverse, even for a philosopher, to demand explanation for a fact that required none. The last three chapters, however, have been attempts to explain and establish the logical and ontological grounds upon which to argue that the 'brute fact' view is untenable.

Among the grounds in question are those established originally in chapter 2 about Fido's being black but which, consequent upon existence having now been shown to be a real property of individuals, can now be accepted as equally valid for Fido's existing:

5.1 In Fido's existing are to be distinguished two ontological categories exemplified by Fido and his existence. Fido and his existence are *constituents* of Fido's existing, i.e. it is from them that Fido's existing is conceptually constructible.
5.2 Fido is a complete entity.
5.3 Fido's existence is an incomplete entity, a property instance. It is simply a feature of, or pattern in, Fido's existing.

Passing reference has already been made to the potential conflict between points (5.1)–(5.3) on the one hand and, on the other hand, the fact that Fido could neither be referred to nor conceived of before he existed. It is this conflict which I shall now argue makes the question 'How ever can it be that Fido does exist?' logically inescapable. The response to the question will be to show just how the conflict can be resolved. These, then, will be the twin concerns of the present chapter.

I THE ARGUMENT

In essence the argument is disarmingly simple.

Fido and his existence are constituents of Fido's existing.
If Fido and his existence are constituents of Fido's existing, then, given the foregoing points about Fido and his existence, Fido's existing cannot be a brute fact.
Therefore, Fido's existing cannot be a brute fact.

Fido and his existence are constituents of Fido's existing

This point is made in (5.1) listed above. While it would be superfluous to repeat the supporting argument given in chapter 2, it may not go amiss to recall briefly what it means to be a constituent of Fido's existing. The ontological distinction between constituents and components is one between parts from which an ontological whole can be *built up*, and parts into which it can be *broken down* or decomposed but which are not required in its construction. The former may be called 'constituents' and the latter 'components'. The building up and decomposition of which I have been speaking are of course only conceptual, not physical. Expressed differently, *constituents* of an ontological whole are any of its parts which would need to be recognized under pain of not knowing what the whole was in itself (as contrasted with knowing it merely in its relation to something else). Thus, to say that Fido and his existence are constituents of Fido's existing is to say that, according to one legitimate ontological analysis of Fido's existing, Fido and his existence are exemplifications of categories (viz. complete entity and incomplete entity) that must be recognized under pain of not knowing what Fido's existing is. Correspondingly, *components* of an ontological whole would be any of its parts that need *not* be recognized in order to know what the whole is in itself. Thus, Fido and his existence would have been components of Fido's existing, had it been possible to know what Fido's existing was in itself, while being quite oblivious to the presence therein of Fido and his existence.

It is essential to understand that the foregoing account does *not* presuppose that there be only one legitimate way of analysing Fido's existing. So far as the present argument is concerned, it is completely irrelevant whether there be one or many such analyses: although that is an interesting question, it is not one that I am required to address here. The nub of the argument is that a legitimate analysis cannot generate an insoluble paradox. Obviously, therefore the paradox generated by the present analysis cannot be an insoluble one. The task is to determine what would have to be accepted in order to resolve it.

If Fido and his existence are constituents, Fido's existing cannot be a brute fact

In regard to the relations between Fido and his existence, we have noted not only that Fido's existence is individuated by Fido but that Fido is inconceivable until he has completed his existence. Between them, therefore, we find the following interdependence:

5.4 On the one hand, Fido's existence could not be the property instance which it is except it have been individuated by Fido.

5.5 On the other hand, Fido could not even be conceived to be the concrete individual that he is except he have individuated his existence.

The reciprocal priorities expressed in (5.4) and (5.5) would have been entirely acceptable and unproblematic had Fido and his existence been components of Fido's existing. A problem arises only because the reciprocal priorities obtain despite Fido and his existence not being components of Fido's existing, but constituents of it. Being constituents, it must be possible conceptually to construct Fido's existing from them; and therein lies the problem posed by (5.4) and (5.5).

Any conceptual construction of Fido's existing can begin only with a complete entity, a requirement which eliminates Fido's existence as a starting point and means that the construction can begin only with Fido. Obviously, the next step in the construction would be for Fido to complete his existence. Equally obviously, that presupposes that Fido be *able* to complete his existence. Yet, the Fido who would be required for the first stage in the conceptual construction of Fido's existing would be a Fido conceived of as *able* to complete his existence without however having actually done so. But we know that a Fido which has not actually completed his existence is a Fido that is not conceivable at all, let alone conceivable as *able to complete* his existence. Hence Fido is disqualified from forming the basis for the conceptual construction of Fido's existing, a construction which now seems impossible to begin, let alone to finish. To repeat, the fact that Fido and his existence were constituents meant that Fido's existing should be conceptually constructible from them. The mutual priorities between them noted in (5.4) and (5.5) has meant first that Fido's existence could not be the starting point (since it is an incomplete entity), and second that not even Fido could be the starting point since at that stage there could be no possibility of *his* completing his existence.[1] The required construction could not therefore even get started. Our dilemma can therefore be summarized as follows:

5.6 Fido and his existence are constituents of Fido's existing, which should thus be conceptually constructible from them.

5.7 Fido's existing seems not to be constructible from them, since only Fido could be the first stage in the construction and he seems to be disqualified from that role because even his ability to complete his existence is not conceivable until he actually completes it.

The conflict between (5.6) and (5.7) bears directly on the brute fact view of Fido's existing which claims that there is no *logical* compulsion to ask how ever it can be that Fido does exist. On that view, it would be logically acceptable to hold that Fido is simply there, and 'that is all there is to it'.[2] The immediate effect of the antinomy between (5.6) and (5.7), however, is to expose such a view to the following *reductio ad absurdum*:

Let us assume the brute fact view that Fido's existing logically raises no questions.

1 This is an instance where it is important to heed Prior's advice that, when considering whether something is possible, we should always ask *when* the possibility is supposed to hold.
2 Cf. Russell's similar claim about the existence of the Universe: 'There is nothing puzzling about the existence of the Universe. It just does exist, and that is all there is to it. That is simply a brute fact' (B. Russell and F. Copleston, 'A Debate on the Existence of God', reprinted in J. Hick (ed.), *The Existence of God* (London: Macmillan, 1965), p.174).

But, if Fido's existing logically raises no questions, then neither are any questions raised by the implications of Fido's existing, viz. that both (5.6) and (5.7) are true.

But, the conjunction of (5.6) with (5.7) is self-contradictory, and therefore implies anything at all, including that Fido's existing logically does raise a question, e.g. 'How ever can it be that Fido does exist, given that (5.6) and (5.7) are contradictory?'

Therefore, if the brute fact view were true, Fido's existing would logically both raise and not raise that question.

Therefore, the brute fact view is false.

Clearly, the contradiction between (5.6) and (5.7) renders inescapable the question, 'How ever can it be that Fido does exist?' Equally clearly, however, the impasse between them ought not to be inescapable since Fido undoubtedly does exist, which would be impossible were the contradiction more than a merely apparent one.

Summary of the argument so far

Before attempting to reconcile (5.6) with (5.7), it might be helpful to sketch the course of the argument so far.

5.8 Fido exists.

5.9 According to a Fregean way – which is not necessarily the only legitimate way – of understanding Fido's existing, instances of two categorial parts are to be distinguished in it, viz. Fido and his existence.

5.10 Either these two parts are related to Fido's existing as its constituents or they are related to it as its components.

5.11 But, they cannot be its components; since their being components of Fido's existing would entail that it had *no* components (cf. chapter 2).

5.12 Therefore they are constituents of Fido's existing.

5.13 Therefore Fido's existing should be conceptually constructible from Fido and his existence.

5.14 But there seems to be no starting point for such construction, since Fido's existence is disqualified by being an incomplete entity and Fido is disqualified by being inconceivable until he has completed his existence.

5.15 (5.13) and (5.14) cannot both be true.

5.16 Therefore, there must be some way of resolving the dilemma posed by (5.13) and (5.14).

Reconciling Fido's existing with Fido and his existence being its constituents

Were the dilemma irresoluble, Fido could not exist. Since he does exist, one or other of its horns must be false; and since Fido and his existence are undeniably constituents of Fido's existing, the only conclusion is that, despite not being conceivable until he existed, Fido can indeed be the first step in the conceptual construction of Fido's existing. Let us therefore see how that might be:

Fido can be the first step in the construction only if he is *able* to complete his existence.

However, while Fido has the capacity to complete his existence only *coincidently* with that capacity's being employed, he cannot have it *in virtue of* its being employed. Why? Because, to have that capacity in virtue of its being employed would be to have it in virtue of Fido's existing; and thus Fido's existing would be ontologically prior to Fido, which is contrary to Fido's being a constituent of his existing. Nor, however, can Fido have that capacity simply in virtue of his status as a concrete individual, otherwise he would have been conceivable even before he existed.

But, if he has that capacity neither in virtue of his status as a concrete individual nor in virtue of his being an *existing* concrete individual, he must have it in virtue of something other than either his being a concrete individual or his being an existing concrete individual. Let that 'something' be *a*.

So, the dilemma presented by (5.6) and (5.7) can indeed be resolved, the key to its resolution being to recognize that it is one thing to say that Fido's being able to complete his existence *coincides* with the exercise of that ability, but quite another to say that he has the ability *in virtue of* exercising it. Once it is recognized that the former can be accepted without the latter, Fido is no longer disqualified from being the starting point in the conceptual construction of Fido's existing, which could then proceed quite straightforwardly. The consequence, however, is that Fido's existing cannot be a brute fact, but is dependent upon something other than either it or its constituents. This has to be accepted under pain of saying that Fido cannot exist when he quite plainly does exist.

Explaining the role of a

Although we know *that a* is that in virtue of which Fido is able to complete his existence, it is not yet clear just *how* that is consistent with Fido's not being conceivable until he existed. To clarify that point we need to determine how *a* is related to Fido. Consider therefore the relations as depicted in figures A and B.

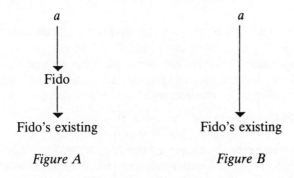

Figure A   *Figure B*

As depicted in Figure A, *a* would be that in virtue of which Fido was able to complete his existence. Only subsequently, however, would Fido actually do so. This is clearly not how they are related, since it would result in Fido being conceivable before he existed. As a minimum, *a* needs to be depicted as that in virtue of which Fido's ability to complete his existence *coincides* with his actually doing so. In this respect, therefore, Figure B would be more acceptable than Figure A. None the less, Figure B remains ambiguous as to whether or not Fido's ability to complete his existence is ontologically prior to his existing. Figure C has the merit of removing the ambiguity by making clear not merely that Fido's ability to complete his existence coincides with his actually doing so, but showing also that it is ontologically prior to Fido's existing.

As depicted in Figure C, *a* is that in virtue of which Fido is able to complete his existence and *conjointly* is that in virtue of which Fido's existence is actually completed by him. This ensures that the following claims (5.17) and (5.18) are both satisfied.

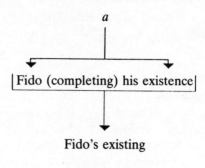

Figure C

5.17 That Fido can be the first step in the conceptual construction of Fido's existing because, despite being *coincident* with his existence, his being able to complete his existence is not *in virtue* either of his existence or of his existing,

5.18 That Fido was inconceivable before he existed.

It should be remembered, however, that Fido's role in the whole discussion has been that of an arbitrary individual, which means that the conclusion drawn in regard to him is one that holds equally for any existing individual whatever. That is to say, any existing individual exists if and only if its existing is caused by something external to its existing.

Possible misconceptions of the argument

Lest the foregoing argument be misunderstood, I should stress that it does not rest on there being any necessary connection between Fido and his existence, nor does it rest on the Principle of Sufficient Reason. Had the former been the case, the argument would have been of the following form.

There is a necessary connection between Fido and his existence: there can be no Fido without his existence, nor any Fido's existence without Fido. (It is, of course, not necessary that Fido exist.)

But that necessary connection can be explained only in terms of a *tertium quid* to which Fido and his existence are each related.

Therefore, there is a *tertium quid* to which Fido and his existence are each related.

This particular argument assumes that it is the necessity of the connection between Fido and his existence which requires explanation. Equally obviously, the assumption is false and the argument unsound. While my argument does indeed turn on the connection between Fido and his existence, the particular aspect of their connection that finally generates concern is not its necessity but, rather, their being so related as to render impossible any conceptual construction of Fido's existing. For precisely that reason Fido's existing could not be accepted as simply a brute fact. The brute fact view was therefore untenable not because of any necessary connection between Fido and his existence, but because of the contradiction between (5.6) and (5.7).

Much the same can be said about any suggestion that the argument employs the Principle of Sufficient Reason or a variant of it, the Principle of Intelligibility. Had it done so, it would have been along roughly the following lines:

If the dilemma posed by (5.6) and (5.7) were not resolvable and had therefore to be accepted as a brute fact, Fido's existing would be *unintelligible*.

But, according to the Principle of Intelligibility, it is intelligible why whatever exists does exist.

Therefore, Fido's existing cannot be unintelligible.

Therefore, the dilemma cannot be accepted as a brute fact: there must be some way of resolving it.

The reasoning in my argument was quite different: it was based not on the need to eschew the unintelligible, but on the need to eschew the *contradictory*, viz. (5.6) and (5.7).

II OBJECTIONS

Further misconceptions might be avoided by considering various objections that could be raised against the argument.

The humble dog owner

Appeal might be made to the fact that the humble dog owner can go through his whole life knowing that Fido is an individual dog, knowing that Fido both undergoes changes and produces changes in his environment, and of course knowing (though hardly remarking) that Fido exists. Despite his considerable familiarity with Fido, however, he would be bemused by the suggestion that there was anything remotely paradoxical about Fido's existing. So, how can there really be any paradox if Fido's owner finds his existing utterly unparadoxical, despite knowing quite well how to speak of Fido, of Fido's existing and even (if need be) of Fido's existence?

The first response to this animadversion is to recall what I have already noted on more than one occasion, namely, that although I am committed to the Fregean-style analysis or understanding of Fido's existing being one legitimate analysis, I am certainly not committed to its being the *sole* legitimate analysis. Hence, it would be a matter of no consequence even if no other analysis, whether by philosophers or by the humble dog owner, should fail to engender any paradox at all. My point is merely that, if an analysis is unquestionably a legitimate one, then a problem arising from it cannot be dismissed simply by appealing to the alleged fact that there are other legitimate analyses from which that problem fails to arise. One cannot concede that an analysis is a legitimate one, while at the same time allowing that it could engender an irresoluble paradox. Nor, having allowed that an analysis is a legitimate one, can one abandon it at the first sign of its engendering a paradox – unless it be quite clear that the paradox could be resolved in no other way.

The objector might press his point by denying that there could be more than one legitimate analysis of Fido's existing, and insisting not only that a choice must be made between the humble dog owner's and a Fregean-style analysis but that the former must be preferred to the latter. This choice would be compelling, however, only if either the humble dog owner could be shown to recognize the full implications of his understanding of Fido's existing, or if the Fregean-style analyst could be shown to have drawn the wrong inferences from his understanding of it. The relative merits of the two views, however, are not to be determined simply on the basis of whether they do or do not *appear* to generate a paradox: the issue can be settled only by examining the respective arguments.

The paradox would not arise if Fido's existing were conceived of as having more than two parts

This is a variant on the objection that the Fregean-style analysis is not the only possible one, an objection which I have pre-empted earlier in the chapter. I might now add, however, that so far as generating a paradox is concerned the number of parts in Fido's existing is of no consequence. What does count is whether the parts are constituents and, if so, whether Fido's existing can be conceptually constructed from them. As to the first point, I think it is clear from chapter 2 that the parts would have to be constituents, no matter what kind of analysis was employed. As to the second point, there are good grounds for saying that the constituents would be a mixture of complete and incomplete entities, and that these might very well give rise to our paradox, given that Fido could not be conceived of until he existed. So, the chances of avoiding a paradox are not good, irrespective of what kind of analysis is used. However, even if it were avoidable by some analyses, that would have simply no bearing on the implications of the paradox generated by the Fregean-style analysis.

The argument proves not that *a* does exist, but merely that we have to think that it does

This point has been raised by Peter Forrest on the grounds that it is not clear whether two of the argument's key premises reflect the way things are or merely the way we have to think that things are. One of the premises is that concrete individuals cannot be referred to before they exist; and the question raised about it is whether the failure of reference might not be due entirely to our human limitations. Might it not be that such individuals are already 'there' to be referred to, but that it is merely our human limitations that prevent our doing so. The other premiss is that existence is a real property of concrete individuals; and the question raised in this case is whether it merely reflects the tensed character of time and hence is valid only for such beings as may be unable to avoid tenses.

In regard to the first question, let us suppose that future individuals are indeed already 'there' to be referred to, but that we humans are not equipped to refer to them. If they are already 'there', then they are there either as concrete or as abstract, i.e. either as able to cause or to be changed or both, or as unable either to cause or to be changed. If they are 'there' as concrete, then they already exist; and what might seem to be their coming to *exist* would be simply their coming to be *known* to exist. But Socrates' coming to exist was obviously not simply an epistemological event: it was in principle possible to observe the physical process by which he emerged from gametes to embryo and further. So, if future individuals were 'there' at all, it could only be as abstract entities. Any reference to *them*, however, could be the *same* as reference to the concrete individuals in which they come to be exemplified only if the former were identical with the latter; and that would be impossible since the former are abstract and latter concrete.

Well, if reference to the abstract entities cannot be the *same* as reference to the concrete ones, perhaps it could be a *means* of referring to the concrete entities in which the abstract entities come later to be exemplified. That, however, would be possible only if exemplification of the abstract entities were restricted necessarily to those concrete entities in which they did as a matter of fact come to be exemplified. As the discussion of Plantingian haecceities in chapter 3 showed, they cannot be thus restricted. Indeed, had there been any such entities, they could just as readily have been exemplified in rhinoceroses or amoebas as in men. So, even if future individuals were somehow already 'there', they would offer simply no grounds for saying that any superior being could refer to the concrete individuals that come later to exemplify the abstract ones. In that particular regard no other being would be any better off than we are.

So far as concerns the second question – that the argument for existence as a real property rests on our inability to avoid tenses – it must be pointed out that the argument rests not on the existence of tensing but on the existence of temporal order; and it is immaterial to it whether the temporal order be expressed in terms of tenses or of dates. So, the question is not whether God or any other being could avoid tenses in conceiving of the Universe, but whether they could conceive of it as *not* temporally ordered. If God could do so we should have a problem, for presumably we should want to say that at least some of our temporal propositions are true. Moreover, the God of classical theism could not be mistaken about anything, which he would be if he could conceive of our Universe as not ordered temporally, despite some of our temporal propositions about it being true. To escape this dilemma we have two options. One is to say that God could indeed conceive of our universe as temporally ordered; the other is to say that he could conceive of it without conceiving of it as temporally ordered (though also without conceiving of it as *not* temporally ordered). Obviously, the first alternative would not threaten the argument for existence being a real property. Nor would the second alternative pose any threat, since it is quite compatible with *our* conceiving of our universe as temporally ordered. Finally, neither alternative would impute temporality to God himself. The first alternative is to be preferred, however, since the second would impute ignorance to God.

I conclude therefore that neither of the two premises in question can be interpreted as simply reflecting the limitations of the human condition. Consequently, the argument is innocent of the charge of proving not that *a* exists, but merely that we are compelled to think that it does.

III FURTHER CONCLUSIONS

Does Fido's existing require a sustaining cause?

It might be suggested that dependence on *a* was required only at the first instant of Fido's existing, but not thereafter. Well, is *a* merely an initiating cause of Fido's existing or it is it also a sustaining one? Why should Fido's existing not be like a building which, once erected, could continue to stand without further help from its builders? Why, once Fido has begun to exist, could he not continue to do so without any subsequent dependence on *a*?

At this point we need to observe a distinction between Fido's *coming* to exist, and Fido's *actually* existing. The former would be a process terminating in Fido's beginning to exist, an outcome sharply to be distinguished from the process itself. The argument in this chapter was based not on the fact that Fido came to exist, but only on the fact that he *does* exist: so far as the argument was concerned, it was immaterial whether Fido's existing did or did not have a beginning. And the conclusion was that Fido's *actually* existing, his actually completing his existence, was dependent on *a*. Fido's completing his existence is, however, not something fleeting, but perdures for the whole of his life: to say that he was no longer completing his existence would be to say that he was dead. Hence, to say that *a* is a condition of Fido's completing his existence is to say that there is no time during his life when his continuing to exist is not conditional on *a*.

What we may conclude, therefore, is not that a's existing is required for Fido's *coming* to exist; for about that point the argument had nothing to say. Indeed, it would have been quite consistent with the argument if Fido had never come to exist, but had existed eternally. It would have been quite inconsistent with the argument, however, had Fido's existing ever *not* been conditional on a, even for so much as an instant.

'Fido exists' is an elliptical proposition

Although it is a truism that 'Fido exists' is made true by Fido's existing, it is a truism that is rather less than the whole truth; for it carries not the faintest suggestion of Fido's existing being conditional on something external to it. On the face of it, therefore, the proposition 'Fido exists' is ambiguous as to whether it is made true simply by Fido's existing, or by Fido's existing *and* the existence of something external to Fido's existing. The task is to determine just how to remove the ambiguity, by ensuring that 'Fido exists' is understood in such a way as to be closed to Fido's existing being understood as a brute fact, and open only to its being understood as conditional on something external to it.

It might be suggested that our requirements would be met simply by 'Fido exists' being understood as elliptical for 'Fido exists only if a exists'. Clearly, that will not do, since 'Fido exists' is a categorical proposition whereas the suggested replacement is hypothetical. No such difficulty would arise, however, if the replacement were to be 'Fido exists & Fido exists only if a exists'. Yet this would be like the doctor's prescription that did nothing to vaccinate a patient against the flu, but tried simply to counter the disease once the infection had taken hold. The present suggestion does nothing to vaccinate 'Fido exists' against the ambiguity itself, but merely offers some addendum (viz. 'Fido exists only if a exists') to counter the effect of the ambiguity with which 'Fido exists' is infected. This is entirely the wrong treatment, for, by expanding 'Fido exists' to 'Fido exists & Fido exists only if a exists', nothing is done to change the self-contradictory implications of a non-elliptical 'Fido exists': that proposition continues to be ambiguous, albeit now as a logical part of the larger one. What we are offered is a complex proposition, the grasp of which presupposes a grasp of its constituent propositions, including 'Fido exists'. What has happened, therefore, is not that 'Fido exists' has been rendered unambiguous by the complex proposition, but rather that the complex proposition has been rendered ambiguous by containing 'Fido exists'.

Reflecting on the ineptness of these suggestions, it appears that at least three conditions must be met if 'Fido exists' is to be rendered unambiguous.

5.19 'Fido exists' must be so expanded as to make it clear that Fido's existing is conditional on something external to it.

5.20 The expanded expression must continue to be a categorical proposition; and it must also be one from which 'Fido exists' can be inferred. That much follows from the failure of the first suggestion.

5.21 The expanded expression cannot contain the proposition 'Fido exists' as a logical part, otherwise the ambiguity would not be removed but simply extended to the larger proposition as well. Thus, if the ambiguity is to be tackled at its root, the resulting expression cannot *presuppose* any grasp of 'Fido exists', and hence cannot contain it as a logical part. Now, that can be achieved only by some change within the logical unit 'Fido exists', and hence some change to the logical subject expression, or to the predicate, or to both. That much follows from the failure of the second suggestion.

All three criteria are satisfied by using a reduplicative construction, namely, 'Fido exists inasmuch as his existing is conditional on *a*', or 'Fido exists *qua* being conditional on *a*'. This clearly satisfies (5.19). Moreover, in accordance with (5.20), the expanded proposition continues to be a categorical one. In addition, '____ exists' expresses no mere ability to exist (as, for example, '____ swims' in 'Fido swims' might express merely the ability to swim rather than Fido's actually swimming), but is to be understood as saying that Fido exists *now*. Thus, from the expanded proposition we can infer both 'Fido exists' and 'Fido's existing is conditional on *a*', inferences such as could be drawn from any proposition of the form *b*, *qua H*, is *F*. For example, from 'Tom signed the document *qua* Prime Minister' we could similarly infer both 'Tom was Prime Minister' and 'Tom signed the document'. Thus, condition (5.20) is met by the proposed expansion of 'Fido exists'.

Condition (5.21) requires that 'Fido exists' not remain intact as a logical part of the expanded proposition. Now, two analyses have been suggested for '*b* qua *H* is *F*', in one of which '*qua H* is attached to the subject expression '*b*', viz. '(*b* qua *H*) is *F*' or '(Tom *qua* Prime Minister) signed the document'. In the other analysis, proposed by Aristotle and endorsed by Geach, the '*qua H*' is attached to the predicate, viz. '*b* (is, *qua H, F*)' or 'Tom (signed, *qua* Prime Minister, the document)'. In neither case however does the proposition '*b* is *F*' or 'Tom signed the document' form a logical part of the expanded proposition. Precisely the same holds for 'Fido exists *qua* conditional on *a*'. If analysed in the first way, it would be '(Fido *qu*a conditional on *a*) exists'; or the second analysis it would be 'Fido (exists *qua* conditional on *a*)'. In neither case does 'Fido exists' form a logical part of the expanded proposition.

It was already clear that, if 'Fido exists' were not to be inherently inconsistent, it would have to be treated as an elliptical expression and our task has been to discover what form the ellipsis should take. Whatever that form might be, it would have to satisfy conditions (5.19), (5.20), and (5.21); for which reason the appropriate ellipsis proved to be '*qua* conditional on *a*'. Hence, 'Fido exists' is to be understood as elliptical for 'Fido exists *qua* conditional on *a*' This entails our earlier conclusion, 'Fido exists only if *a* exists' or 'Fido exists only conditionally on *a*'; of course, the converse does not hold.

It might now be objected that I have rejected the Fregean analysis of 'Fido exists' in requiring it to be interpreted elliptically and hence am no longer entitled to rely on the premiss that the Fregean analysis is a legitimate one. In denying this charge I merely point out that it is not the Fregean analysis that I am impugning but simply the proposition to which the analysis is to be applied. The Fregean analysis is that any singular simple proposition can be analysed into a complete expression and an incomplete one (name and predicate, related as complete to incomplete). That point remains untouched, irrespective of whether it is applied to 'Fido exists' or to 'Fido exists *qua* conditional on *a*'. The fact that its application to 'Fido exists' leads to the conclusion that the latter is elliptical reflects not on the analysis that was employed but merely on what the analysis was applied to.

Finally, our conclusion can now be generalized to become 'Any existing individual exists *qua* conditional on something external to it'[3] or 'Any existing individual exists inasmuch as something external to it exists'. As was to be expected, this is stronger than our earlier conclusion – 'Any existing individual exists only if something external to it exists' or 'Any existing individual exists only conditionally on something external to it' – which it entails, without being entailed by it in return. Although stronger, however, it is still only the penultimate conclusion, for it does not preclude the same questions being asked about *a* as were asked about Fido. The ultimate conclusion will be sought in the next chapter.

3 Hereinafter *a* will be called a cause rather than a necessary condition. Nothing turns on the change: it is purely a matter of terminological convenience though not entirely arbitrary, for 'cause' is commonly used in this way in a number of everyday situations. Thus, to the question 'What caused the fire in the container?' the reply might be 'The leaking of oxygen into it', or to 'What caused the skid?' the answer might be 'The lack of tread on the tyres'. Although it is not always possible to substitute 'cause' for 'necessary condition', it is at the very least as possible to do so in regard to *a* as in the two instances just cited. Anyone uneasy about doing so may reverse it for themselves without the slightest effect on the argument.

Chapter 6

Why existence? The *ultimate* answer

The preceding chapter offered no final answer to our question 'How ever can it be that Fido does exist?'; for if a is a concrete individual the same kind of question and answer will be as appropriate to it as it was to Fido. And, if a exists *qua* conditional on concrete individual b, the same kind of question and answer would be appropriate to b. We are therefore forced to ask whether our answer could be anything but a preliminary one. More particularly, would the question of Fido's existing be answered ultimately by saying that it was caused by a series of causes[1] a, b, c, etc., which need never be terminated? The answer to this question requires us to determine under what conditions, if any, a causal series would have necessarily to be terminated. Although Hume and many others have thought that there are no such conditions, theirs is not a view that will survive close examination.

In his *Dialogues Concerning Natural Religion* Hume has Cleanthes argue that there is nothing amiss with a series of causes being infinite, since in such a series 'each part is caused by that which preceded it, and causes that which succeeds it'. 'Where then', he asks, 'is the difficulty?' To the suggestion that the difficulty lies not with any part of the series but with the series as a whole, Cleanthes replies that 'did I show you the particular causes of each individual in a collection of twenty particles of matter, I should think it very unreasonable should you afterwards ask me what was the cause of

---

1 In the preceding chapter I noted that the substitution of 'cause' for 'necessary condition' was purely a matter of convenience, though sanctioned by common usage. The convenience of doing so in discussing whether Fido's existing could be conditional on an infinite series of a, b, c, etc. is simply because that is a question that happens to be posed most often in the language of causes.

the whole twenty'.[2]

The same kind of argument is offered by Paul Edwards[3] who, in considering the example of a pile of books stacked one on top of the other, has pointed out that even if the pile were infinite there would be no book that was not supported by another. But if no book were unsupported, there would be no danger of the pile collapsing, and hence no need of any 'unsupported supporter' to underpin the pile as a whole. Contrary to what proponents of the contingency argument might say, therefore, it is only a finite pile that would need support in order to avert a collapse; an infinite pile would require no support at all.

The points made by Hume and Edwards, and later endorsed by Antony Flew[4], have also been underlined by Ronald Hepburn:

> But what exactly are we doing if we take away the first cause and posit instead an infinite succession of causes and effects? There is no specific cause whose existence or efficacy as a cause is being removed: no phenomenon is being robbed of its being. For all that is being said is that no matter what phenomenon you mention, that phenomenon will have a cause, which itself has a cause.[5]

In each of the cases mentioned it is worth noting that the conclusion is presented as applying not just to some, but to all causal series. To support so sweeping a conclusion one might reasonably have expected first some attempt to specify what a necessarily terminating causal series would have to be like, and second some argument to show that a series of *that* type would be quite impossible. We have been offered nothing of the kind. Instead, having considered only the familiar types of causal series, and without questioning whether those might be the only types conceivable, a conclusion has been reached by employing an inference that has only to be stated to be recognized as invalid.

None of the familiar types of causal series need to be terminated.

Therefore, no type of causal series need be terminated.

2 D. Hume, *Dialogues Concerning Natural Religion*, part IX.
3 P. Edwards, 'The Cosmological Argument', reprinted in D. Burrill (ed.), *The Cosmological Arguments* (New York: Doubleday, 1967), pp.101–24.
4 A. Flew, *God and Philosophy* (London: Hutchinson, 1966), p.90.
5 R. Hepburn, 'The Cosmological Arguments for the Existence of God', in P. Edwards (ed.), *Encyclopaedia of Philosophy* (New York: Macmillan & The Free Press, 1967), vol. 2, p.235.

The hidden premiss in that argument is that none but the familiar types of causal series is even conceivable, which was perhaps thought to be so self-evident as scarcely to be worth considering. However, it is precisely this hidden and seemingly innocuous assumption that I shall be contesting. I shall be concerned to show not merely that a necessarily terminating causal series is conceivable, but also what form it would take, as well as its obvious relevance to our contingency argument. I shall therefore proceed as follows:

6.1 Specify the conditions a causal series would have to satisfy if it were necessarily to be terminated.

6.2 Discuss the implications of those conditions as regards the *logical form* of such a series, noting how it would need to differ radically from that of a series which had only contingently to be terminated.

6.3 Indicate how the findings in (6.2) bear importantly upon the contingency argument, an argument to which the possibility of necessarily terminating series has rightly been regarded as integral.

I shall conclude that Hume and those of like mind have succeeded in establishing not that no causal series has necessarily to be terminated, but only that no causal series of *certain types* have necessarily to be terminated. A different type of causal series – one that would satisfy the conditions for being necessarily terminated – is not only conceivable, but would be quite untouched by the Humean criticisms. Hume, however, did not think of it; nor even do proponents of the contingency argument seem to have considered it, notwithstanding its indispensability for the defence of their own position.

I CONDITIONS FOR A NECESSARILY TERMINATING CAUSAL SERIES

Before proceeding with this topic I should clarify what I mean by a necessarily terminating series, as compared with a contingently terminating one. The necessity in question is to be understood as an intrinsic one, and thus to stem not from anything extrinsic to the series, but from the very nature of the components that go to form the series. As I am using the phrase, therefore, a necessarily terminating series would have to be terminated simply because its components were of a kind that would allow of no other option. An example taken from the non-causal area would be a series of logical operators like 'the father of .....'. Because they can be operators only inasmuch as they are operating on an appropriate argument (namely, a singular term), it is obvious that the only series they could form would be one in which the gap in each operator was filled by just such a term, e.g. by 'Bill' in the gap in the last operator of the series, by 'the father of Bill' in the penultimate operator, by 'the father of the father of Bill' in the preceding one, and so on.

A different kind of series, however, might have components compatible with the series being open, no less than with its being terminated. Such a series would be only contingently terminating. An example would be '(*a* is begotten by *b*) & (*b* is begotten by *c*) & . . .', which may be either open or terminated. Its components dictate neither option, but are consistent with either.[6]

Since I am concerned with the form to be taken by a necessarily terminating causal series, my question is this. What conditions would a causal series have to meet *if* it were necessarily to be terminating purely in virtue of its being causal? Well, one obvious condition of any account's being a causal one is that it be explanatory. For, although not all accounts that claim to be explanatory may have to be causal, those that claim to be causal must be explanatory, at least to some extent. If, then, the linguistic expression of a causal series can perform its explanatory task while being open, it clearly need not be terminated. But if it can do its job only by being terminated, then it has necessarily to be terminated: to allow that it could be open would be to allow that it be both causal and non-causal.

Now, it is a truism that an expression which cannot *say* anything, cannot *explain* anything either. But only closed sentences can say anything.[7] Consequently, if the linguistic expression of a causal series is to explain anything, either it as a whole or at least some part of it must be a closed sentence. However, not all

---

6 Of course, if perchance *c* were unbegotten the series would contain no succeeding members, and in *that* sense it would be necessarily terminating. In the sense in which I am using the phrase, however, the series would remain a contingently terminating one, since the causes that compose it are quite compatible with its *not* being terminated.

7 By a *closed* sentence I mean a sentence containing no unquantified variables.

closed sentences can be explanatory. Those which, like questions and commands, lack a truth-value cannot be explanatory. And, although conditionals do have a truth-value, not even they taken alone can properly be said to be explanatory – a car crash is not explained by saying '*if* there were oil on the road the car would have crashed'. Properly speaking, categoricals are the only closed sentences that can be explanatory. Thus, a very simple and straightforward criterion for determining whether a causal series has necessarily to be terminating is that either the whole or some part of its linguistic expression must be a sentence that is both closed and categorical. A series that passes it while being open need not be terminated; a series that can pass it *only* by being terminated has necessarily to be terminated.

The first point to be made about our criterion is that it is not based on any principle of sufficient reason, nor on the principle of intelligibility (according to which everything must be intelligible or explicable), nor on the assumption that everything must be causally explicable, as some versions of the principle of causality might maintain. I stress this because it has frequently been objected against the contingency argument that the need to terminate a causal series can be justified only by invoking one or other of the principles just mentioned. The foregoing criterion, however, relies on no principle other than that of non-contradiction; for it expresses the purely analytic point that a non-explanatory proposition has no claim to being a causal one.

The second point is that our criterion exposes the limitations of a claim frequently made about the nature of explanation. I refer to the claim that at 'every stage explanation is in terms of something else which, at that stage has to be accepted as a brute fact. In some further stage that fact itself may be explained; but still in terms of something else which, at least temporarily, has to be accepted'.[8] Now, to assert that the intermediate stages of explanation have to be facts (whether brute or otherwise) is to assert that they must be expressible by sentences that, logically, are closed. That can be maintained, however, only by neglecting the possibility of an explanation whose stages might have properly to be expressed by sentences that are *not* closed logically, even if they seem to be closed grammatically. Hence what has been proposed as a consequence of the 'essential nature of explanation' is at best

8 A. Flew, *God and Philosophy*, p.83.

a consequence of but one kind of explanation, namely, the kind whose stages are properly speaking to be framed in sentences that logically are closed rather than open.

Having made these points about our criterion for a necessarily terminating series, we can draw out its implications by considering the following three types of causal series:

> I (*a* is caused by *b*) & (*b* is caused by *c*) & (*c* is caused by *d*) & . . . .

Series I leaves it an open question whether each cause is simply causing without being caused to do so, or whether it is being caused to cause. An example of the first interpretation would be a series of progenitors *e*, *d*, *c*, *b*, *a* in which *e* was dead before *d* generated *c*, and *c* was dead before *b* generated *a*. An example of the second interpretation would be a series of railway trucks coupled to a moving locomotive, and where truck *b* not merely causes *a* to move but is caused to do so by truck *c*, and so on. The latter kind of series, in which the causes are caused to cause, might be written thus:

> I.i (*a* is caused to move by *b*) & (*b* is caused to cause *a* to move by *c*) & (*c* is caused to cause *b* to cause *a* to move by *d*) & . . . .

Expressed in more general terms the series becomes:

> II (*a* is caused to G by *b*) & (*b* is caused to cause *a* to G by *c*) & (*c* is caused to cause *b* to cause *a* to G by *d*) & . . . .

A series stronger than (II), and one to which I shall be referrring later is:

> III (*a* is caused to G by *b*) but only on condition that (*b* is caused to cause *a* to G by *c*) but only on condition that (*c* is caused to cause *b* to cause *a* to G by *d*) . . . .[9]

I mention the three series not for their intrinsic interest but merely to illustrate the point that they have at least one thing in common –

---

9 In canonical language 'if and only if' would be used instead of the ordinary language 'but only on condition that'. I prefer the latter, even though the difference may be only one of Fregean tone (*Farbung*).

each of them can be explanatory without having to be terminated. Let us take (I) for example. Must it be terminated? Would it pass our test, if it were not? Some might argue that it would not, since no conclusion can be inferred from an incomplete set of premises. But if the series were open, it would be incomplete; and from it we could therefore never infer what it is its job to explain, namely, that *a* obtains. Series I, therefore, could not be open.

This objection is question-begging in conflating incompleteness of the linguistic expression of the series with incompleteness of the premises needed to conclude that *a* obtains. On the contrary, the latter, even if incomplete, may well contain sufficient premises for the required conclusion. For, given the existential assumption for *b*, '*a* obtains' can be inferred simply from '*a* is caused by *b*', not to mention from '(*a* is caused by *b*) & (*b* is caused by *c*)', or from any longer set of conjuncts. Precisely the same is true of series II and III. In all three series each component beyond the first ('*a* is caused by *b*' or '*a* is caused to *G* by *b*') serves not to render explanatory what was not explanatory at all, but simply to render more complete an explanation that previously was merely less than complete, though still an explanation for all that. To conclude otherwise one would have to draw upon some such premiss as, 'nothing can be explained at all unless it is explained completely'. Since that premiss is unsustainable, the conclusion remains that series I, II, and III are able to be open, without having to be so. It is about series of these types that Hume was entirely right: there is indeed no difficulty about such an endless succession of objects, each part of which 'is caused by that which preceded it, and causes that which succeeds it'.

Now, to have understood why I–III are contingently terminating is by implication to have understood the converse, namely, the conditions required for a causal series to be a necessarily terminating one. The reason for I–III being able to be open is that the linguistic expression of each is composed of closed sentences (and of course sentential connectives). Since even the first of those sentences is explanatory in its own right, failure to terminate the series could never render its expression non-explanatory. It is therefore not difficult to see just what conditions must be met by the expression of any series that is to be necessarily terminating precisely in virtue of its being causal. For the series to be causal its expression must be explanatory, which means that either the whole or some part of it must be a closed categorical causal sentence. For the causation to be such that the series is necessarily terminating, however, no proper part[10] of its expression could be a closed categorical sentence, for otherwise the expression need *never* be closed. The consequences are twofold. One is that the expression as a whole would have to be a closed categorical causal sentence; the other is that no proper part of it could be a closed categorical sentence.

It now remains to show how these two conditions affect the *logical form* required by the expression of any causal series that would satisfy them. Such a series I shall call series IV; and I shall suppose that the final effect produced by it is *a*, which is preceded by *b*, *c*, *d*, each of which is both an effect of its predecessor and a cause of its successor.

II LOGICAL FORM OF A NECESSARILY TERMINATING CAUSAL SERIES

Of themselves the two points noted at the end of the previous section leave us almost entirely ignorant about what logical form the linguistic expression of series IV would take. As a first step towards dispelling that ignorance let us note two rather obvious points.

6.4 The linguistic expression of the series must begin with '*a* is caused to *G* by ____' or its equivalent. This is so simply because what the series purports to explain is just how *a*'s being *G* is caused.

6.5 Except in the limit case of a one-member series, the linguistic expression of the series must contain *repeated* instances of '.....is caused to G by ____'. This is so because it purports to be the expression not of one instance of causation, but of a *series* of causations.

Although these points fail to provide all the answers we need, they do suggest pertinent questions to ask, the first of which is: just what kind of expression is to fill the gap in '*a* is caused to *G* by ____'? Since *a* is in some way caused to *G* by *b*, it is clear that '*b*', or some singular term designating *b*, must occur in the

10 A proper part of an expression is a part of it which is not identical with that expression.

gap. But if '*b*' (or some term designating *b*) were to occur *alone* in the gap, the result would be the closed sentence '*a* is caused to *G* by *b*', which we have seen would preclude the series from being a necessarily terminating one. The question of how to fill the gap in '*a* is caused to *G* by ____' therefore becomes one of how to ensure that '*b*' does occur in it, though without thereby converting it into a closed sentence.

To say that '*b*', though not '*b*' alone, must occupy the gap is simply to say that it can occur only as part of some larger expression that fills the gap. We need therefore to know what that larger expression could be. Clearly, no logical predicate, whether of first or of any higher level, could fit the gap; only a logical subject could do so.

Among logical subjects, however, the only ones suitable would be those which,

6.6 were logically complex (because having to contain '*b*' as a logical proper *part*), and
6.7 which would make possible a series that had necessarily to be terminated.

What kind of expression could satisfy those conditions? To meet condition (6.6) it would have to be an expression in which '*b*' was the argument expression, and the rest of the expression a functional expression. One kind that comes immediately to mind is something of the form 'the *H* of *b*', in which 'the *H* of ____'[11] would be a functional expression taking '*b*' as its argument expression. Yet that would fail to satisfy condition (6.7), since the series resulting from its use would be of the form,

(*a* is caused to *G* by the *H* of *b*) & (the *H* of *b* is caused to *G* by the *K* of *c*) & . . . ',

which we have seen to be a form that need never be terminated.

Fortunately, that is not the only kind of functional expression that could combine with '*b*' to constitute a logical subject. A different kind is one with the form '..... inasmuch as it is *K*', which I might call a reduplicative functional expression because it contains the reduplicative term 'inasmuch as' that has been

11 Examples of common functional expressions are 'the father of ____' and 'the capital of ____', where the gap in the former could be filled by 'John' and in the latter by 'Australia'.

introduced already in chapter 5.[12] Now, if '*b*' were part of a reduplicative expression, say '*b* inasmuch as it is *K*', it could fill the gap in '*a* is caused to G by ____' thus:

a is caused to G by *b* inasmuch as it is *K*

In doing so it clearly meets condition (6.6). But does it also meet condition (6.7), i.e. could it contribute to the forming of a causal series that had necessarily to be terminated? 'The *H* of *b*' could not; but would '*b* inasmuch as it is *K*' fare any better?

There are two questions here, the first being whether '*b* inasmuch as it is *K*' can contribute to forming a causal series, and the second being whether that series would have necessarily to be terminated. To answer the first in the affirmative we have only to substitute 'is caused to G by *c*' for 'is *K*', thereby obtaining,

IV *a* is caused to G by *b* inasmuch as it is caused to G by *c*.

Here we have the expression of a two-stage causal series involving *c* and *b* as causes. The question then is whether such a series has necessarily to be terminated.

We have seen that a causal series would be necessarily terminated if at any stage its linguistic expression were an open sentence, but not if at every stage its linguistic expression were a closed sentence. So, the question becomes whether (IV) is composed of closed sentences. The temptation to think that it is might stem from mistaking it for a mere variant of,

a is caused to G by *b* *but only on condition that b* is caused to G by *c*,

which itself is merely a variant of series III, and is indeed composed of closed causal sentences, thus:

(*a* is caused to G by *b*) *but only on condition that* (*b* is caused to G by *c*).

Why, then, should (IV) not have a similar logical form, viz.

12 While Aristotle made use of reduplicative terms (*Prior Analytics* I, 38, 49a pp. 23–7), it was the mediaeval logicians who seem first either to have designated them as such or to have treated them at any length. They did so in their discussion of 'exponible propositions', a good example of which occurs in Peter of Spain's *Summulae Logicales*. Mediaeval theologians placed considerable weight on reduplicative terms in treating of such topics as the incarnation of God in Christ. Later, Leibniz was to recognize their relevance to the substitution of terms *salva veritate*, and Bolzano to the semantics of names.

(a is caused to G by b) *inasmuch as* (b is caused to G by c)?

Being thus composed of closed sentences, it would have never to be terminated.

This suggestion would overlook the fact that, whereas '.....only on condition that ____' is a propositional connective, '..... inasmuch as ____' is not. The gaps in the former are to be filled by propositions, those in the latter are to be filled by *sub*-propositional parts. It is for that reason that the logical form of (IV) cannot be as above, but has rather to be,

a is caused to G by [b inasmuch as it is caused to G by (c)].

Now, for a series of that form to be extendable, its round brackets would need to be filled not by 'c', but by 'c inasmuch as it is caused to G by ____', viz.

a is caused to G by [b inasmuch as it is caused to G by {c inasmuch as it is caused to G by (. . .'

Now, that is plainly an open sentence. So, if (IV) were to be extendable at every stage, its linguistic expression would have always to be an open sentence and hence could never be explanatory as the linguistic expression of a causal series is required to be. To be a *causal* series, therefore, series IV has necessarily to be terminated at some stage. Sooner or later the gap has to be filled not by the reduplicative use of a singular term but solely by a non-reduplicative use, e.g. by 'm' in the following:

a is caused to G by [b inasmuch as it is caused to G by {c inasmuch as it is caused to G by (d inasmuch as it is cause to G by (m))}].

One final point to be settled about this series is whether it should be read as tensed or tenseless. This amounts to asking whether the connection between b's causing and b's being caused is a temporal one: would it really matter if b's causing and b's being caused were not concurrent? Here we continue to be guided by the key fact that in the linguistic expression of (IV) the gap in 'a is caused to G by ____' cannot be occupied by 'b' alone. Consequently, any suggestion that would allow 'b' alone to fill the gap has to be rejected.

Let us then consider the result of allowing b's being caused to precede *b*'s causing. In that case, whatever *c* did to *b* would occur before *b* caused *a* to *G*. It would then be perfectly correct to say, without any qualification, that *a* was caused to *G* by *b*, and hence that '*b*' alone could occupy the gap in '*a* is caused to *G* by ____'. Since that is inadmissable, so also is the suggestion that *b*'s being caused could precede *b*'s causing – which, unless one were to allow backward causation, is the same as saying that *b*'s being caused must be concurrent with *b*'s causing. Since our earlier way of expressing series IV was ambiguous in that respect, the ambiguity should be removed by making it clear that the various occurrences of 'is' are not tenseless, but tensed. Thus modified, the series should be rewritten:

IV *a* is being caused to *G* by [*b* inasmuch as it is being caused to *G* by {*c* inasmuch as it is being caused to *G* by (*d* inasmuch as it is being caused to *G* by (*m*))}].[13]

Can we say that here is what we have been seeking, namely, a form to be taken by the linguistic expression of a causal series that not merely may be terminated, but has necessarily to be terminated? Well, not quite; for so far we have taken no account of a view mentioned in the last chapter, namely, that in '*b* as *H* is *F*' the reduplicative expression forms part of a predicate rather than of a subject expression. On that view, the proposition would be held to attach the complex predicate 'is, as *H*, *F*' to the simple subject expression '*b*'. Hence it would be a mistake to treat '*a* is caused to *G* by *b* inasmuch as it is *K*' as if '*b* inasmuch as it is *K*' were a complex subject expression, and *b*-inasmuch-as-it-is-*K* as what causes *a* to *G*. Rather, the cause would be simply *b*, and what is predicated of it would not be '*a* is caused to *G* by .....', but would be '*a* is, inasmuch as *b* is *K*, caused to *G* by .....'. Let us therefore consider the consequences of adopting this kind of analysis.

Applying it to '*a* is being caused to exist by *b* inasmuch as *b* is being caused to exist by *c*' results in:

6.8 *a* is, inasmuch as *b* is being caused to exist by *c*, being caused to exist by *b*.

For simplicity let us rewrite this as:

6.9 *a* is, inasmuch as *b* is R*c*, R*b*,

___

13 Use of the continuous present is neutral as to whether the causation is instantaneous or continuous, episodic or a process.

where 'R' does duty for 'being caused by'. Of course, if c too were an individual, and thus were caused to exist by something else (say, d), then (6.9) would have to be expanded as follows:

6.10 a is, inasmuch as b is [inasmuch as c is Rd]Rc, Rb

And, if d too were an individual, a further expansion would be required:

6.11 a is, inasmuch as b is [inasmuch as c is (inasmuch as d is Re) Rd]Rc, Rb.

As so written, however, each of (6.9), (6.10), and (6.11) belies the fact that it contains a gap which can be filled either by a singular term or by a reduplicative operator of the form, '[inasmuch as c is Rd] Rc'. Properly speaking, therefore, (6.9) should be written:

a is, inasmuch as b is ..... Rc, Rb

Mutatis mutandis, the same goes for (6.10) and (6.11), which likewise are shown to be open sentences.

Moreover, if our attempts to close the gap were confined to iterating more and more reduplicative operators, they would inevitably fail; for we should succeed only in transferring the gap from one point to another, without ever eliminating it altogether. Thus, if the series were to be extendable at every stage, its linguistic expression would have always to be an open sentence, and hence could never be explanatory as the linguistic expression of a causal series is required to be. To be a causal series, therefore, our series has necessarily to be terminated at some stage or other. Sooner or later the gap in its linguistic expression has to be filled not by a reduplicative operator, but solely by a singular term, e.g. by 'm' in the following:

V a is, inasmuch as b is [inasmuch as c is (inasmuch as d is caused to exist by m) caused to exist by d] caused to exist by c, caused to exist by b

It is to be noted that our conclusion was the same, irrespective of which analysis of reduplicative expressions was employed. Whether that analysis was the Aristotelian (which does seem preferable) or whether it was the one more in accord with surface grammar, we had to conclude that any causal series whose linguistic expression requires the use of reduplicative expressions not merely may be terminated, but has necessarily to be terminated.

This proved to be the case with series V no less than with series IV. Hardly surprisingly, their linguistic expressions emerged as quite radically different from the expression of those series that were only contingently terminating.

III CAUSAL SERIES AND THE CONTINGENCY ARGUMENT

Many proponents of the contingency argument will doubtless wonder at my giving so much attention to objections which in their view arise only from a failure to appreciate the centuries-old distinction between *per se* subordinated causes and *per accidens* subordinated causes. The objections, so they might claim, may hold against the latter but certainly not against the former. The first point I want therefore to establish is that such confidence is entirely misplaced, for the Hume/Edwards objections are valid no less against a series of *per se* than of *per accidens* subordinated causes, as can readily be shown after a few explanatory remarks about the contingency argument as well as about the distinction between *per se* and *per accidens* causes.

The contingency argument in broadest outline is, like the argument I am attempting in this book, one that begins with the quite unexceptionable premiss that something exists, a something which I have taken to be Fido. Its next step is to argue both that Fido is caused to exist and that there must be an uncaused cause of his existing, it being contended that Fido could not exist unless the causal series ending with Fido's being caused to exist were terminated at the other end also. What kind of causal series is this? Well, in many forms of the argument it is acknowledged that not any kind of series would do, e.g. a series of *per accidens* subordinated causes (causes *in fieri*, as they are sometimes called) would not do, for it need never be terminated. It is often claimed, however, that another kind – one composed of *per se* subordinated causes (causes *in esse*) – does have necessarily to be terminated. And on that claim the success of the contingency argument is thought to rest.

What then is this distinction between *per se* and *per accidens* subordinated causes? It is one deriving from Aquinas and Scotus, and explained by the latter thus:

in essentially ordered causes, the second depends upon the first precisely in its act of causation. In accidentally ordered causes this is not the case, although the second may depend upon the first for its existence or in some other way. Thus a son depends upon his father for existence but is not dependent upon him in exercising his own causality, since he can act just as well whether his father be living or dead.[14]

The expression 'the second depends upon the first precisely in its act of causation' is far from clear, being ambiguous as to whether the causal series is of type II, or of some other type. The ambiguity can be resolved, however, with the help of examples of *per se* subordinated causation used by Aquinas and others:

6.12 that a stone be moved by a stick, and the stick by the hand.[15]

6.13 [A goods train in which] each truck is moved and moves by the action of the one immediately in front of it.[16]

A critic of the possibility of necessarily finite causal series has offered another example in similar vein:

6.14 A series where the fire heats the pot and the pot in turn heats the stew, causing it to boil is . . . essentially ordered; for the warmth of the pot is both caused by the warmth of the fire and cause of the warmth of the stew, while the warmth of the stew is both caused by the warmth of the pot and cause of the stew's boiling.[17]

Clearly, Aquinas' example may be expressed as:

(The stone is being caused to move by the stick) & (the stick is being caused to move by the hand).

The other two examples take a similar form, thus indicating that all are instances not of series IV or V, but of series II. As such, they need never be terminated, notwithstanding their being instances of *per se* subordinated causation. Thus, Humean criticism of necessarily terminating causal series stems neither from ignorance of *per se* subordinated causation nor from a misunderstanding of

14 Duns Scotus, *Philosophical Writings*, ed. and trans. Allan Wolter (London: Nelson, 1962), pp.40–1.
15 Aquinas, *Summa Theologiae*, I, 46, 2 ad 7um.
16 R.P. Phillips, *Modern Thomistic Philosophy* (Westminster, MD: Newman, 1959), II, p.178.
17 P. Brown, 'Infinite Causal Regress', *Philosophical Review* 75 (1966), p.517.

it. At least on that point it is the defence of the series, and not the criticism, that has been misconceived.

To say that the defence has been misconceived is, however, not to deny that the Hume/Edwards objections too have been misconceived; and that is my second point. Hume and Edwards were correct in thinking that a series of *per se* subordinated causes was not proof against their criticisms; they were incorrect in assuming that no conceivable causal series could be proof against them, for the main point of this discussion has been show that such a series is indeed quite conceivable.

The forms of series IV and V not only show that the series have to be terminated, but suggest just why the arguments of Hume and Edwards are ineffectual against them. Crucial to their arguments was the premiss that each part of a causal series 'is caused by that which preceded it, and causes that which succeeds it'. Series IV and V, however, are cases of causal series in which each part *neither* is caused by that which precedes it, *nor* causes that which succeeds it: b, for example, could properly be said to be caused to G by c alone only if 'c' alone could fill the gap in 'a is being caused to G by b inasmuch as it is being cause to G by ___'. Likewise, b alone could properly be said to cause a to G only if 'b' alone could fill the gap in 'a is being caused to G by ___'. But, as we have seen, these gaps cannot be filled by 'c' and 'b' respectively. Hence, b can neither cause a to G nor can it itself be caused to G by c. Obviously, precisely the same conclusion could be drawn if the Aristotelian analysis of reduplicative propositions were adopted, and series V were substituted for series IV.

This explains why the earlier comments of Hume, Edwards, and Hepburn are simply irrelevant to any causal series of types IV and V. Hume, you will recall, remarked that 'did I show the particular causes of each individual in a collection of twenty particles of matter, I should think it very unreasonable should you afterwards ask me what was the cause of the whole twenty'. Edwards proposed the case of a group of Eskimos standing at the corner of 6th and 50th Streets in New York, and of our knowing why each member of the group was in New York. He considers the reasonableness of our asking, 'All right, but what about the group as a whole; why is *it* in New York?' This, he observes, would 'plainly be an absurd question'. Although these points are undeniably true of causal series in which each member is caused by the one preceding it, they have just no bearing on series IV and

V since, properly speaking, each of their members is not caused by the preceding one.

In IV, for example, what causes a to G is not b, but b inasmuch as it is caused to G by c inasmuch as it is caused to G by d inasmuch as it is caused to G by m. About such a series, moreover, it is wrong to suggest that we could take away the First Cause and posit instead an infinite series of causes and effects. By replacing 'm' with 'e inasmuch as it is caused to G by ____' we should be converting the expression of the series from a closed sentence to an open one, and thus changing the series from a causal one to one that quite literally could cause nothing.

The objections of Hume and Edwards, and Mackie as well, fail to impugn series IV or V, but succeed only in showing that their authors had too restricted a view of the forms that a causal series could take. And, being wrong about that, they were wrong too about whether any conceivable causal series had necessarily to be terminating. The same blinkered vision has been shown by proponents of the contingency argument, which is why even the defence of necessarily terminating causal series has been no less astray than has the criticism.

The question for defenders and critics alike was not whether a necessarily terminating causal series is conceivable – for it is – but whether such a series is ever instantiated. For us, that question now presents no difficulty, for it has been shown already in the latter part of chapter 5 that the kind of causation occurring in series IV and V is precisely the kind that causes Fido to exist, i.e. Fido exists only *inasmuch as* he is caused to do so by something external to him. Moreover, the same applies to b, to c, and to any other individual that might be part of the causal series causing Fido to exist. That being so, the series in question has necessarily to be a terminating one. If m is the cause that terminates the series, then m will be something that causes members of the series to exist without itself being caused to exist. A necessarily terminating causal series is not only conceivable, it is instantiated in as many cases as there are concrete individuals.

Thus, for an ultimate, rather than a merely penultimate, answer to the question 'How ever can it be that Fido does exist?', we shall have to expand our earlier conclusion that Fido exists inasmuch as he is caused to do so by something external to him. We shall have to say, 'He exists inasmuch as he is caused to do so by something external to him, *and ultimately by a cause that is itself not caused to exist*'. The same holds for every existing individual, without exception. That this conclusion has been reached is further evidence, if such were needed, that the question it answers is, contrary to the opinions cited in chapter 1, neither gratuitous nor improper.

Finally, I should add that the argument just concluded rather undercuts Quentin Smith's contention[18] that, if the classical Big Bang Theory or some relevantly similar theory is true, 'our universe exists without cause and without explanation' (p.65). This, he claims, provides 'a valid argument for God's non-existence, not a sound one' (p.49). Modest though his claim is, it is not modest enough; for our argument is quite unaffected by whether the Universe did or did not have a beginning. It is unaffected also by just what kind of beginning, if any, the Universe may have had, whether it were that of the classical Big Bang Theory or not.

18 Q. Smith, 'Atheism, Theism and the Big Bang Theory', *Australasian Journal of Philosophy* 69 (1991), pp.48–66.

Chapter 7

The uncaused cause

From the previous chapter we know *that* there is an uncaused cause of Fido's existing, but as yet do not know *what* can be said about it. In this and the following chapters I want to dispel at least some of that ignorance. Before doing so, however, I should put to rest two disparate, though not unrelated, objections to the very notion of an uncaused cause.

I OBJECTIONS TO THE NOTION OF AN UNCAUSED CAUSED

The first objection claims that it is not even reasonable to suggest that any explanation of Fido's existing could ever be exhaustive:

> [One] is making an unreasonable metaphysical demand on the universe by insisting that it must be such that a final completion of this process [of explanation] is possible in principle . . . there are various grades and modes of rationality and . . . we can hold the universe to be rational in some ways, for example, ordered causally, without making such extreme demands as this. It would seem that at this point we have come up against one of those rock-bottom philosophical oppositions about which nothing further can be said.[1]

This objection is based on the common, though mistaken, view that every form of the contingency argument for the existence of God must be based on the principle of sufficient reason or of intelligibility, according to which it must be intelligible why everything which occurs or exists does in fact occur or exist.

1 W.P. Alston, *Religious Beliefs and Philosophical Thought* (New York: Harcourt, Brace & World, 1963), p.20.

The view mentioned by Alston suggests that this requirement of intelligibility is itself unreasonable, if it is pressed so hard as to require a complete, rather than a merely partial, explanation of why Fido exists.

J. Morreall provides a more recent instance of the view cited above when he states confidently that 'the basic principle which leads us to God in the first place, at least in our philosophical theology, is the Principle of Sufficient Reason. . . . Without this principle the cosmological and teleological arguments could not even begin.'[2] No less confident is Hick's claim that the cosmological argument 'rests upon a fundamental act of faith, faith in the ultimate "rationality" of existence and hence can only be probative to those who need no proof'.[3] Undoubtedly, many versions of the contingency argument do employ the principle of sufficient reason, two famous examples being from Leibniz and Samuel Clarke, not to mention a well-known contemporary instance in Copleston's debate with Russell. My point, however, is that notwithstanding how many are the versions of the contingency argument using the principle of sufficient reason, the argument I have proposed makes no appeal whatever to it; and, consequently, it remains untouched by objections like the one cited by Alston.

Furthermore, no unreasonable metaphysical demand could ever be fulfilled. Hence, had the demand for a complete explanation of Fido's existing been unreasonable, it should have been impossible to reach the conclusion that was drawn at the end of the previous chapter. It would be pointless to object that its conclusion must be false because it purports to fulfil an impossible demand. On the contrary, whether the demand is an impossible one is to be determined by whether it can be fulfilled. And that, in turn, is to be decided not in advance, but only after the argument has been carefully examined.

The previous objection was directed against the possibility of proving there to be any uncaused cause of Fido's existing. The second objection is directed not against the possibility, but against the utility, of doing so. It makes the point that if our concern was to avoid having to accept the existence of anything as a brute fact, then all we have succeeded in doing has been to postpone the evil

2 J. Morreall, 'God as Self-Explanatory', *Philosophical Quarterly* 30 (1980), pp.206–14.
3 J. Hick (ed.), *The Existence of God* (London: Macmillan, 1965), pp.6f.

day. Even if it is true that Fido's existing cannot be a brute fact, it must surely be admitted that the existence of the uncaused cause is a brute fact. The upshot is that there comes a point when we surely have no choice but to accept some fact as beyond explanation, and hence a brute fact. Our exertions, therefore, have been largely in vain.

Like the previous objection, this one too labours under the misapprehension that all forms of the contingency argument rely on the principle of sufficient reason. If that principle really were the mainspring of the argument, it would be natural to think of the pursuit of the uncaused cause as nothing more than a flight from brute facts. It might then be at least arguable, though unsuccessfully in my view, that the existence of an uncaused cause is a brute fact, and hence that brute facts have proved inescapable after all: ultimately the existence of Fido or even of the Universe would be unintelligible, inexplicable.

Well, whatever the relevance of that objection to most forms of the contingency argument, it has none to the present one. Since that argument makes no use of anything like the principle of sufficient reason, it would be misguided to regard it as prompted by a flight from brute facts. What prompted the argument was not any aversion to brute facts as such, but the recognition that to accept Fido's existing as a brute fact would be to accept that Fido and his existence were simultaneously *both* constituents and non-constituents of Fido's existing. Since, however, the uncaused cause cannot be an individual in any more than an analogical sense, it would not generate that contradiction even if it were a brute fact. Only if the rationale of the argument had been the avoidance of brute facts *as such* could its conclusion make the argument suspect, or lay it open to the present charge of inconsistency.

II ELABORATING ON THE UNCAUSED CAUSE

An uncaused cause is not distinct from its existence

Following the failure of objections both to the possibility and to the utility of admitting an uncaused cause, we might now ask what more can be said about m, other than that it is the uncaused cause of Fido's existing. There must surely be something about m in virtue of which it is uncaused. Just what is that 'something'? The question can be answered by comparing m with those causes – a, *b*, *c*, and *d* – which were not uncaused, and by recalling why it was that they, no less than Fido, did require a cause.

As noted above, the reason was that *a*, *b*, *c*, and *d* could have been accepted as uncaused only if they and their existence were at the one time both constituents and non-constituents of Fido's existing. This situation arose because, as individuals, they were distinct from their existence. Obviously, therefore, the uncaused cause would have to lack any distinction between itself and its existence.[4] Equally obviously, the difference between *m* and *a–d* is not merely their place in the series; for while *a-d* might well exchange places with each other, the uncaused cause could not swap places with any of the caused causes. Between them and it there is a quite radical difference: they are distinct from their existence whereas the uncaused cause is not. But, if *m* is *not distinct* from its existence, it must be the *same* as its existence; it must be that *m* is its existence. For that reason *m* is called Subsistent Existence.

Objections to the notion of subsistent existence

Since the notion of Subsistent Existence is often deemed to be rather bizarre, it is scarcely surprising that it has come under heavy fire, though admittedly more in discussions of the proposition 'God is his existence' than of 'The uncaused cause is its existence'. Still, whatever the objections to the former, they are equally applicable to the latter. Kenny sums them up as follows:

> The objections . . . which have been made during the centuries to Plato's theory of Ideas apply to Aquinas' theory of God as subsistent being. But this is not all that is wrong with the theory; for the predicate to which the Platonic extrapolation is applied

4 Commenting on Aquinas' Tertia Via, Mackie has suggested correctly that it rests on the view 'that anything whose essence does not involve existence must, even if permanent, depend for its existence on something else'. He has further suggested that 'Aquinas would need something like the principle of sufficient reason to support' this view (*The Miracle of Theism* (Oxford: Oxford University Press, 1982), p.91). This happens to be wrong in so far as Aquinas is concerned, as is evident from his *De Ente et Essentia* (c.4) and from Joseph Owens's 'The Causal Proposition – Principle or Conclusion?' *The Modern Schoolman* 32 (1954–5), part I, pp.159–71; part II, pp.257–70; part III, pp.323–39. More importantly for our purposes, however, it is wrong in so far as the present argument is concerned, firstly because no such position has been assumed, but has been argued for; and secondly because the argument has rested not on the principle of sufficient reason but on the principle of non-contradiction.

is . . . a very extraordinary predicate. Either it is understood as a predicate which holds of all substances; in which case it is too uninformative to constitute the essence of any entity; or it is understood as a variable expression which permits of no substitution, in which case it is an ill-formed formula. The notion of *Ipsum Esse Subsistens*, therefore, so far from being a profound metaphysical analysis of the divine nature, turns out to be the Platonic idea of a predicate which is at best uninformative and at worst unintelligible.[5]

The comparison between objections against the theory of an uncaused cause as Subsistent Existence and those against Plato's theory of Ideas is prompted by the fact that the predicate '＿＿ is existence' is an abstract expression whereas any predicate said of the uncaused cause should be concrete. As Prior once said, 'that's just bad grammar, a combining of words that fails to make them *mean* – like "Cat no six"'.[6] Were we to accept this line of argument, however, we should be hard put to account for the success of so many advertisements in print, radio, and TV. If such claims as 'Brand X puts the whiteness back in your sheets' were meaningless because their benighted authors combined abstract with concrete expressions, advertising companies would long since have gone out of business. That their businesses are booming is due to the fact that even those who may well be affronted by grammatical and logical howlers in advertisements are also perfectly well aware of what they mean. 'Brand X puts the whiteness back in your sheets' translates very simply into 'Brand X makes your sheets white again'.

Before dismissing 'The uncaused cause is its existence' as unintelligible we might try doing with it what we can do so readily with TV advertisements: we might try translating it into a form which does not offend either our grammatical or our logical susceptibilities. All that the offending proposition does is to put positively what is expressed negatively by 'The uncaused cause is not distinct from its existence'. There may be some dispute as to whether the latter proposition is true or not, but it is not difficult to show that it is intelligible. We have only to recall that a predicate '*F*' cannot be meaningful unless 'not-*F*', too, is

5 A. Kenny, *The Five Ways* (London: Routledge & Kegan Paul, 1969), p.95.
6 A.N. Prior, 'Can Religion be Discussed?', in A. Flew and A. Macintyre, *New Essays in Philosophical Theology* (London: SCM Press, 1955), p.5.

meaningful. 'Red' cannot be meaningful unless 'non-red' is, nor 'intelligent' unless 'stupid' (i.e. 'non-intelligent') is, nor 'adroit' unless 'clumsy' (i.e. 'non-adroit') is. Similarly, '____ *is* distinct from its existence' cannot be meaningful unless '____ is *not*-distinct from its existence' is also. Now, the former occurs in 'Socrates is distinct from his property of existing', a proposition which is far from unintelligible, since it implies simply that 'Socrates does not exist' is not self-contradictory. Obviously, then, the predicable '____ is *not* distinct from his property of existing' must be meaningful also. Now, 'God is identical with his property of existing' is simply another way of saying precisely what is said by 'God is not distinct from his property of existing'. And, because the latter employs a meaningful predicate, the former does too.

The preceding argument might be summarized as follows, in which '*F*-ness' does duty for 'existence' and 'being *F*' does duty for 'property of existing':

7.1 'The uncaused cause is his *F*-ness' is intelligible if 'The uncaused cause is his being *F*' is intelligible.

7.2 'The uncaused cause is his being *F*' is intelligible if 'The uncaused cause is not distinct from his being *F*' is intelligible.

7.3 'The uncaused cause is not distinct from his being *F*' is intelligible if the predicable '____ is not distinct from his being *F*' is intelligible.

7.4 The predicable '____ is not distinct from his being *F*' is intelligible if the predicable '____ is distinct from his being *F*' is intelligible.

7.5 The predicable '____ is distinct from his being *F*' is intelligible if the proposition 'Socrates is distinct from his being *F*' is intelligible.

7.6 But, the latter is intelligible, since it implies merely that 'Socrates is not *F*' is not self-contradictory.

7.7 Therefore, all the foregoing conditions have been met for 'The uncaused cause is his *F*-ness' or 'The uncaused cause is his being *F*' to be intelligible.

7.8 Therefore, 'The uncaused cause is his existence' and 'The uncaused cause is his property of existing' are intelligible.

If the foregoing argument is correct, it would be entirely inappropriate at this point to insist that the notion of anything being identical with its existence is *inconceivable*. Of course, if 'inconceivable' were being used merely loosely to mean 'unimaginable', the claim would be incontestable, for there are many situations that are unimaginable without being also inconceivable. Thus, a non-existing Socrates is unimaginable, even though perfectly conceivable, since that is just what we do conceive of when we say 'Socrates does not exist'. Again, although we cannot imagine black swans being simultaneously non-black, we have no difficulty in conceiving of it, as we do in saying 'Black swans are non-black': although false, self-contradictory propositions are not meaningless. The same kind of point can be made in regard to something being identical with its existence. We need to distinguish between imagining it and conceiving it; and, though the former is impossible, the latter is not. Indeed, that is exactly what we do when we attach to 'God' the predicable '____ is not distinct from his existence'. Conceivability is independent of imaginability, no less than it is of truth. And God's being identical with his existence is quite conceivable, irrespective of whether it be true or false, imaginable or unimaginable.

If there is a puzzle about 'The uncaused cause is its existence', it is not because it is *like* the advertisement in intermixing abstract with concrete, but because of the way in which it is *unlike* our advertising example. In order to remove the abstract term from 'The uncaused cause is its existence' we had to express it in terms of what it was *not* saying: 'Not (the uncaused cause is not identical with its existence)'. In the advertising example, however, there was no question of having to say 'Not (Brand X does not make your sheets white)'. While there was no difficulty with expressing 'Brand X puts the whiteness back in your sheets' both concretely and positively, it might seem impossible to do the same for 'The uncaused cause is its existence'. Although there is no difficulty about saying 'The uncaused cause exists', our language seems incapable of expressing positively the fact that the referents of 'the uncaused cause' and of '____ exists' are one and the same.

The problem is that the language we use is suitable for speaking about things that are distinct from their existence; and hence, when used about the uncaused cause, its very structure gives the misleading impression that the uncaused cause, too, is distinct from its existence. The impression could be avoided only if language were to contain a proposition or propositions devoid of any distinction between subject expression and predicate, i.e. propositions that were logically simple in the sense of containing no *sub*-propositional logical parts. If, however, no such proposition were even conceivable, then it might be plausible to object that there is surely something wrong with an ontological claim that, to escape being misleading, needs for its expression a proposition with a logical form that is not even conceivable. This, I should think, would be a rather more substantial objection than the one based on the intermixing of abstract and concrete terms. I shall, however, try to show that it too fails, for logically simple propositions are by no means inconceivable.

If the notion of a proposition with no sub-propositional logical parts seems bizarre, the reason may lie in our accepting unquestioningly that propositions must always say something *about something* – that not only must predications always be propositions, but propositions must always be predications. This claim has only to be stated explicitly to be recognized as rather less than tautological, for what suffices to characterize a proposition does not suffice for a predication. To be a proposition it is enough that an expression be a bearer of truth-value; to be a predication, however, an expression has not only to be a bearer of truth-value, but has also to say something about something. All predications, of course, must be logically complex, containing at least two logical parts, either a subject and predicate, or predicable and higher-level predicate. But, what of the converse? Are *all* propositions predications, expressions saying something about something, and hence logically complex? Or, could there not be propositions that merely said something (with truth-value), though without saying something *about* something? In approaching these questions we might ponder the warning implicit in Waismann's remarks that,

> by growing up in a certain language, by thinking in its semantic and syntactical grooves, we acquire a certain more or less uniform outlook on the world – an outlook we are scarcely aware of until (say) by coming across a language of a totally different structure we are shocked into seeing the oddity of the obvious, or what seemed to be obvious.[7]

A proposition might be said to have sub-propositional logical parts (i.e. be logically complex) on three grounds:

7.9 If it were saying something about an individual or individuals, e.g. 'Tom is tall', 'The Robinsons are crossing the

7 F. Waismann, *How I See Philosophy* (London: Macmillan, 1968), p.174.

street'. Here a logical subject is employed with a first-level predicate.

7.10 If, instead of logical subject and first-level predicate, the parts were first-level predicable and second-level predicate (or second-level and third-level, etc.)

7.11 If it were in some tense other than the simple present: such tenses are a composite of the simple present with one or more tense inflectors.

Now, I do not suggest that a proposition containing a logical predicate could be anything but logically complex. But I do suggest that a proposition could be logically simple if it fulfilled the following conditions:

7.12 If it were to employ no predicates at all, not even a first-level one, *and*

7.13 If, though tensed, it were in the simple present.

To support this position I offer a number of examples, the first of which is the Rumanian 'fulgură' (literally, 'lightens'), which is not only grammatically simple, but, as I shall argue, logically simple as well. Our interest, however, is not grammatical, but logical; for we want to know whether there are any grounds for analysing the proposition in terms of singular term/first-level predicate. The question, therefore, is whether there are any parts of 'fulgură' that signify separately. This, of course, is not the same as asking whether the proposition contains separate expressions, for expressions like 'The Bull and Bush' may contain separate expressions, though none that *signify* separately. On the other hand, an expression like 'ambulat' ('He is walking') may contain no *separate* expressions, even though containing expressions that do signify separately: the 't' inflection signifies for 'he', and the verb stem 'ambula' signifies for walking. Unlike 'ambulat', 'fulgură' contains no inflection at all, but is nothing more than the verb stem. Thus, not only does it contain no separate expression, it contains no expression that even *signifies* separately. But, in the absence of any expression that signifies separately, the Rumanian proposition offers no grounds for analysis into singular term and first-level predicate, nor into any other (proper) logical parts.[8] Here, therefore, is one proposition that is logically simple.

8 This is not simply a point of ordinary grammar; it is a point of philosophical logic.

The same can be said of the German 'es klappert' (literally, 'it rattles'), as can be seen from one context in which it appears, e.g. 'Grossmutter, da ist eine Maus drin! hört wie es klappert! da ist eine Maus drin!'[9] To be a grammatical subject 'es' ought to refer back to 'Maus', and hence should have not the neuter, but the feminine form 'sie'. 'Es', therefore, is not a subject, but a mere grammatical filler, which could well be omitted were we (or the Germans) not so bound by convention as to require a dummy subject term where a genuine one was lacking. So, despite the 'es', 'es klappert' contains no expression that might even purport to refer to a Fregean object. Since it contains no referring expressions, it admits of no singular term/first-level predicate analysis. Like 'fulgură', therefore, 'es klappert' also is a logically simple proposition.[10]

It might be objected that perhaps 'fulgură' and certainly 'es klappert' are in the present tense. But, if tensed, they are surely complex because constituted from two elements – one a tense inflector and the other a proposition in the tenseless present. Ought not the logical structure of 'it is rattling' therefore be 'Pr (it *is* rattling)', where 'Pr' is the present tense inflector and '*is*' is the tenseless present?

It is a disputed question whether this is, or even could be, the logical structure of 'it is rattling'. In Prior's view it could not be:

> For suppose we do take the view that tensed utterances can be formed by attaching some sort of modifier to timeless propositional contents, e.g. that 'I shall see John' amounts to something like '(Me seeing John) future', where the element in brackets is supposed to be a non-temporally characterized 'content'. Then if attaching 'future' to such a content forms a future-tensed sentence, '(Me seeing John) future' will not itself be the sort of thing 'future' or 'past' can be attached to, since

9 'Grandmother, there is a mouse inside! Hark at the rattling! There is a mouse inside!' (C. Brentano, *Geschichte vom braven Kasperl and dem schönen Anmerl*).

10 As in the case of 'fulgură', this conclusion is drawn not from a grammatical premiss but from a logical one, namely, the absence of any possible referring expression. I should add that, although even one example suffices to establish the possibility of logically simple propositions, there is a whole range of propositions in English and German which, I should argue, are logically simple despite being grammatically complex, e.g. 'It is raining (snowing, hailing, thundering)', 'It is quiet', 'It is draughty', 'es brennt' ('Fire!'). Cf. my 'Logically Simple Propositions', *Analysis* 34 (1973–4), pp.123–8.

it is not a content but a tensed sentence. The building up of sentences that have *complex* tenses requires that tensing be an operation of which the subjects are themselves tensed sentences, and when we have got inside all other tensing to the 'kernel' of the complex, *its* tense will have to be the present.[11]

Prior's view rests on two premisses. The first is that, contrary to Quine, Smart, and others, tensed discourse is irreducible to tenseless discourse; the second is that tenses may be iterated. It is unnecessary to argue whether these points are true or false, since it suffices for my purposes not that they be true, but merely that they make sense. Now, the ineliminability of tenses is not a nonsensical notion, nor therefore is the iteration of tenses. But their iteration requires that the first of the iterated tense inflectors should operate on an expression of the same logical type as does the last inflector of the group. The last inflector operates on a tensed sentence. Hence the first must do likewise. So, the basic unit of tensed discourse is not a tenseless proposition, but one in the present tense.

On this view, then, although tensing introduces logical complexity into 'it *was* rattling' and into many other tensed propositions, it not only does not, but cannot do so where the tense in question is the simple present. And that is precisely the case with 'it is rattling'. If this is correct, some propositions seem clearly to be logically simple. These include 'fulgură' and 'es klappert'. Lingering doubts about their logical simplicity would seem to stem from the dispute as to whether or not tenses are eliminable in favour of dates and the like. However, even if they were, talk of propositions being tensed would not be nonsense; and so the notion of propositions in the present tense being logically simple would still make good sense. That is the minimum I want to claim, and it is the least I think I have shown – that the nature of propositions does not preclude their being logically simple. I claim not that there could be a language composed *exclusively* of such propositions, but only that there is no reason why a language with logically complex propositions should not include simple ones as well.

It might be urged that no one of the allegedly simple propositions *has* to be construed as simple, but that all are equally

11 A.N. Prior, *Past, Present and Future* (Oxford: Oxford University Press, 1967), p.15.

construable as logically complex. I shall not debate the point here, nor need I do so, since for present purposes it does not matter whether they are construable as logically complex, provided there is nothing against their being also construable as logically simple. All I need claim to have established here, and in the article mentioned in note 10, is merely that the notion of a logically simple proposition is an acceptable one, and acceptable indeed as one that may well be instantiated in quite ordinary creature-talk. At least that much has been done.

This discussion of logically simple propositions was prompted by the suggestion that the notion of subsistent existence was suspect because it was expressible only by propositions whose logical structure carried misleading ontological implications. As I noted earlier, the objection would carry weight only if it were impossible even to conceive of logically simple propositions, i.e. those propositions with a structure appropriate to the task of expressing for the uncaused cause the analogue of what is expressed for Fido by 'Fido exists'. Such a proposition might be written simply as 'Exists', using the upper case 'E' to distinguish the propositional use of 'exists' from its predicative use. Since it has turned out that logically simple propositions are at least conceivable, the objection lapses.

So much for difficulties arising from the fact that 'The uncaused cause is its existence' contains a concrete subject but an abstract predicate. Kenny, however, has offered two other objections purporting to show the proposition as either unintelligible or uninformative, depending on how the predicate '____ exists' is construed. To construe it as a predicate variable would mean that the proposition 'The uncaused cause exists' would be an open sentence, and therefore unintelligible. Since I have shown in the Appendix to chapter 4 that '____ exists' is not a predicate variable, I need dwell no longer on that particular option. Kenny's alternative is that '____ exists' be understood as a predicate which holds of all individuals and hence, he thinks, is the 'thinnest' and least informative of predicates. Moreover, since it is common to all individuals, it 'could hardly constitute the particular essence of any subject'.[12] However, what follows from the premiss that existence is common to all individuals is not that it could hardly constitute the particular essence of any subject, but that any

12 A. Kenny, *The Five Ways* (London: Routledge & Kegan Paul, 1969), p.95.

essence it did constitute would not be particularly interesting. Yet even that conclusion is suspect, for it rests on the dubious and unargued premiss that if – which I do not necessarily concede – the *predicative* use of 'exists' really is the thinnest possible kind of predicate, then its *propositional* use must be the thinnest possible kind of proposition. If the notion of subsistent existence is to be rejected, it will have to be for reasons other than these or the ones considered earlier.

There can be only one uncaused cause

So far, although I have spoken of Fido's existing being caused by an uncaused cause, I have not considered whether there would be many uncaused causes or only one. However, now that *m* is known to be Subsistent Existence, it is not difficult to show that there could be no more than one uncaused cause. Let us assume the contrary to be true, and that in addition to *m* there was another uncaused cause, *n*. Then, since an uncaused cause is subsistent existence, *m* and *n* would be two instances of subsistent existence. But, to say that they are two is to say that they are individuated, each being an individual instance of subsistent existence. But, if they are individuated, then *m* and *n* must each be distinct from its existence. But to say that would be to embrace a contradiction; for it would be saying that something which *cannot* be distinct from its existence (because uncaused) *is* distinct from its existence (because an individual). It is impossible therefore that there be more than one uncaused cause. Cause *m* is not merely *an* uncaused cause, it is *the* uncaused cause – the ultimate cause not only of Fido's existing but of that of every other individual as well .

The uncaused cause is not an individual in an univocal sense

Considered in itself, the conclusion that *m* is the ultimate cause of every individual might seem to carry Spinozian overtones, at least to the extent of suggesting that *m* is not only *causa omnium rerum* but also *causa sui*. That would follow, of course, only if *m* were itself a concrete individual, something which is precluded to it in virtue of there being no distinction between it and its existence, whereas that distinction does hold for all concrete individuals. Thus, although *m* is indeed a concrete *entity* (because it is capable of causing), it cannot be a concrete *individual*, or at least it cannot be an individual except in an analogical sense of that term. A corollary is that the *m* is not a body of any kind. These conclusions serve to emphasize just how radical is the difference between *m* on the one hand and Fido, *a*, *b*, *c*, *d*, and any concrete individual on the other.

Extraordinary as the conclusion might seem, it is far from novel. Aquinas, for example, had already said as much in the thirteenth century when he noted: '"substance" means that which is possessed of a nature such that it will exist of itself. But this nature is not the thing's existence. So it is plain that God does not belong to the genus of substance.'[13] Paul Tillich, belonging to a different tradition, makes much the same point in claiming that 'the being of God cannot be understood as the existence of a being alongside others or above others. If God is *a* being, he is subject to the categories of finitude, especially to space and substance.'[14]

Is the Universe the uncaused cause?

Granted that Fido could not exist unless ultimately he was caused to do so by an uncaused cause, why should the Universe not be that cause? Or, putting it another way, why should the Universe be caused to exist? This question has been answered in various ways:

7.14 In view of the nature of explanation, the question would be senseless.

7.15 In view of the nature of explanation, the theistic hypothesis is more probable than that the existence of the Universe should be uncaused.

7.16 The reason is that the Universe is not the kind of being which could exist without being caused to do so.

Among statements of the first position it would be difficult to find any more explicit that those from Matson and Scriven. The former claims that 'the universe is the framework within which causal explanations operate. And although these explanations show the linkage of one part of the universe to another, it is quite beyond their scope to link the universe to anything else. To ask for the

---

13 Aquinas, *Summa Theologiae*, I, 3, 5 ad 1um
14 P. Tillich, *Systematic Theology*, (Chicago: Chicago University Press), I, part II, IIB, 3b.

cause of the universe is to ask a question similar to "When is time?" or "Where is space?"'[15] Unlike Matson, who argues from the nature of *causal* explanation, Scriven bases himself on what he considers to be the nature of explanation in general:

> We know that either the sum of all explanations or the final theory cannot itself require explanation . . . . There is no point in asking *why* the chain of explanations does not have a beginning, if it does not; or why it has *this* beginning rather than another, if it has this beginning; or why it is only as old as it is, if it is only that old, for we have passed into the realm where explanations are no longer indigenous. . . . Some questions just do not make sense in the limit, and so it is with the present question, Why does the Universe exist? If it is pushed to the limit and answers about the function and relation of the parts of the Universe are rejected, it simply becomes an improper question.[16]

At first sight it is puzzling why anyone should think that either of these views is what they purport to be – an effective counter to the theistic position that the Universe is caused to exist by God. To the theistic claim that the Universe is to be viewed within the further context provided by the existence of God, Matson and Scriven reply in effect by denying the possibility of any such further context. However, it is one thing for them to claim that there is a limit beyond which it is senseless to ask for further explanation of why Fido should exist, but quite another thing to claim that that limit is reached when explanation extends as far as the existence of the Universe[17] – for that is the very point supposed to be at issue.

Matson's and Scriven's position is more understandable if taken to be assuming that the argument to show that the Universe is caused to exist must appeal to the Principle of Sufficient Reason or of Intelligibility. In that case they might be saying not only that there is a point at which that principle is no longer applicable, but that such a point is reached with the existence of the Universe.

15 W. Matson, *The Existence of God* (Ithaca: Cornell University Press, 1965), p.83.
16 M. Scriven, *Primary Philosophy* (New York: McGraw-Hill, 1966), pp.124–5.
17 It is possible that Matson could defend himself by saying that he is claiming not that explanation could not go beyond the existence of the Universe, but only that *causal* explanation could not do so, the reason being that the very notion of a cause would then become meaningless. I shall discuss this point in chapter 9.

Even this, however, would be to overstate their case, for they are not entitled to state *that* the limit is reached with the existence of the Universe: all they are entitled to ask is *why* the limit is *not* reached at that point. In other words, it is perfectly proper to challenge the theist to prove that the Principle of Sufficient Reason is applicable to the existence of the Universe; it is presumptuous to deny its applicability, at least on the grounds of the nature of explanation. They should be claiming not that the existence of the Universe requires no explanation, but merely that it has not been shown to require any. Framed in this way, they would only be making the modest and entirely reasonable point that the theist cannot simply assume that the existence of the Universe as a whole needs to be explained.

Swinburne neither overreaches himself as do Matson and Scriven, nor accepts the Principle of Sufficient Reason as offering any answer to whether the Universe is caused to exist. Recognizing that his 'choice is between the universe as stopping-point and God as stopping-point', he suggests that the matter can be resolved 'only by an *a posteriori* [argument] from the simplicity and explanatory power of a postulated *explanans* in comparison with the complexity of the *explanandum*'.[18] He himself provides a simple summary of his argument.

> There is quite a chance that if there is a God he will make something of the finitude and complexity of the universe. It is very unlikely that a universe would exist uncaused, but rather more likely that God would exist uncaused. The existence of the universe is strange and puzzling. It can be made more comprehensible if we suppose that it is brought about by God. This supposition postulates a simpler beginning of explanation than does the supposition of the existence of an uncaused universe, and that is grounds for believing the former supposition to be true.[19]

Whether or not Swinburne's estimates of the relative probabilities are correct, his approach is at least innocent of the mistakes of either Matson or Scriven on the one hand, or of the proponents of the Principle of Sufficient Reason on the other. There is, however,

18 R. Swinburne, *The Existence of God* (Oxford: Oxford University Press, 1979), p.129.
19 ibid., pp.131–2.

another approach which, either wittingly or unwittingly, both he and they seem to have overlooked; and that is the direct approach of examining whether the Universe is the kind of thing which, like Fido, does need to be caused, under pain of its existing having contradictory implications. If that can be settled, there will be no need to approach the problem indirectly either via probability theory, or via the theory of explanation, or via appeal to principles that are not obviously appropriate to the task.

Discussion of whether Fido was caused to exist turned on what it meant for Fido to be an individual, namely, that he was distinct from his real property of existence. Similarly, discussion of whether the Universe has a cause will depend on whether the Universe too is an individual.

Is the Universe itself an individual?

To answer this question, the meaning of 'the Universe' needs to be defined in such a way as to favour no particular answer to the question 'Why does the Universe exist?' Having to be quite neutral in that regard, our notion of the Universe must satisfy the following two conditions:

7.17 it must not *presuppose* either that the Universe does have a cause, for then it would be guilty of prejudging the answer to the issue in question,

7.18 it must not *exclude* the possibility of the Universe having a cause, for that too would be prejudging the issue in question, though in the opposite way.

One definition to be considered comes from Leibniz:

The Universe is everything that exists, other than God.

This clearly offends against (7.17), for it assumes what it has no right to assume at this stage, namely, that there either is or could be a God. In effect, it defines God *into* existence. The remedy might therefore seem to lie in omitting all mention of God, thus:

The Universe is everything that exists.

However, while this certainly satisfies (7.17), it now offends against (7.18). For, by defining the Universe as *everything* that exists, it excludes the possibility of there being anything other than the Universe, and defines God *out of* existence.

In order to meet not only (7.17) but (7.18) as well, I propose the following definition:

The Universe is everything existing which either is a concrete individual or is individuated by individuals.

I choose this for several reasons. The first is that the question 'How ever can it be that Fido exists?' arose because Fido was a concrete individual, and it seems desirable that the Universe should include everything that might give rise to such a question. It should therefore include all individuals – stars, planets, humans, brute animals, plants, trees, stones, mountains, atoms, molecules, etc. It is impossible, however, to include all individuals without also including whatever they may individuate – properties, relations, thoughts, fields of force, etc. So, if the Universe is to include all individuals, it must include also whatever they individuate. Although it may be debated just where the line of demarcation should be drawn between individuals and what are merely individuated by individuals (on what side of the line would space and time fall?) my definition would be unaffected, whatever the outcome of that debate. For present purposes I am not interested in whether something is an individual rather than merely individuated by an individual. All that matters for the moment is that it be accepted as *either* an individual *or* as individuated by an individual, for in either case it would still fall within the Universe.

On the one hand, the proposed definition includes everything that an atheist would include in the Universe – but no more. On the other hand, it does not close off any possibility that a theist might want left open, e.g. the possibility of the Universe having a cause. Of course, some theists, might object that it does close off that possibility, since it excludes the possibility of there being any *individual* other than the Universe and its contents. This, they might say, is tantamount to excluding the possibility of the existence of God, for surely the very least to be said of God is that he is an individual of some sort. The objection could be sustained, however, only if God were taken to be an individual in the *same sense* of 'individual' as is used in saying that mountains, bees, and humans are individuals; and that would be to anthropomorphize God. Since most theists are anxious not to anthropomorphize God, but to insist on his transcendence (i.e. his radical difference from the Universe and everything in it), they cannot reasonably object to my definition of the Universe.

Having defined how the term 'Universe' will now be used, we may return to the question of whether the Universe is an individual. The answer is yes, it is an individual. Why? Simply because it is composed of individuals and what is individuated by individuals. Of course, it might be objected immediately that what is true of parts need not be true of the whole that they compose. Just because the members of a team are men, it does not follow that the team itself is a man. And just because the parts of the Universe are individuals, it does not follow that the Universe itself is an individual. To think otherwise, it might be said, would be to commit the fallacy of composition.

Certainly, one must be alert to the possibility of committing that fallacy. However, the invalidity of an argument schema shows not that the conclusion is *false*, but only that it cannot follow simply in virtue of that particular schema. Hence, from the invalidity of the schema 'If the parts of the whole are F, then the whole itself is *F*' it does not follow that a whole may *never* have the same property as its parts – a table is of course wooden if all its parts are wooden, and a society is wealthy if all its members are wealthy. Moreover, it is always the case that whatever is composed of individuals is itself an individual. Although a raft is not a plank because its parts are planks, it is an individual (raft) because its members are individuals, albeit individual planks. An army may not be a man because its members are men, but it is an individual because its members are individuals. What kind of individual is it? An individual army. The Eighth Army is one army, the Fifth Army another. Similarly, although the Universe would be neither a man nor a mouse even if all of its parts were men or mice, it is an individual (universe) if its parts are individuals[20] (of various sorts).

Even though that point is innocent of the fallacy of composition, there may still be some unease about regarding the Universe as an individual. One reason is its sheer size, another is that it is all-encompassing. The sheer size of the Universe could represent a problem if we were to think that every individual must be delimitable. If that were true, then an infinite Universe could not

---

20 I am not saying that the Universe is individuated *solely* by its individual parts, any more than the Eighth Army is. The Eighth Army remains the Eighth Army (and not the Fifth), even when some of its members have been replaced; and the Universe would remain the Universe even if some of its members were replaced. But neither the Universe nor the Eighth Army could be an individual at all unless some of their parts were individuals.

be an individual, since *ex hypothesi* it would not be delimitable. Let us therefore consider whether every individual really must be delimitable. Let us assume there to be an infinitely long mountain range, and ask whether it would be any less an individual than a finite range would be. Of course, neither we nor even a light ray could ever traverse or in any other way delimit the whole of the infinite range, whereas the finite one could be either traversed or otherwise delimited. But delimitability cannot be a condition for being an individual range, for many ranges have been named and known to be individual ranges long before they had been delimited, and even before it was known whether they were or were not infinitely long. So, even an infinite mountain range would still be an individual range. It is not necessary that the range itself be delimited, but suffices that some of its parts be delimited, and that it be identifiable in some such way as 'the mountain range containing parts *a*, *b*, *c*' (where *a*, *b*, and *c* are merely *some* parts of the range: those that have been delimited).

Again, consider an infinite pile of books. To know that it was an *individual* pile there would be no need to be able to peer to the 'top' of it. On the contrary, it could be identified as 'the pile of books of which the three bottom members are *d*, *e*, *f*'. Likewise with an infinite Universe. Here, too, it is not required that it be delimited, but simply that it be identifiable in some such way as 'the Universe containing individual galaxies *g*, *h*, *k*,' where *g*, *h*, and *k* may be only some of innumerable galaxies in the Universe. Our solar system is an individual (solar system), the galaxies are individual (galaxies), and so too is our Universe an individual (universe).

As for the fact that the Universe is all-encompassing, the objection may go like this:

7.19 A prerequisite of individuality is distinguishability: nothing could be an individual unless distinguishable from other individuals.

7.20 But, since the Universe is the *totality* of all that is individual or individuated by individuals, there could be nothing from which it could be distinguished.

7.21 Therefore, it would make no sense to regard it as an individual.

If we accept (7.19), the whole weight of the argument will rest on (7.20), i.e. on whether there really could be nothing from which the Universe could be distinguished. Well, admittedly there could never be two universes co-existing; for then neither of them would encompass *all* individuals, and hence neither could be a universe. However that does not settle the matter, for while two universes could not exist concurrently, they could exist successively, e.g. the ceasing to exist of Universe *A* could be followed by the beginning to exist of Universe *B*, which would be distinct from *A*. In claiming *A* and *B* to be distinct I am not relying on their being temporally distinct, for in a tightly curved time there might be no such distinction. Even in such a time, however, they would be distinct if none of the individuals in *A* were at all continuous with those of *B*. So, even universes may be distinguishable.

Of the three objections against the Universe being an individual none has been valid, and so our earlier conclusion stands. It is in fact confirmed by the findings of mereology in which 'Universe' has been defined thus:

> *A* is the Universe if *A* is the mereological class of all existing objects.[21]

The key notion here is that of a mereological class, a notion which Leśniewski, the founding father of mereology, was at pains to distinguish from Russell's notion of a class which he regarded as defective in failing to distinguish between the distributive and collective senses of class expressions.[22] Had we been restricted to the distributive sense of 'class' it is doubtful whether the Universe could have been regarded as a class, for in the case of a distributive class it must always be possible to specify the *kind* of objects that form it: such a class is always a class of objects that are *F*, or at least of objects that are *F* or *G* or *H*, etc. Since it is doubtful that we could ever give a disjunctive list of the kind of objects in the Universe, it is equally doubtful that the Universe could ever be considered as a distributive class. Yet, even if it could, it would have to be an abstract rather than a concrete object; and that would debar us from inferring that a class containing concrete objects must itself be a concrete object.

21 B. Soboçinski, 'Atomic Mereology', *Notre Dame Journal of Formal Logic* 12 (1971), p.83.
22 J. Leśniewski, 'O podstawach matematyki', *Przeglad Fiolficzny* 310 (1928), pp.261–91. Translation taken from M. Munitz, *Existence and Logic* (New York: New York University Press, 1974), p.175.

We are unencumbered by these and other difficulties by treating the Universe not as a distributive class, but as a collective one in Leśniewski's sense of that term. For one thing, since a collective class does not have to be comprised of parts of only one kind nor even a finite disjunction of kinds, there is no bar to the Universe being a collective class. Moreover, a collective class of objects not only is itself an object, but is an object of the same type as its members. In particular, if its members are concrete objects then so too will the collective class be a concrete object, and not an abstract one as is the case with distributive classes. Finally, there is no need for the parts of a collective class to be continuous: there may even be spatial and temporal gaps between them. And that point too is relevant to considering the Universe as a (collective) class.

What all this means for our notion of the Universe is that it may quite properly be considered as a collective class of concrete objects, as Soboçinski defined it. Moreover, there is no distinction of type between the Universe *qua* object and any one of the objects that comprise it. Furthermore, the Universe may be conceived no less properly as a class of individuals (which is how I have conceived it) than as a class of objects. As a class of individuals it itself will be an individual of the same type (concrete) as are any of its parts, including Fido.[23]

The Universe is not the uncaused cause

Since the Universe itself is an individual, it will be no less distinct from its existence than are Fido and all other individuals distinct from their existence. Whatever is distinct from its existence, however, can exist only if caused to do so. Hence, the Universe cannot be the uncaused cause – Matson, Scriven, Russell, Mackie, and many others notwithstanding.

23 After writing these pages on the Universe as an individual, I came across a similar conclusion drawn by D.M. Armstrong in his *Nominalism and Realism* (Cambridge: Cambridge University Press, 1978) in which the following points are made:

It is worth noting that the totality of things – the universe – is a particular (p.155, n.1).

A collection of particulars (scattered or not) will also be a particular, and so a substance. If the world consists simply of particulars having properties and relations, then we can say not only that all particulars are substances but also that all substances are particulars (p.132).

Penelhum once wrote: 'Somewhere there must be an unexplained and inexplicable being: either the world we live in, or a being that created it, or another being that created the creator, and so on. But the cosmological argument does not help us to know where to stop'.[24] Whatever might be said about such forms of the cosmological argument as he was considering, it cannot be said that the present argument 'does not help us to know where to stop'. The criterion is very clear: a stop both must, and can only be made, with a being that is not distinct from its existence. That is why a stop just cannot be made with the Universe. The same answer can be given to Mackie's question, 'Why should there not be a permanent stock of matter whose essence did not involve existence but which did not derive its existence from anything else?'[25] Since any such stock of matter would be distinct from its existence, it would be self-contradictory to suggest that it did 'not derive its existence from anything else'.

24 T. Penelhum, *Religion and Rationality* (New York: Random House, 1971), p.44.
25 J. Mackie, *The Miracle of Theism* (Oxford: Oxford University Press, 1982), p.91.

Chapter 8

Necessary existence

If the previous arguments have been sound there is something which, although causing Fido and even the Universe to exist, does not itself have a cause. Being uncaused, it cannot be distinct from its existence, and thus is not an individual in anything but an analogical sense of that term. Moreover, not being distinct from its existence, it is unique: neither successively nor concurrently could there be any uncaused cause other than the one there is. These various conclusions point to its being what H.P. Owen has called the God of classical theism. However, one of the tenets of classical theism is that God is not merely Subsistent Existence but is also Necessary Existence, a notion often dismissed as absurd and as therefore constituting a *reductio ad absurdum* of any argument which concluded, even by implication, that there was something which existed necessarily. Naturally enough, the contingency argument is thought to be self-refuting in this way. So, since the argument in this book is a contingency argument in the broad sense of that term, we need to determine not only whether the notion of necessary existence is proof against the absurdity charge, but whether the uncaused cause is such that it does indeed exist necessarily.

I THE NOTION OF NECESSARY EXISTENCE

Logical necessity?

A common objection to the notion of necessary existence is that necessity is not a property of thing, but only of propositions. When we say that a proposition is necessary, we mean that it is necessarily true or false. But things cannot be true or false, and *a fortiori* they cannot be necessarily true or necessarily false. On this view, therefore, to say that some *thing* exists necessarily makes as little sense as saying that a stone falls intelligently, or that the sun rises wisely, or that a race is run melodiously. Mackie suggests that once we concede that it is not *logically* impossible 'that the alleged necessary being might not have existed, we have no understanding of how it could be true of this being that it is not the case that it might not have existed'.[1]

Mackie's claim will be addressed later in the chapter. At this point, however, we might well wonder what could justify a claim that restricted necessity to propositions. It certainly could not be maintained that *nothing* said of propositions can be said of things. For 'complex' may be said of things no less than of propositions: a proposition is complex if composed of parts (whether of other propositions or of subject and predicate), and a car is complex if composed of parts. Indeed, not only does there seem no good reason for restricting necessity to propositions, there seems to be positive reason for *not* doing so. For, as Geach has remarked, 'since what is "necessary" is what "cannot" not be, to say that "necessary" can only refer to logical necessity is equivalent to saying that whatever cannot be so, logically cannot be so – e.g. that since I cannot speak Russian, my speaking Russian is logically impossible: which is absurd'.[2] This of course is merely a conceptual point, that can be made without begging the question as to whether there really is anything answering to the notion 'necessary existence'. It merely explains what would be meant by such a being, if there were one.

'___ exists' as requiring something to be true of?

Even if we were to change our question from 'Does the uncaused cause exist necessarily?' to 'Is the proposition "The uncaused cause exists" necessarily true?', the objector would still not be

---

1 J. Mackie, *The Miracle of Theism* (Oxford: Oxford University Press, 1982), p.84. Hume would certainly agree: 'The words . . . *necessary existence* have no meaning at all or, which is the same thing, none that is consistent' (*Dialogues Concerning Natural Religion*, part IX).

2 G.E.M. Anscombe and P.T. Geach, *Three Philosophers* (Oxford: Blackwell, 1969), p.114.

placated. For he would then point out that, while an affirmative answer may not be meaningless, it is nevertheless false; since 'The uncaused cause exists' is an existential proposition, and no existential proposition can necessarily be true.

The point is well taken, although the grounds for it are sometimes mistakenly thought to be peculiar to existential propositions. In fact, however, neither '____ exists' nor any other first-level predicable has necessarily to be true of anything, and nowhere is that more so than in those propositions that are often proposed as being paradigms of necessity: analytic propositions. In 'Man is an animal', for example, the predicable '____ is an animal' is not being affirmed or denied of anything: what *is* being affirmed is that if anything is a man it is an animal. But this does not fully meet the objection, for there are some analytic propositions in which a first-level predicate (and not merely a first-level predicable) does occur, e.g. 'This man is an animal'. In such cases one might well be tempted to think that '____ is an animal' is surely a necessary predicate.

In fact, there is nothing about the predicable '____ is an animal' that requires there to be any man for it to be true of. And the same holds in the case of 'Fido is a dog': there is nothing about the predicable '____ is a dog' that requires there to be any dog for it to be true of. Of course it is necessary that 'this man' can have '____ is an animal' attached to it as a predicate; and it is necessary that 'Fido' can have '____ is a dog' attached to it as a predicate. But it is not necessary that '____ is an animal' have any man to be predicated of, nor that '____ is a dog' have any particular dog to be predicated of. This may seem like labouring the obvious, but it is worth saying lest the predicates in analytic propositions be regarded as necessary ones. There is indeed a sense in which they can be said to be necessary, but it is not the sense in which we are interested. Whether in analytic or in synthetic propositions, no predicate whatever is necessary in the sense that there has to be something for it to be predicated of.

In the foregoing respect '____ exists' is no different from any other first-level predicable. Consequently, although it could make sense to say that *b* exists contingently, it would make no sense whatever to say that *b* exists necessarily, if that were to mean that the predicable '____ exists' were such that it just had to be true of *b*. Similarly, if we contrast '*b* exists contingently' with '*b* exists necessarily'. From the former we can infer not only that it is a contingent matter whether *b* exist, but that *b*'s existence is a contingent one. From the latter, however, we can infer only that it is a necessary matter that *b* exist, but not that *b*'s existence is a necessary one. Considered in itself, *b*'s existence might well be only contingent, for the fact that *b* cannot cease to exist might be explained by some determination *ab extrinseco*. If all that prevented *b*'s ceasing to exist were merely some extrinsic intervention, then *b*'s existence would still be contingent, even though one could rightly say '*b* exists necessarily'.

An obvious bar to such extrinsic determination would be if '____ exists' were part of the notion of '*b*', and '*b* exists' were analytic. Even this, however, would not allow us to infer that *b*'s *existence* was an inherently necessary one, but only that *b* was a necessary *entity*. The difference between the existence of *b* in non-analytic and analytic examples would not be its being inherently contingent in the first case but inherently necessary in the second. Rather, the kind of existence would be the same in each case; only the kind of entity having it would be different.[3] Thus, talk of inherently necessary existence would be no less inappropriate if '____ exists' were part of an analytic proposition than if it were part of a synthetic proposition. Or, to put it in terms used earlier, even if there were in fact something of which it had to be predicated, that still would not mean that '____ exists' positively required there to be something of which it was true.

It is quite correct, therefore, to say there is nothing about the predicable '____ exists' (nor about any other predicable) that requires there to be something for it to be true of. However, while that particular sense of necessity is relevant to predicates, it really has nothing to do with whether the proposition in which the predicate occurs is necessarily true. To admit that '____ exists' need have nothing to be true of is quite consistent with 'The uncaused cause exists' being necessarily true.

3 Similarly, the kind of attribute bespoken by 'The Polar bear is white' does not differ from that bespoken by 'The dog is white', even though the first proposition might be analytic and the second synthetic. The difference lies not in the *attribute* of being white, but in the kind of *entity* possessing that attribute, i.e. polar bear *vs* dog.

Self-explanatory existence as necessary existence?

Another suggestion for what might be meant by necessary existence is implicit in Penelhum's account of what he considers to
be the rationale for the theist's demand that God's existence be
necessary:

> If it is puzzling that *anything* exists, it should seem puzzling
> that *God* does; if a certain feature's presence in the universe
> is puzzling, then it should seem puzzling that it, or that which
> gives rise to it, should be present in God. In neither case is the
> explanation complete. To complete it more has to be built in:
> the being referred to has to be one whose existence, or whose
> possession of the relevant attributes, is self-explanatory. The
> potentially endless series of 'Why?'-questions has to end in an
> answer that covers not only the last 'Why?' but the next one
> too. So we have the doctrine of a being who necessarily is,
> or necessarily is what he is. It is very important to see that
> exactly the same theoretical move is involved whether it is
> said that the divine existence or nature is self-explanatory to
> us or merely in itself; what is essential is that the explanation
> should be said to lie in the divine being, even if we do not
> know it.[4]

It should be noted that Penelhum conflates the notions of necessary existence with that of self-explanatory existence, his strategy
being to argue that because the latter is absurd so too must be the
former. Arguing for the absurdity of self-explanatory existence,
he claims that the distinctive character of the concept of existence
is that it cannot be 'a quality which a perfect being might have,
since it is not a quality at all'. Hence the very notion of existence
'precludes our saying that there can be a being whose existence
follows from his essence; and also precludes the even stronger
logical move of *identifying* the existence of anything with its
essence'.[5] With these options denied us, the only other way of
God's existence being self-explanatory would be for God to be
the cause of his own existence, a suggestion which Penelhum
rightly regards as manifestly absurd. He concludes that the notion
of a being whose existence is self-explanatory is a 'logically

4 T. Penelhum, 'Divine Necessity', *Mind* 69 (1960), p.176
5 ibid., p.180.

impossible' one, and that 'this is still logically impossible when it is softened by its user's saying that we personally do not know the explanation'.[6] From this it is supposed to follow that the notion of a being whose existence is necessary is likewise logically impossible.

Why does Penelhum consider it proper to conflate 'necessary existence' with 'self-explanatory existence'? Because, like Mackie,[7] he mistakenly thinks that a puzzle is supposed to arise not merely as to why Fido or the Universe exists, but as to why *anything at all* exists. If existence is a puzzle no matter where it is found, then it is of course right that God's existence should be no less puzzling than Fido's or the Universe's. And if the puzzle in regard to the latter two entities was solved by invoking God's existence, then an infinite regress could be blocked (assuming of course that it really did have to be blocked) only by claiming God's existence to be not puzzling at all, but self-explanatory. The absurdity of this move lies in saying that God's existence is self-explanatory, after saying previously that existence, no matter where it was found, was not self-explanatory. On that supposition, if God's existence were self-explanatory, then so too should be Fido's existence; but if Fido's existence were *not* self-explanatory, then neither should God's existence be self-explanatory. The one thing quite impossible would be for God's existence to be self-explanatory while Fido's was not.

The difference between our argument and the one Penelhum and Mackie seem to have in mind is that our puzzle was not 'Why does *anything at all* (including God, if there be a God) exist?', but 'Why does any existing concrete *individual* exist?' What prompted our question was that contradictory implications seemed to follow from saying that Fido exists, implications that would have been associated not with every existent, but only with such as were distinct from their existence. Hence, while there was a logical demand on us to ask why Fido or anything else distinct from its existence should exist, there was absolutely no such demand to ask why something *not* distinct from its existence should exist. Such a question

6 ibid., p.182.
7 Surprisingly, Mackie (*The Miracle of Theism*, p.232) fails to distinguish 'Why is there *anything at all*?' from the more restricted question, 'Why should there be any *world* rather than none?'

would indeed have been entirely gratuitous,[8] whereas in the argument apparently considered by Penelhum and Mackie it would have been entirely mandatory. Moreover, since we did not proceed from the premiss that existence, no matter where it was found, needs to be explained, there was no inconsistency in not requiring any explanation of the existence of the uncaused cause.

Necessary existence as question stopping?

Plantinga has taken a different tack by attempting to explain the necessity of 'God exists' in terms other than necessary *truth*. In its stead he once suggested that to say 'God exists' is necessary is to say that, if it were true, a certain kind of question necessarily could not be asked. Both he and Hick, for example, interpret 'God exists' as being necessary in the sense that it is the point at which questions of the kind 'Why is that such-and-such exists?' cannot sensibly be asked.

This suggestion can be criticized, however, as treating the existence of God as simply a brute fact. Any theist who invoked the existence of God because he was unwilling to accept the existence of the Universe as a brute fact would be no better off for doing so, because God himself is being treated as a brute fact. Hence, it would be more in accord with the principle of simplicity just to accept the existence of the Universe as a brute fact, and forget about God.

Plantinga and Hick each have a rejoinder to this kind of objection, though neither to my mind is satisfactory. Plantinga would say that to ask why God exists 'is to presuppose that God does exist; but it is a necessary truth that if He does, He has no cause; hence there is no answer to a question asking for His causal conditions. The question . . . . is therefore an absurdity. A person

8 To say that the question would have been gratuitous is not to say that the existence of the uncaused cause would be merely a brute fact. A fact is a brute one only if there is no reason for asking or for *not* asking why it is so. The existence of the uncaused cause fails to satisfy that condition, for while there is admittedly no reason to ask why the uncaused cause should exist, there is very good reason for *not* asking that question. The reason is simply that between the uncaused cause and its existence there is lacking the distinction which alone could provide the ground for asking why the uncaused cause should exist. Consequently, there is every reason for *not* asking that question; and so the existence of the uncaused cause cannot be a brute fact, despite its being gratuitous to ask why *that* cause should exist.

who seriously asks it betrays a misapprehension of the concept of God.'⁹ On this view, therefore, although it may be a howler to ask why God exists, it is no howler to ask why that question is a howler. And if we can say *why* it makes no sense to ask why God exists, then it would presumably be wrong to regard God's existence as a brute fact.

Plantinga explains that God's 'beginning to exist is causally impossible, for since it is analytic that God is not dependent upon anything, he has no cause; and hence His coming into existence would be an event which would have no causally sufficient conditions. So, if God does exist, He cannot . . . have begun to exist.'¹⁰ To reach such a conclusion, however, he needs to draw upon an unstated premiss; for, if God does exist, the lack of causally sufficient conditions would fail to show that he did not begin to exist, unless it were assumed additionally that every event requires causally sufficient conditions. And since that assumption is a synthetic proposition, it would either have to be accepted as a brute fact or proved in some way. So, by invoking God, Plantinga may not succeed in avoiding accepting a brute fact; and he still has the task of showing that his brute fact is preferable to the atheist's.

Hick, however, does try to do just that. He is prepared to admit that the existence of God would indeed be a brute fact, but sees it as a logically superior one to that of the existence of the Universe. The latter 'can function as a *de facto* terminus of explanation; but God can, in addition, function as a *de iure* or logical terminus.' He explains that 'the existence of God (defined as eternal, independent, and as the creator of everything that exists other than himself) . . . is an uniquely ultimate fact, behind or beyond which it is logically impossible to go; whereas the existence of the physical universe does not have this totally ultimate character'.¹¹ According to this account, what makes the difference between God and Universe as ultimate explanations is that the former is independent and eternal

9 A. Plantinga, *God and Other Minds* (Ithaca: Cornell University Press, 1967), p.182.
10 A. Plantinga, 'Necessary Being', in *Faith and Philosophy* (Grand Rapids: Eerdmans, 1964), p.107.
11 J. Hick, 'Comment' (in reply to D.R. Duff-Forbes, 'Hick, Necessary Being, and the Cosmological Argument'), *Canadian Journal of Philosophy* 1 (1971–2), pp.486–7.

and creator of everything other than himself, whereas the latter is not.

Although Hick lists three characteristics which make God superior to the Universe as an ultimate explanation, only one of them really matters. The question of eternity[12] is not one that need distinguish God from the Universe. If created, the Universe need not have had a beginning, but could be co-eternal with God, even though dependent upon him. Nor is being a creator a *sine qua non* for an ultimate explanation. If there were grounds for taking the existence of the Universe to be the ultimate explanation of Fido's existing, they would not be vitiated simply because the Universe was *not* 'creator of everything other than itself', for the *ex hypothesi* absence of anything other than itself would make creation a non-question. Of the characteristics mentioned by Hick the only one that matters, therefore, is independence. It is this, apparently, which makes the difference between being a *de facto* and a *de iure* terminus of explanation. It is this which would make it a necessary being in the special sense proposed by Hick.

We are entitled to ask why we should not ascribe independence to the Universe rather than to some entity called 'God'. On this point Hick's position is quite clear:

> Given a beginningless universe it is logically possible to ask whether it exists in dependence upon the will of a God who is creator of everything that exists other than himself. But given such a God, it is not logically possible to ask whether his existence is dependent upon the existence of the physical universe, or of anything else; for his relationship to anything that exists, other than himself, has been defined asymmetrically as that of creator to creature.[13]

Obviously, the possibility of asking whether God exists dependently on something has been eliminated by definition, i.e. by stipulation. But if stipulation could be employed at that point, why could it not have been employed at an earlier point, namely,

---

12 I am using 'eternity' here in the loose sense of 'everlasting existence'. Although 'eternal existence' and 'everlasting existence' may be synonymous in the popular mind, they ought not to be in the philosophical mind. At least since the time of Boethius 'eternity' has had the technical sense of '*interminabilis vitae tota simul et perfecta possessio*' (the complete possession all at once of illimitable life).
13 J. Hick, 'Comment', p.486.

in connection with the Universe? There is, of course, no reason. Only if the Universe were demonstrably a dependent entity would we be blocked from stipulating that it be the terminus of explanation. But, while that option is open to us and some theists, it is not open to Hick who, while he believes that the Universe is a dependent entity, does not think that is *demonstrably* so.

Two conclusions might be drawn about Plantinga's and Hick's understanding of 'necessary existence'. The first is that neither of them is able to avoid admitting at least one brute fact. The second is that it is only in a very attenuated and oblique sense that the necessity, as they envisage it, could be ascribed to *existence* or even to a *truth*, viz. the truth of an existential proposition. Properly speaking, it should be ascribed to the effect which a certain proposition ('God exists') has on the posing of a certain question, namely, the question 'Why is it that the Universe (or some part thereof) exists?' That, however, is not to explain 'necessary existence', but merely to explain it away.

II DOES THE UNCAUSED CAUSE EXIST NECESSARILY?

So far we have discussed three unsuccessful attempts to deny that the notion of necessary existence could apply to anything, and one strained attempt to show that it could. Hence, if that were all we had to guide us in answering the present question, we should be in a miserable quandary as to what to reply. We really ought therefore to consider whether anything we know about the uncaused cause could lead us to conclude that it exists necessarily.

Those, like Hepburn, who take the notion of uncaused cause to be 'rather like "surfaceless sphere", and not far from "non-canine dog"'[14] would naturally answer 'no' to this. There is of course a sense in which they are right, namely, the sense in which an event *e* follows necessarily upon conditions *c* if a statement of their occurrence entails the occurrence of *e*. This is the sense

14 'Following Kant we could argue that we make good sense of the idea of necessity, when we are told of the conditions under which whatever is necessary is necessary. Given such conditions, then such and such is necessarily the case. But the notion of God, we are told, is an "*unconditionally* necessary" being. And this phrase, although *grammatically* unimpeachable, is logically vacuous; rather like "surfaceless sphere", and not far from "non-canine dog"' (R. Hepburn, *Christianity and Paradox*, p.173).

in which *e* is said to be physically necessary. However, since *m* is uncaused and hence lacks any causal conditions, its existence cannot be physically necessary. Indeed, its existence can be neither physically necessary nor physically contingent: the notion of these *physical* modalities is simply inapplicable to it.

Still, just to say that the uncaused cause cannot be physically necessary is not to say that it is not necessary *tout court*, for it is no less presumptuous to regard physical necessity as exhausting the notion of necessity than to regard logical necessity, or logical necessity and physical necessity, as doing so. Swinburne, for example has distinguished six senses of 'necessity',[15] and even his list is not a complete one. As yet, therefore, it remains an open question whether the uncaused cause can be said to exist necessarily in a sense of 'necessarily' that would be acceptable to classical theism.

Before trying to settle that question I should mention two further unacceptable suggestions of what it might mean to say that the uncaused cause exists necessarily. One is Swinburne's fifth sense of 'necessity', which he expresses in the formal mode thus: 'A proposition is necessary if and only if things will be and always have been as it states they are at the time'.[16] While that may well be a satisfactory account of *everlasting* existence, it is not an account of necessary existence except in the quite equivocal sense of 'necessary' which, as I noted earlier, has regretably acquired currency in the phrase 'necessary condition'. Of an entity existing in that manner, it would be no contradiction whatever to say that, although it as a matter of fact neither began to exist nor will cease to exist, neither its beginning nor its ceasing to exist is precluded as a matter of necessity. If the uncaused cause is to be identified with the God of classical theism, however, its existence will have to be necessary in a sense of that term which is modal rather than merely factual.

Swinburne does not endorse the previous view, but suggests rather that the necessity attributed to God is 'that God does not depend for his existence on himself or on anything else'.[17] The implications of this suggestion are brought out by his explaining that

15 R. Swinburne, *The Coherence of Theism* (Oxford: Oxford University Press, 1977), chapter 13.
16 ibid., p.251.
17 ibid., p.267.

if there is no God or any similar being, 'The universe exists' would be a necessary proposition, for in that case the universe would not depend for its existence on anything else. The existence of the universe would be an *ultimate brute fact*. Also, if there were no God or similar being and atoms were indestructible and there were exactly ten billion billion of them, then 'there are ten billion billion atoms' would be a necessary proposition on [the aforementioned] criterion.[18]

This proposal calls for three comments. The first is that, if the argument in the last two chapters is correct, then in considering the Universe as not being dependent for its existence on anything else, Swinburne would unwittingly be entertaining an implicitly self-contradictory proposition, namely, the proposition that 'The universe, which is distinct from its existence and hence is caused to exist, is not dependent on anything and hence is not caused to exist'. From a self-contradiction, however, any conclusion at all can be drawn: not only could we conclude that '"The Universe exists" *is* a necessary proposition', we could equally conclude that '"The Universe exists" is *not* a necessary proposition', and likewise for the proposition 'There are ten billion billion atoms'. If we are to explain the notion of necessary existence, therefore, it will not be in terms of causal independence but in terms of the more basic notion of something's lacking any distinction from its existence.

The second comment is that Swinburne's suggestion no more contains any modal notion than does the earlier proposal to equate necessary existence with everlasting existence. Even were we to allow that the uncaused cause did not as a matter of fact depend for its existence on itself or anything else, we should not thereby be prevented from asking whether it *could not* be so dependent. Yet, only if it could not be so dependent would its existence be necessary in the full-blooded (i.e. modal) sense of that term.

Thirdly, it is scarcely surprising to find that this criterion results in necessary existence being identified with an ultimate brute fact, for a brute fact cannot be modally necessary whether it be ultimate or no. Since a brute fact is one for which there is no explanation as to why it should hold, it must also be a fact for which there is no reason why it should not hold. Why then should it be regarded as a fact that *could not* be otherwise? There is no reason at all: if the uncaused cause were necessary in the sense that Swinburne thinks appropriate to the God of classical theism, it would be a being which *could* not-exist. Consequently, this cannot be the sense of 'necessary existence' that would allow the uncaused cause to be identified with God, for the least that is meant by saying that God exists necessarily is that he exists and could never have not-existed.

As to whether the uncaused cause *could not* not-exist, there is clearly one sense in which it could not: if the Universe exists, then the uncaused cause could not not-exist. However, it is equally clear that we are interested not in an existence which is necessary only in a conditional sense, but in whether the uncaused cause could ever not not-exist even if there were no Universe at all, i.e. whether the uncaused cause is absolutely necessary rather than merely conditionally so. Now, the most noteworthy thing about the uncaused cause, and what makes it so radically different from the Universe and all its contents, is its being not distinct from its existence. Does it follow therefrom that it is impossible that the uncaused cause either will ever not-exist or did ever not-exist? In other words, could it be that the uncaused cause so exists as to be unable either to cease to exist or to have begun to exist?

Let us consider, therefore, the consequence of its being possible that the uncaused cause should have begun to exist? So far as this possibility is concerned, there is of course no restriction on just when it might have been realized; and so it would be no less possible that the uncaused cause should have begun to exist before the Universe existed than concomitantly with that event. Let UC_1 be the uncaused cause that would begin to exist before the Universe, and UC_2 the one that would begin to exist concomitantly with the Universe. Since it was established in the previous chapter that there could be no more than one uncaused cause, whether together or successively, UC_1 and UC_2 would have to be identical with each other. For that same reason they would be not merely that same *kind* of thing, but numerically the same. None the less, they would not be identical in all respects, since they would differ in regard to their life histories. Now, this combination of numerical identity with difference over time is not to be found in abstract entities, but only in concrete ones and, specifically, in concrete individuals. So, the supposition we have been entertaining commits us to allowing that the uncaused cause *is* an individual, even though the identity between it and its existence has been shown to *preclude* its being an individual.[19] We should be committed to accepting precisely the same consequence were we to suppose that the uncaused cause could have ceased to exist. Both suppositions being untenable, therefore, it must be affirmed that the uncaused cause not merely *does* not begin or cease to exist, but that it *cannot* do so: it exists necessarily.

III CONCLUSION

The notion of necessary existence that has now emerged differs from those discussed earlier in the chapter. Obviously, it is not the notion of logical necessity, as it is has so often been misconceived to be. At the same time it shows the error in Mackie's claim that 'we have no understanding of how it could be true of this [uncaused] being that it is not the case that it might not have existed'. Moreover, since it is not self-contradictory to say 'The uncaused cause does not exist', the notion of necessary existence, as I am using it, provides no grounds whatever for any ontological argument for the existence of God. What *would* be self-contradictory would be to say that the existence of the uncaused cause was physically necessary, since that would imply that its existence depended on certain conditions obtaining, and thus that the uncaused cause was, after all, caused to exist. Hence, it was already clear that the existence of the uncaused cause was not physically necessary; and the preceding account is entirely in accord with that contention.

With the exclusion of both logical and physical necessity, it was not perhaps unsurprising that other notions should have been explored. What should be surprising, however, is that so many of them are consistent with the existence of the uncaused cause being simply a brute fact. Swinburne's suggestion that the necessity in question was that of independence is a case in point, for that view would entail that even a Universe without a cause could be said to exist necessarily. Similarly, the suggestion that to say that existence of the uncaused cause was necessary would be to say that a certain kind of question could not sensibly be asked: 'Why is it that the uncaused cause exists?' Now, it is certainly true that that question

19 While precluded from being a concrete *individual*, it is not precluded from being a concrete entity; for a concrete entity is one that can either cause or be caused or both. Since Subsistent Existence is a cause, it is a concrete entity even though not an individual except in an analogous sense of that term.

could not sensibly be asked. However, it is equally true that the
same question could not sensibly be asked of brute facts (if such
there be). Thus, no one claiming the existence of the Universe to
be a brute fact could sensibly ask, 'Why does the Universe exist?'
Not only would this consequence not satisfy the theist, it would
also be a Pickwickian use of 'necessary', for the point about the
putative brute facts is simply that they just do obtain; and if there is
no reason why a brute fact should obtain, there is equally no reason
why it should not obtain. Hence, it would be an intolerable strain
on language to say that a brute fact, thus understood, obtained
necessarily.

Although Penelhum was equally concerned with understanding
why a 'potentially endless series of "Why?"-questions has to end',
he rightly took it as self-evident that a brute fact could have no
claim to being necessary. Thus, the being that he thought to
be the theist's choice for ending the series of 'Why?'-questions
was not a brute fact, but a being whose existence was self-
explanatory. Penelhum, of course, rejected this notion because
he believed, wrongly, that existence was not a real property of
individuals. That, however, is not the point of my recalling his
view here. I recall it simply to show that, even if the notion of
a self-explanatory being is not open to Penelhum's objections, it
is not to be equated with the notion that does in fact put an end
to the series of 'Why?'-questions. In chapter 5 it was shown that
what was needed to terminate that series was a being that was not
distinct from its existence, i.e. Subsistent Existence. We saw earlier
that the notion of Subsistent Existence was not the notion of an
independent being, for the former notion includes the latter, but
not conversely. Precisely the same can be said about the notion of
a self-explanatory being: it is included in the notion of Subsistent
Existence, but not conversely.

Thus, the notion of Subsistent Existence – a being which is not
distinct from its existence – has turned out to be indispensable. The
series of 'Why?-questions had to be blocked, for otherwise Fido
could not have existed: his existing would have had contradictory
implications. It could be blocked only by a being that, unlike
individuals, was not distinct from its existence. Such a being
was uncaused, and thus independent. However, such a being
was also unique in the sense that its notion did not admit of its
being instantiated in any but one way. For that reason, it *could*
neither begin to exist nor cease to exist. In other words, it could

not not-exist, which is to say that it exists necessarily. That is to say, once that being was understood to be Subsistent Existence, it was self-explanatory why its existence was necessary. Moreover, its existence was necessary not in the anaemic (i.e. non-modal) sense that has sometimes been applied to existence, but in the full-blooded (i.e. modal) sense applied to an existence that could neither begin nor end.

Chapter 9

Objections to the contingency argument

My claim to have proved the existence of a being which is Subsistent Existence, unique, and the cause of the Universe, and which I have called 'God' flies in the face of the prevailing wisdom of which perhaps the most uncompromising expression comes from Hepburn:

> a great many philosophers are convinced that the Cosmological Argument was once and for all demolished by Kant and Hume, and that restatements of it are no more significant of life than the twitching of a body already dead. I believe, moreover, that these philosophers are more nearly right than wrong. The Cosmological Argument did receive at least crippling wounds from Kant and Hume.[1]

Speaking more generally, and not confining his remarks to the cosmological argument, Swinburne makes much the same point:

> [Hume and Kant] produced principles designed to show that reason could never reach justified conclusions about matters much beyond the range of immediate experience, and above all that reason could never reach a justified conclusion about the existence of God. In recent years many others have argued in the same spirit, so that both among professional philosophers and outside their narrow circle, there is today a deep scepticism about the power of reason to reach a justified conclusion about the existence of God.[2]

1 R. Hepburn, *Christianity and Paradox* (New York: Pegasus, 1966), p.156.
2 R. Swinburne, *The Existence of God* (Oxford: Oxford University Press, 1979), p.2.

Theists who hold such views are confronted with the problem of whether their theism is philosophically justifiable. One response has been to argue that, although their theism may not be demonstrable, belief in it can be shown to be at least reasonable. Thus, in his *God and Other Minds* Plantinga argues that it is no less rational to believe in the existence of God than in the existence of minds other than our own. In *The Nature of Necessity* he offers further grounds for the rationality of belief in God's existence, these grounds being reformulated versions of St Anselm's ontological argument, about which he concludes that they 'cannot, perhaps, be said to *prove* or *establish* their conclusions. But since it is rational to accept their central premiss, they do show that it is rational to *accept* that conclusion. And perhaps that is all that can be expected of any such argument.'[3] In a still more recent piece he has argued that there seems to be no reason why belief in the existence of God should not be among the foundations of a person's noetic structure.[4] Efforts by several others to prove the rationality of belief in the existence of God purport to show not that there is any conclusive evidence for his existence but that the weight of evidence renders it more likely than not. This is the very general line taken by Mitchell,[5] Schlesinger,[6] and Swinburne[7] each in their different ways.

Considered in themselves, there is much to be said for some of these approaches, for it is no small thing to show that it is at least reasonable to believe in the existence of God. If their diffidence about the possibility of proving the existence of God is prompted by tacit acceptance of the Humean and Kantian objections, however, I think that they are misguided; for the applicability of those objections has been much exaggerated. They are commonly presented not as being limited to one or other form of argument for the existence of God, but as fatal to all such arguments without exception. That, as I hope now to show, is a view that cannot be sustained.

3 A. Plantinga, *The Nature of Necessity* (Oxford: Oxford University Press, 1974), p.221. Cf. also his *God, Freedom and Evil* (London: Allen & Unwin 1975), pp.85–112.

4 A. Plantinga, 'Is Belief in God Rational?', in C. Delaney (ed.), *Rationality and Religious Belief* (Notre Dame: University of Notre Dame Press, 1979), chapter 1.

5 B. Mitchell, *The Justification of Religious Belief* (London: Macmillan, 1973).

6 G. Schlesinger, *Religion and Scientific Method* (Boston: Reidel, 1977).

7 R. Swinburne, *The Existence of God.*

I COMMENT ON PARTICULAR OBJECTIONS

'The Universe exists & God does not exist' is not self-contradictory

This familiar and ambitious claim is simply another version of the brute fact view of Fido's (or the Universe's) existence. It has been refuted by the argument developed in chapter 5, in which even the innocuous claim that Fido (or the Universe) exists was shown to have implications which would have been contradictory had Fido (or the Universe) not been caused to exist.

The contingency argument presupposes the ontological argument

It is commonly claimed, though Mackie[8] is a notable exception, that Kant effectively demolished the contingency argument by showing that it tacitly presupposed the ontological argument, and that since the latter was invalid so must be the former. Kant of course spoke not of a 'contingency' argument but of a 'cosmological' one; but for present purposes that is merely a terminological point. He sketched the argument thus:

> If anything exists, an absolutely necessary being must also exist.
>
> Now I, at least, exist.
>
> Therefore, an absolutely necessary being exists.[9]

The argument is quite valid. In Kant's view, however, even if it could prove that an absolutely necessary being exists, it could in no way determine the nature of that being – unless it employed the ontological argument to do so. Thus, while not denying the contingency argument's ability to prove the existence of a necessary being, he did deny that it provided us with any idea of what that being was like. It would therefore leave us totally ignorant of whether the necessary being would or would not be God. Only if we already knew from the ontological argument that there was a most perfect being (*ens realissimum*), that the most perfect being was a necessary being, and that no other being than the *ens realissimum* could be necessary would we be able to say

8 J. Mackie, *The Miracle of Theism* (Oxford: Oxford University Press, 1982), pp.82–4
9 I. Kant, *Critique of Pure Reason*, B632.

that the contingency argument proved the existence not merely of a necessary being but of God. Thus, this tacit employment of the invalid ontological argument would effectively undermine the validity of the contingency argument.

My first comment is that we need to distinguish, as Kant did not, between two notions of necessity and, correlatively, between two kinds of contingency argument. According to one notion, a necessary being is such that the denial of its existence – 'God does not exist' – is self-contradictory. There have been arguments that do conclude to just such a necessary being, Leibniz's and Samuel Clarke's being cases in point. In other arguments, however, the necessary being is *not* such that denial of its existence is self-contradictory. The (non-logical) necessity of such a being is said to consist in its existing now, and of being incapable of either ceasing to exist or of having begun to exist. This is the notion employed by Aquinas, and it is doubtful whether Kant, whose work was done against a Leibnizian and Wolffian background, was at all familiar with it.

Whatever the accuracy of that little piece of historical speculation, what can safely be said is that while Kant's criticism may be effective against the Leibnizian form of the argument, it is quite ineffective against those forms which employ a notion of necessary being other than a logically necessary one. This is notably so in our present argument, where the key conclusion is not that there is a necessary being (whether of the logical or non-logical kind). Rather, the key conclusion is that there is an uncaused cause, from which conclusion it is then possible to infer what kind of being that must be, namely, one which is not distinct from its existence. It is only *after* establishing both the existence and nature of the uncaused cause that it can be shown to exist necessarily. That much is perfectly clear from the previous chapter, and it renders the particular Kantian criticism simply irrelevant.

The principle of causality is unusable by the contingency argument

As regards using the principle of causality in the contingency argument, Hume was no less critical than Kant, though for reasons that ultimately are quite different. Kant, in virtue of his complex epistemological theory, restricted knowledge to the realm of what he called 'phenomena'. Whether there could be anything apart from phenomena (viz. a 'noumenon') was, from the nature of the case, unknowable. Moreover, even if there were a noumenon, the principle of causality would be inapplicable to it. Why? Because, when 'so employed, the principle of causality, which is only valid within the field of experience, and outside this field has no application, nay, is indeed meaningless, would be altogether diverted from its proper use'.[10]

Hume's criticism is based not on any epistemological theory, but on his regularity theory of causation, according to which the only justification for saying that an event a is the cause of event b is for events like a to be conjoined always with events like b – whenever events like a occur, then events like b occur. On this view, the notion of causation presupposes not simply *one* occurrence of an event like a conjoined with an event like b but many such occurrences. Consequently, the notion of being caused could be applied to the Universe only if there were more than one instance of the existence of a universe accompanying the existence of some other being. Since there is only one universe, however, it would be quite impossible for us to observe a number of universes and uncaused causes, and hence quite impossible also for us ever to be justified in proposing the Humean-type causal principle 'Whenever universes exist so too do uncaused causes'. On this view, therefore, it could make no sense to speak of the Universe as being caused.

What are we to say to these objections? Well, when the Kantian objection is divorced from its distinctive epistemology, it has a certain plausibility. Indeed, it might even be compelling against a contingency argument that did in fact rely on a principle of causality which was simply *assumed* to apply to everything that existed (including God, if there were a God). In that case one could very well ask how such an assumption could be justified. The fact of the matter, however, is that the argument in earlier chapters had no need to justify any such assumption, since the principle of causality played just no part in it.

As I have stressed more than once, the nub of the argument is neither the principle of causality nor even the principle of sufficient reason, but is simply the fact that the implications of Fido's existing present us with a well-defined choice – either to allow that Fido cannot exist without being caused or to accept that his existing has

10 I. Kant, *Critique of Pure Reason*, B664.

contradictory implications, and thus that 'Fido exists' is true while being also self-contradictory. That, of course, is really no choice at all. Yet, it is useless accepting that 'choice' without accepting too that there must be an uncaused cause; for, as was evident in series IV and V of chapter 6, it would be self-contradictory to accept that Fido was caused to exist while at the same denying that ultimately he was caused to exist by an *uncaused* cause. So, the Kantian is presented with yet another dilemma – either to accept that there is an uncaused cause or to allow that a Fido who cannot exist without being caused does exist without being caused.

Since the price of rejecting the second option is to accept the existence of something beyond the realm of phenomena, it would disturb a Kantian; but it need not disturb *us*, provided we recognize that part of the job of relative terms like 'cause' is precisely to transcend the universe within which they have application. This point has been made by Geach:

> if we form a general term with the relative term 'smaller than' and the general term 'visible' which both apply to members of the directly visible universe, the term 'smaller than any visible thing' can have no such application, and if it applies at all it applies outside the logical limits of that universe. . . . Now obviously what goes for 'smaller than any visible thing' goes for 'cause of every mutable thing'; so long as 'cause of' and 'mutable' have application within our familiar universe, we may introduce the term 'cause of very mutable thing', and reason as to what other predicates this term implies, without a sense of having fallen into gibberish – even though this term could not itself apply to anything within the familiar universe. Such reasoning will indeed as Quine says involve analogy and extrapolation, but that need not frighten us. *Per Deum meum transilio murum* – by my God I leap over the wall.[11]

11 P.T. Geach, *God and the Soul* (London: Macmillan, 1964), pp.80–1. As Geach notes, Quine makes the same point:
  Such a compound . . . does not even purport to denote things to which we could point and give individual names if they came our way. The relative term 'smaller than' has enabled us to transcend the old domain, without a sense of having fallen into gibberish. The mechanism is of course analogy, and more specifically extrapolation (W.V. Quine, *Word and Object* (Cambridge, MA.: Massachussetts Institute of Technology Press, 1960), p.109).

Since what Geach says about 'cause of every mutable thing' is equally true of 'cause of everything that is distinct from its existence', the Kantian objection lapses.

The Humean objection is like the Kantian one in its strategy of trying to dismiss the contingency argument by showing it to have an unacceptable consequence, which in this case is taken to be a denial of the regularity theory of causation. Just whether that is an unacceptable consequence is quite debatable, for many philosophers would hold no brief for the regularity theory. Some, like Ducasse, deny that regularity is even a necessary condition for a given event to be a cause; for this, they would insist, can sometimes be known from just a single instance. Others, like P. Hare, Madden, and Harré, deny that regularity is a sufficient condition for a given event to be causal, and criticize Hume for rejecting any necessary connection between cause and effect. On these views it might even be regarded as a point in favour of the contingency argument that it should entail a denial of the regularity theory. Certainly, however, the controversial character of the regularity theory makes it a rather dubious ground for rejecting our present version of the contingency argument. That is the first and most charitable thing to be said about the objection.

To be less charitable and more brutal, it must be said that the objection is demonstrably invalid, for the present argument does something which the regularity theory merely assumes, but cannot prove, to be impossible. Hume's assumption is that whether something is an effect cannot be determined by anything intrinsic to it; on the contrary, it is to be determined only on such purely extrinsic grounds as regularity. As I said, no kind of proof has been offered for the assumption, nor is it easy to see that any is possible. In any case, the crucial move in our contingency argument has had the effect of proving Hume wrong, for it has shown it to be quite possible to demonstrate that something is an effect, not on any extrinsic grounds – such as regularity, or even the principles of sufficient reason or of causality – but on purely *intrinsic* grounds offered by the relations between Fido, his existence, and Fido's existing. Thus, unless the Humean can invalidate those grounds, his regularity objection simply misses the mark, while if he could succeed in invalidating those grounds his regularity objection would be superfluous. In either case it would be pointless even to raise it.

No eternal succession of objects can have a cause

Hume makes this point by remarking that 'in tracing an eternal succession of objects it seems absurd to inquire for a general cause or first author. How can anything that exists from eternity have a cause, since that relation implies a priority in time and a beginning of existence?'[12] The objection is based on the assumption that the Universe has no beginning, but is eternal. And that, thinks Hume, is incompatible with its having a cause. Why? Because, in his view, a cause must always *precede* its effect. But, if preceded by its cause, the Universe could not be eternal. For, since there would be something existing before it, the Universe would have a beginning, and hence could not be eternal at all.

Now, from a purely philosophical point of view, the existence of an uncaused cause of the Universe is no less compatible with the Universe having a beginning than with its having none. Hence, no philosophical exception can be taken to Hume's assuming 'an eternal succession of objects'. Exception can, however, be taken to his conceiving a cause as having to precede its effect. Although that may be how the popular mind conceives it, it is a misconception none the less, for the truth of the matter is that a cause can be contemporaneous with its effect. For example, the cause of my writing these words is the movement of my hand holding the pen. That movement does not precede the making of marks on the paper, but is simultaneous with it. Cause and effect are in this case not separated in time; they are temporally coincident. This is also the case with the series of causes that causes Fido to exist.

Since a cause does not have to precede its effect, the cause of the Universe would not have to exist before the Universe, but could be co-eternal with it. Thus, since the eternity of the Universe would not preclude its being caused, Hume's objection must lapse.

If each link in a causal chain has a cause, the chain as a whole requires no cause

Immediately after raising the previous objection, Hume adds:

In such a chain, too, or succession of objects, each part is caused

12 Hume, *Dialogues Concerning Natural Religion*, part IX.

by that which preceded it, and causes that which succeeds it. Where then is the difficulty? But the *whole*, you say, wants a cause. I answer that the uniting of these parts into a whole, like the uniting of several distinct countries into one kingdom, or several distinct members into one body, is performed merely by an arbitrary act of the mind, and has no influence on the nature of things. Did I show you the particular causes of each individual in a collection of twenty particles of matter, I should think it very unreasonable should you afterwards ask me what was the cause of the whole twenty.[13]

In the light of the discussion of necessarily terminating causal series in chapter 6 this objection can be rebutted quite briefly. The point is that Hume's remarks are apposite only to those series in which, as he states, each member of the chain causes that which succeeds it. Such is of course the case in series I–III of chapter 6, in each of which series it can be said without any qualification that *b* causes *a*, *c* causes *b*, and *d* causes *c*. It is not the case, however, in series IV and V about which it is false to say without qualification that *b* causes *a*, and so on. Rather, we have to add the qualification that *b* causes only inasmuch as it itself is being caused to exist. The effect of that qualification is to leave us logically no choice but to enquire at every point (except *m*) as to what causes the whole series of preceding causes to cause Fido to exist. Thus, while entirely apposite to series I–III, Hume's remarks are simply inapplicable to series IV and V, which are the series employed in the present contingency argument.

Fido's existence can be explained either by a finite series or by an infinite one

The objection is that the contingency argument overstates its case by insisting that Fido's existing could be caused *only* by a series that terminated in an uncaused cause. All that it is entitled to claim is that Fido's existing is caused *either* by such a series *or* by one that is not terminated at all. Thus, Paul Edwards, citing the example of a pile of books, argues:

A *finite* series of books would indeed come crashing down, since the first or lowest member would not have a predecessor

13 ibid.

on which it could be supported. If the series, however, were infinite this would not be the case. In that event every member would have a predecessor to support itself on and there would be no crash. That is to say: a crash can be avoided *either* by a finite series with a first self-supporting member *or* by an infinite series.[14]

This, though a neat point, is one to which chapter 6 provides a ready answer. To put it briefly, Edwards would be absolutely right if the series in question were of types I–III. The causal series required to cause Fido to exist, however, is none of these, but is of type IV or V, concerning which we have seen there to be no choice about whether the series is terminated: it has to be terminated under pain of not being causal.

The uncaused cause is not identifiable

The objection goes thus:

9.1 For there to be an uncaused cause it must be identifiable in some way.

9.2 But the uncaused cause is not identifiable at all.

9.3 Therefore, there can be no uncaused cause.

Using the term 'God' where I have used 'uncaused cause', Penelhum explains the difficulty in his way:

> It is commonly regarded by logical theorists as a necessary feature of well-formed assertions, not only that one should be able to understand the sort of statement about the subject of the sentences used, but also that one should be able to identify that subject successfully. Any statement . . . involves both an act of referring to a subject and an act of saying something about that subject. . . . How can the speaker and hearer of statements about God share a clear idea of what subject these statements are about, when God, an immaterial being, occupying no particular place or time, cannot be picked out and identified in the way things and persons can be?[15]

Flew made the same point in observing that 'until and unless [the question of God's identifiability] can be answered there can be no

14　P. Edwards, 'The Cosmological Argument', reprinted in D. Burrill (ed.), *The Cosmological Arguments* (New York: Doubleday, 1967), p.112.

15　T. Penelhum, *Religion and Rationality* (New York: Random House, 1971), pp.145–6.

question of existence or non-existence: because there has been no proper account of what it would be for him to be or not to be; of what, in short, he would be'.[16]

Now, Penelhum suggests that the question could be answered – provided there be no more than one incorporeal being with mental states and properties.[17] His point is simply that if God were an incorporeal being with mental states and properties, and if there were only one such being, then there could be no ambiguity about the use of the term 'God', since there would be only one being to which it could possibly refer. Obviously, this answer would be unsatisfactory to anyone like Plato and Leibniz who thought there could be incorporeal beings other than simply God. Penelhum, however, argues that the very notion of a plurality of bodiless individuals is 'incoherent, since there is no device supplied for meaningfully using the notion of one such bodiless person being distinct from another'.[18] Flew takes a similar line in speaking of 'the difficulty – amounting, it might be thought, to impossibility – of supplying appropriate means of identification and criteria of identity for incorporeal personal substances'.[19]

About this view I make two comments. The first is that if it were incoherent to suggest (as I have no need to do) that there could be a plurality of incorporeal entities no one of which could be distinguished from the others, then I should argue that it must likewise be incoherent to suggest that there could be a plurality of *corporeal* entities no one of which could be distinguished one from another. But, since the latter suggestion is not demonstrably incoherent, neither can the former be demonstrably incoherent.

In drawing that conclusion I am endorsing the views, though not necessarily all the arguments, of those who reject the doctrine of the Identity of Indiscernibles. I do so for reasons based on the claim in chapter 3 that no concrete individual could be conceived of before it existed:

If the Identity of Indiscernibles were true, what is distinctive of an individual would be a universal property.

But, there is no time at which a universal property would be

16 A. Flew, *God and Philosophy* (London: Hutchinson, 1966), p.31.
17 T. Penelhum, *Religion and Rationality*, p.156.
18 ibid.
19 A. Flew, *God and Philosophy*, p.33.

inconceivable,[20] whereas there is a time at which what is distinctive of an individual (i.e. its individuality) is inconceivable, viz. at the time before it existed.

Therefore, the Identity of Indiscernibles is false.

What follows from all this is that Flew's and Penelhum's concern with the alleged impossibility of providing identifying criteria for God sits rather uneasily with their unconcern that such impossibility cannot be excluded even in the case of corporeal entities. What could have excluded it in the latter case was the Identity of Indiscernibles. Since it is false, it is theoretically possible (though in practice highly improbable) that two *corporeal* individuals be described completely by one and the same description. Thus, even if the same were true of *incorporeal* entities, it could hardly be grounds for any reasonable objection to there being a plurality of such entities.

My second comment is that the same is decidedly not true of the incorporeal entity that is God, for there is no difficulty at all in providing the uncaused cause with a criterion of identification. In making that claim, however, I distinguish a criterion of *identification* from one of *recognition*. To say that something has a criterion of identification is to say merely that the thing in question can be talked about without there being any ambiguity as to precisely which thing is being talked about. For example, the phrase 'the first man on the moon' provides us with such a criterion of identification, for it allows us to talk unambiguously about Neil Armstrong. However, it provides us with no means of *recognizing* Neil Armstrong should we pass him in the street.

Now, even though the uncaused cause might not be the only incorporeal entity, it alone would or could be *not* distinct from its existence. Hence, if 'the uncaused cause' is used to mean 'the being that is not distinct from its existence' there can be no ambiguity as to what is being talked about. Consequently, it is false to say, as premiss (9.2) did, that the uncaused cause lacks any criterion of identification. Thus the objection must fail.

---

20 The properties to which this applies are, or course, only those whose designations include *no* singular term. For example, although the property of being hit by Socrates would not be conceivable before Socrates existed, the property of being hit by a man would be always conceivable.

It is conceivable that an individual's beginning to exist be uncaused

Hume and Mackie are among the many who claim that there is no difficulty in conceiving of something's beginning to exist without its being caused to do so.[21] Well, is there no such difficulty? If by 'conceive' they mean 'imagine', then of course one could readily imagine, for example, a room being empty at one moment and at the next moment being full of people (who had not existed previously). These would be but two successive 'frames' in our imagination; and their being successive need raise no question at all about whether the people in the second 'frame' were caused to exist. Alternatively, 'conceivable' might mean merely 'able to be thought about'. Here again there would be no difficulty in thinking about an entity's beginning to exist without being caused. Even if it were acknowledged to be self-contradictory, we could still think about it, no less than we can think about round squares, and about such contradictions as occur in *reductio ad absurdum* arguments.

However, for 'conceivable' to carry the weight that Hume and Mackie place on it, the proposition 'Fido begins to exist without being caused to do so' would have to carry no contradictory implications. Yet, that is precisely what we have seen that it does carry. So, all that 'conceivable' could mean in this case is the entirely innocuous 'not *known* by the objector to be self-contradictory'. Thus understood, the objection is merely a biographical point masquerading as philosophical.

The concept of self-explanatory existence is 'indefensible'

Even though, as I have stressed, the contingency argument is to be construed neither as a search for intelligibility nor a flight from brute facts, it would still be rather odd if the argument had the consequence of allowing God's existing to be a brute fact after arguing that Fido's was not. But, if God's existing is not a brute fact, that can only commit us to its being self-explanatory, a notion that Mackie dismisses as 'indefensible'.[22] We need therefore to examine more closely what is meant by saying that God's existing is not a brute fact. As we saw in the previous chapter, a being that is not distinct from its existence exists necessarily. That is to say, it

21 D. Hume, *A Treatise of Human Nature*, book I, part II, section 3.
22 J. Mackie, *The Miracle of Theism*, p.232.

is the nature of the uncaused cause which explains *why* that cause exists necessarily. Again, we saw earlier both why it was that the causal series had to be terminated and what kind of being would be needed to do that job, namely, one lacking any distinction from its existence. So, the nature of the uncaused cause explained *why* it could terminate the series. We have seen, too, that the question 'How can it be that *a* does exist?' had to be asked only if *a* were distinct from its existence. So, the fact that the uncaused cause was not distinct from its existence explained *why* that question had not to be asked about it itself. Finally, it was that same lack of distinction from its existence that explained *why* there could be no more than one uncaused cause.

Here, then, are at least four points that have been established about the uncaused cause, all of which follow from (are *explained* by) its not being distinct from its existence. There is thus a genuine sense in which its existing can be said to be self-explanatory; and it is in marked contrast with what might be said about any being whose existing was claimed to be a brute fact. About such a being there would be no grounds whatever for

9.4   saying whether or not it existed necessarily,
9.5   saying whether it alone must or even could terminate the causal series,
9.6   asking or not asking 'How ever can it be that it does exist?',
9.7   for saying whether it need or need not be unique.

For these reasons, the notion of a being whose existing is self-explanatory proves to be readily defensible, and by no means to be confused with that of a being whose existing was a brute fact.

The argument would prove too much

The conclusion of the present argument has been denied on the grounds that it proves too much. If from the true proposition 'Fido exists' we can conclude that Fido is caused to exist, then from '7 exists' we should conclude also that the number 7 is caused to exist. But, 7 is an abstract object, and hence cannot be caused to exist, for it is a necessary entity. Any argument for the conclusion that it is caused to exist must therefore be unsound, and consequently may not be used – as it has been used – in attempting to prove that Fido is caused to exist.

On the contrary, even if the first-level use of '___ exists' really were predicable of 7, the kind of argument used to prove that Fido is caused to exist would still be quite inapplicable to prove the same of 7. The point is that we should never have been forced to draw that conclusion about Fido, had not Fido been an entity that was inconceivable before it existed. In the case of 7, however, no such thing can be said; for it would make no sense to speak of there being any possible time before which 7 did not exist. Consequently, there is no parity between our argument based on the true proposition 'Fido exists' and any argument that might be based on the true proposition '7 exists'. The objection has overlooked the role played in the present argument by the fact that Fido could not be conceived of before he existed.

II CONCLUSION

Apart from the foregoing objections, a number of others have already been considered at different points in earlier chapters. Although I shall not repeat those discussions, it is not inappropriate to recall here just what those objections were:

9.8 'Why ever should the Universe exist?' is an *improper* question, for, while similar questions might appropriately be raised about the parts of the Universe, they cannot be raised about the Universe as a whole. For response see chapter 7.

9.9 'Why ever should the Universe exist?' is a *gratuitous* question, since the existence of the Universe can be simply a brute fact. For response see chapter 8.

9.10 'Subsistent existence' is a meaningless notion. For response see chapter 7.

9.11 'Necessary existence' is an absurd notion. For response see chapter 8.

9.12 The explanation of Fido's existing can never be exhaustive. For response see chapter 7.

9.13 At every stage explanation is in terms of something else which at that stage has to be accepted as a brute fact. For response see chapter 8.

9.14 There is no more reason to terminate the causal series with Subsistent Existence than to terminate it with the Universe. For response see chapter 7.

I have argued that these seven objections have been no more successful against our present contingency argument than have the

Humean and Kantian objections discussed in this chapter. If I am right, there is decidedly less room than might have been thought for Swinburne's 'scepticism about the power of reason to reach a justified conclusion about the existence of God', and decidedly more room for scepticism about Hepburn's claim that the contingency argument 'was once and for all demolished by Kant and Hume'.

Chapter 10

The contingency argument misconceived

At various points in the preceding chapters I have had occasion to remark on the misconceptions of the contingency argument that have grown up over the centuries. They consisted in the main not so much in misunderstanding a particular version of the argument – though there were examples even of that[1] – as in treating features of some one version as if they were features of all versions. How this has arisen is no mystery, for the argument can be described very simply as one that takes as its initial premiss the existence of the Universe or some part thereof, and concludes to the existence of God. The scope for multiplying versions each conforming to that simple pattern is obvious. That in itself would be no bad thing, provided critics and proponents alike were aware of what was, and what was not, essential to the argument, and were not beguiled into thinking that features of merely some versions were mandatory for all. It is this kind of misconception which has beset the argument at each of its stages – whether the question being addressed, or the reason for answering the question, or even the answer to be given to the question.

It is only when the misunderstandings are viewed as a group that it is possible to appreciate how thoroughly the argument has

---

1 Notable exceptions among proponents of the argument are E. Gilson (cf. n.12, chapter 1); G. Grisez, *Beyond the New Theism* (Notre Dame: University of Notre Dame Press, 1975); J. Owens, 'The Causal Proposition – Principle or Conclusion?', *The Modern Schoolman* 32 (1954–5), pp.159–71, 259–70, 323–39; J. Owens, 'The Accidental and Essential Character of Being in the Doctrine of St Thomas Aquinas', *Mediaeval Studies* 20 (1958), pp.1–40, reprinted in J.R. Catan (ed.), *St Thomas Aquinas on the Existence of God* (Albany: State University of New York Press, 1980); J. Owens, 'Aquinas and the Five Ways', *Monist* 58 (1974), pp.16–35, reprinted in J.R. Catan (ed.).

come to be misconstrued. This chapter therefore is an attempt to underline that point, and to show how fundamentally the present argument differs from what recent centuries have come to regard as the contingency argument.

I MISCONCEPTIONS

Misconceiving the question to be addressed

Not uncommonly it is thought that the question addressed by the contingency argument is something of the form 'Why should anything at all exist?' or 'Why should there be something rather than nothing?' These, it will be recalled from the first chapter, are the kinds of questions that perplexed Wittgenstein, Smart, and Tymieniecka amongst others. They are also the kind of questions that many critics seem to think the contingency argument is designed to answer. As has been noted, even Mackie treats 'Why is there *anything at all*?' and 'Why should there be any *world* rather than none?' as merely two forms of the one question. Perhaps nowhere was this confusion more evident than in an excerpt from a passage that I quoted earlier from Penelhum in which he states that 'if it is puzzling that *anything* exists, it should seem puzzling why *God* does; if a certain feature's presence in the universe is puzzling, then it should seem puzzling that it, or that which gives rise to it, should be present in God'. In supposing the theist to be puzzled as to why *anything* exists, Penelhum presumably supposes he must be puzzled by existence *tout court*, i.e. by existence wherever it might be found, whether in God or in creatures. On that supposition, no theist could consistently profess to be puzzled by the Universe's existing but not puzzled by God's existing. However, the supposition was inept, for the theist's concern need not be with existence *as such*, but rather with existence had by *individuals*, i.e. by entities whose existence is a real first-level property. Naturally, had the initial question really been 'Why does anything at all exist?' such objections as Penelhum's would have been unanswerable. As it is, however, the objection is pointless against an argument concerned with the question 'How ever can it be that any existing concrete individual does exist?' for while the first question would have been entirely gratuitous, the second one is demonstrably not.

Misconceiving the reason for answering the question

Among critics and proponents alike, by far the most common, and indeed most seriously misleading, view is of the contingency argument as prompted by a search for intelligibility or for sufficient reasons why things are thus and so. This is the view that, if the argument begins from some such fact as Fido's existing, it cannot move beyond that point except by supposing that every fact must be intelligible or have a sufficient reason for its being as it is. The position is neatly summed up in Hick's remark that the logical form of the contingency argument is the dilemma: 'either there is a God or [the existence of] the world is ultimately unintelligible'. About this conception of the argument he subsequently notes that 'it rests upon a fundamental act of faith, faith in the ultimate "rationality" of existence: and this is part of a larger faith which the atheist refuses'.[2] Many others have made the same point though perhaps less succinctly, presenting the contingency argument as a debate about intelligibility – between those who believe that the existence of the Universe is intelligible (i.e. that there is a sufficient reason for its existing) and those who are at least agnostic about the truth of that belief. The other side of the coin is to present the argument as a debate about brute facts – between those who believe that there can be no brute (i.e. unintelligible) facts and those who are at least agnostic on that point.

A further consequence of taking the contingency argument to be governed by the Principle of Sufficient Reason would be to regard the use of the principle as, in this instance, virtually the same as that of the Principle of Causality. Although that is understandable enough, especially when we recall that the kind of explanation demanded by the Principle of Sufficient Reason often turns out to be a causal one, it would prompt a number of objections of the kind noted already in the previous chapter. Chief among them is the putative inapplicability of the notion of cause beyond the realm of experience, a claim which we have seen to have either a Kantian or a Humean rationale.

I recall these objections because each would be inevitable, were the contingency argument to be construed as having to employ either the principle of sufficient reason or the principle of causality.

2 J. Hick (ed.), *Arguments for the Existence of God* (London: Macmillan, 1970), p.6

In some cases I am inclined to think that they would be not only inevitable but unanswerable as well. However, as noted in the previous chapter, they have no purchase against an argument not ruinously misconceived as based on such principles.

Misconceiving the answer to be given

It is only fifteen years or so since Flew had occasion to reproach some critics of the contingency argument for assuming that all its versions concluded to the existence of a logically necessary being.[3] Even more recently, it is sometimes still overlooked that some versions of the argument conclude that there is a being whose existence is necessary but *not* logically so. As with the misconceptions mentioned earlier, this one too is the basis of an objection which is thought to be decisive, namely, that since the notion of a logically necessary being is absurd, an argument purporting to support the existence of such a being must be unsound. The objectors seem unaware of there being versions of the argument to which that criticism is not relevant.

Considering the misconceptions as a group, it is of more than passing interest that those mentioned so far seem to have a common source. Each one of them, no matter what stage of the argument it may concern, stems from the tacit assumption that all forms of the argument conform closely to those of Leibniz and Clarke. It is Leibniz and Clarke who take the question to be 'Why does anything at all exist?'; it is they who take the principle of sufficient reason to be the linch-pin of the argument by providing the impetus to pursue that question; and it is they too who conclude that the necessity of God's existence is a logical one. Whatever the failings of the present argument, it is at least innocent of perpetuating those of Leibniz and Clarke.

II THE CENTRAL ROLE OF THE PRINCIPLE OF NON-CONTRADICTION

Having earlier been at pains to stress the central role of the principle of non-contradiction in the present argument, I cannot conclude without summarizing the role it has played not just on one occasion but on several. It was first encountered when we

3 A. Flew, *The Presumption of Atheism* (London: Elek, 1976), chapter 4.

had to accept not only that Fido's existing was constructible conceptually from Fido and his existence, but that there seemed to be no way of even beginning such a construction. Faced with this apparent contradiction, there was logically no option but to ask how it could be that Fido did exist. This was the first appearance of the principle of non-contradiction in the argument.

Initially, the question seemed to be answered by recognizing that Fido exists only if he is caused to do so by something else. However, while that was part of the truth, it was soon evident that it could not be the whole truth, since it failed to eliminate the contradiction implicit in 'Fido exists'. The contradiction could be eliminated only by allowing not only that 'Fido exists' was an elliptical expression, but that the ellipsis consisted of a reduplicative expression. Here, then, was the principle of non-contradiction's second appearance in the argument.

Once 'Fido exists' was recognized as elliptical for 'Fido exists inasmuch as he is caused to exist by something else', it was clear that the causal series upon which we were now embarked was of a form quite unlike those to which the Humean considerations were relevant. While it was not self-contradictory to say that the more common series need never be terminated, that was decidedly not the case with the present series, since at no point in it could there be any causation at all if the series were not terminated. Thus, to say it was a causal series which need never be terminated would be to say that it was a causal series which was not a causal series. This, then, was the third appearance of the principle of non-contradiction. It could be avoided only be accepting that the causal series simply had to be terminated at some point, and thus that there is a cause which necessarily is uncaused.

The principle's fourth appearance occurred in regard to the nature of the uncaused cause. It was impossible that it should be distinct from its existence, since it was precisely Fido's being distinct from his existence that was the ground of his being caused to exist. To say, therefore, that the uncaused cause was distinct from *its* existence would be to say that the necessarily uncaused cause was not uncaused. A similar situation arose from denying that the uncaused cause was unique, for if there were more than one such cause, they would be distinct members of the one kind, viz. the kind whose members were necessarily uncaused. Being members of that particular kind, however, they would be concrete individuals, and consequently would be caused to exist. To say that there could be more than one necessarily uncaused cause would therefore be to say that a necessarily uncaused cause need not be uncaused. As at the other crucial stages in the argument, it was the principle of non-contradiction, and not that of sufficient reason, that was decisive. The central role of the principle of non-contradiction suffices to discredit the suggestion that there is no implicit contradiction in affirming both that Fido exists and that God does not, or Swinburne's firm view that 'atheism does seem to be a supposition consistent with the existence of a complex physical universe, such as our universe'.[4]

III CONCLUSION

The argument here presented has indeed been a contingency argument, for it conforms to the most basic outline of that argument. That apart, however, it requires scant insight to see that it bears little resemblance to such arguments as have proliferated under the influence of Leibniz and Clarke. Comparing it with arguments ante-dating theirs, however, our comments have to be more qualified. As will have been evident at various points, there is a real sense in which it has been influenced by Aquinas and Avicenna with their distinction between essence and existence. Nevertheless, it does not follow Avicenna in regarding existence as an accident, nor does it follow Aquinas who, at least in the *De Ente et Essentia*, seems to have confused the first-level existence that would have been indispensable to his argument with the second-level existence that was quite useless to him. Whether the more ancient insights have been preserved by the present argument is however of merely exegetical interest. What matters is whether it is proof not only against the objections that have long been directed against the contingency argument, but also any new ones that may be raised. From the common old objections there is little to fear: their life-span has already far exceeded their philosophical deserts. Any new ones will have to be considered as they arise.

4 R. Swinburne, *The Existence of God* (Oxford: Oxford University Press, 1979), p.120.

Appendix to chapter 2

OBJECTIONS TO PREDICATE INSTANCES

Among objections raised against predicate instances, one maintains that their notion is self-contradictory, and another that the notion conflicts with the Davidsonian point mentioned in part I of chapter 2. The first objection goes thus:

In 'Spot is black' and 'Fido is black', precisely the same is said of Spot as is said of Fido.

But what is said of Spot is the predicate instance in 'Spot is black', and what is said of Fido is the predicate instance in 'Fido is black'.

But the predicate instances are not the same: they are distinct one from the other, as well as being non-interchangeable with each other.

Therefore what is said of Spot is not the same as what is said of Fido.

Having agreed that what is said of Spot is the same as what is said of Fido, the advocate of predicate instances seems forced to accept that it is not the same.

There would be a contradiction only if what is said of Spot and Fido were to be the same and not the same under one and the same respect. Bearing that in mind, let us recall just how the two predicate instances do differ. Certainly, it is not that Fido is being said to be black, whereas Spot is being said to be only very nearly black: each is said to be unqualifiedly black. The difference between them is that one instance of the predicate can occur only in 'Fido is black', whereas the other can occur only in 'Spot is black'. The question at issue, therefore, is whether the predicate indicated by '_____ can occur only in "Spot (Fido) is black"' says anything about Spot (Fido). It could do so, however, only if it were a first-level predicate. So, the question is whether it really is such a predicate. Well, if it were, our two propositions would be elliptical for:

'Spot is black & can occur only in "Spot is black"'.
'Fido is black & can occur only in "Fido is black"'.

If that really were the case, it would be obvious that different things were indeed being said about Spot and Fido. Equally obviously, however, that is not the case. The predicate indicated by '_____ can occur only in "Spot (Fido) is black"' is being said neither of Spot, nor Fido, nor of any other individual. Rather, it is being said of a predicate, viz. the predicate indicated by '_____ is black'. In other words, it is a meta-linguistic predicate.

Once that is allowed, there is little difficulty in answering the earlier objection. To have been effective, the objection had to show that acceptance of predicate instances entailed that what was said of Spot was both the same and not the same as what was said of Fido. It has now emerged, however, that the claim is untenable. The truth is that precisely the same first-level predicate is said of Spot as is said of Fido. The difference between the *instances* of that predicate is one not of first-level predicates, but of meta-linguistic predicates. What is attributed to Spot is neither more nor less than what is said of Fido. The difference is concerned solely with what is predicable of the *predicate instances* said of Spot and Fido respectively. One of them is said to be able to occur only in 'Spot is black'; the other is said to be able to occur only in 'Fido is black'. Consequently, although the predicate instances are admittedly both the same and not the same, they are the same under one respect and different under quite another. Contrary to the first objection, therefore, acceptance of predicate instances carries no commitment to any contradiction.

The second objection claims the admission of predicate instances to be irreconcilable with Davidson's point that the capacity for the correct use of unsurveyably many propositions is explicable only if those propositions are regarded as derived from a base that is not unsurveyable.

The argument for the objection might go as follows:

The capacity for the correct use of unsurveyably many propositions presupposes a base that is not unsurveyable.

But the base for atomic propositions is said to consist of names and predicate instances.

But there are as many predicate instances as there are propositions containing them.

Hence, for there to be unsurveyably many propositions there would have to be unsurveyably many predicate instances.

But, that would contradict the initial premiss that the base presupposed by the propositions be not unsurveyable.

Therefore, there can be no such item as a predicate instance.

One defect in the argument is its failure to distinguish between:

a. the base elements employed in the *forming* of an atomic proposition,

and

b. the base elements contained *in* the proposition thus formed.

The base elements employed in forming 'Fido is black' are 'Fido' and some such instruction as:

The name β is placed adjacent to, and to the left of, the token phrase 'is black'.

The result of following that instruction with respect to the name 'Fido' would be 'Fido is black', a proposition which obviously does not contain the instruction, but does contain a predicate the presence of which is indicated by the phrase 'is black'. Now, it is true that unsurveyably many propositions would contain unsurveyably many predicate instances. It is not true, however, that the capacity to *form* unsurveyably many propositions requires a grasp of any predicate instances at all, let alone unsurveyably many of them. A grasp of just one such instruction as that mentioned above suffices for forming any number of propositions.

Furthermore, it cannot be said that a capacity to use (as distinct from a capacity to form) unsurveyably many propositions presupposes a grasp of unsurveyably many predicate instances. That objection could be sustained only if instances of the same predicate were to say different things about the bearers of the names to which they were attached. In fact, the contrary is the case; for a capacity to use atomic propositions presupposes merely a grasp of what each predicate instance says about an individual. As already shown, although predicate instances do differ from each other, they differ not at all in regard to what each says of an individual. Each instance says exactly the same of an individual as does every other instance of that predicate: what is said about Fido by 'Fido is black' is precisely what is said about Spot by 'Spot is black'.

The second objection has been no more successful than the first. The doctrine of predicate instances, which follows straightforwardly from the incompleteness of predicates (i.e. their undetachability, unquotability) is neither self-contradictory nor in conflict with the Davidsonian claim. Both objections have laboured under the misapprehension that what I have called the semantic version of the Identity of Indiscernibles is true, viz. that the only possible difference between predicate instances is one of sense. There is no more reason to accept that principle than there is to accept its ontological version: quite the contrary.

Appendix to chapter 3

OBJECTIONS TO THE IMPOSSIBILITY OF REFERRING TO FUTURE INDIVIDUALS

The first objection claims that, even if the argument were applicable to worlds in which Socrates did *not* come to exist, it is quite inapplicable to any world in which Socrates did come to exist. Since Socrates did as a matter of fact (though not of necessity) come to exist in our world in 470 BC, we are surely entitled to say that even in 472 BC it was a matter of fact (though not of necessity) that he was going to exist in 470 BC. That being so, it would surely have been possible in 472 BC to refer to this individual that would in fact come to exist two years later.

This objection illustrates perfectly the danger of ignoring Prior's advice that 'it is always a useful exercise (and one insufficiently practised by philosophers), when told that something was possible, i.e. could have happened, to ask "*When* was it possible?" "*When* could it have happened?"'[1] Now the fact is that Socrates did come to exist in 470 BC. Consequently, we can say,[2]

It *is* now the case that Socrates *did* exist.

$$\text{————— E ——} \frac{\text{S}}{\substack{\\ \text{R}}} \text{———}\blacktriangleright$$

470 BC   1991 AD

From this we can infer,

1 A.N. Prior, *Papers on Time and Tense* (Oxford: Oxford University Press, 1968), p.70.
2 The accompanying diagrams illustrate the temporal relations in each case between S the point of speech, R the point from which reference is being taken, and E the point of the event. Two or more of these points sometimes coincide, as happens with S and R in the first example, and E and R in the second.

It *was* the case (e.g. in 470 BC) that Socrates *does* exist.[3]

$$\underline{\hspace{3cm} \overset{\text{E}}{\underset{\text{R}}{\rule{3cm}{0.4pt}}} \text{S} \longrightarrow}$$

470 BC   1991 AD

From this the objector seems to think that we can infer,

It *was* the case (e.g. in 472 BC) that Socrates *will* exist.

$$\text{---- R ---- E ---- S} \longrightarrow$$

472 BC   470 BC   1991 AD

The fallacy in the last step – the only step in which the point of reference precedes the point of the event – can be illustrated by considering my promising to choose a copy of a book for Tom's next birthday, on which day I then select for him a copy of *Twelfth Night*, copy X. Once the selection has been made we can say,

It *is* now the case that copy X of *Twelfth Night* was selected for Tom.

From this we can infer,

It *was* the case that copy X of *Twelfth Night* is being selected for Tom.

However, until the morning of Tom's birthday when I saw *Twelfth Night* in a book display, not even I had any idea which book I would select for Tom, let alone which copy it would be. Concerning the time prior to that, therefore, no one would have been entitled to say,

It *was* the case that copy X of *Twelfth Night* will be selected for Tom.

On the contrary, the most one would be entitled to say is,

It was the case that *a* book will be selected for Tom.

Comparing the last claim with the first two, the points to note are that not only was the last claim about *a* copy rather than about any particular copy, but that this transition from the singular to the

3 Ordinary English usage would replace 'does' with 'did', thereby failing to indicate the tense that would have been used by someone in 470 BC, viz. 'Socrates *does* exist'. In this way English obscures the fact that 'the essence of "presentness" does *not* lie in coincidence with the point of speech; there is a future presentness and a past presentness also'. (A.N. Prior, *Past, Present and Future* (Oxford: Oxford University Press, 1967), p.14. Italics in the original.)

general occurred once the point of reference preceded the point of the event.

The relevance to the Socrates case is clear. In order to know what can be inferred from 'It was the case (e.g., in 470 BC) that Socrates does exist' we have first to ask 'In regard to *which* reference point is the inference to be drawn?' If the relevant reference point coincides with or succeeds the point of the event, we are entitled to draw a singular inference. If, however, the point of inference *precedes* the point of the event, the inference cannot be singular but only general, e.g.

It was the case that a man (described in as much detail as one might please) will be born in 470 BC.

Contrary to the objection, the fact that *our* vantage point after his birth allows us to refer to Socrates and say that *he* was going to exist in 470 BC is no ground for inferring that the same reference and claim could be made from a vantage point that preceded his birth, e.g. 472 BC.

The *second* objection is the claim that the future is no more open to change than is the past. Why? Because the future is simply what takes place *after* all our changes have been made. Hence it would be nonsense to say that anything we do could prevent its occurring, for the future is what will be; and what will be, will be.

The weakness here lies in not distinguishing between *de dicto* and *de re* necessity. In the *de dicto* sense – 'Necessarily (what will be, will be)' – it is of course tautologically true that we cannot change 'what will be'; for, were we to do so, it would no longer be 'what will be'. In that particular sense, therefore, there is rightly said to be no asymmetry between past (and present) and future. However, although we could never change what will be, we certainly have the power to do something such that, had we done it, what will be true would have been false. For example, if something will be F, we may, nevertheless, have the power to have made it G, even though we fail to exercise that power. But, if we have the power, albeit unexercised, to have made the future G, then it cannot be necessary that it be F. That is to say, although the future is necessary in the *de dicto* sense, it is not necessary in the *de re* sense; for it is false to say 'What will be, necessarily will be'.

With the past, however, the position is altogether different, for not only can we not change the fact that what was was, we have now no power to do anything such that, were we to do it, what was true of the past would now become false. Thus, if what it was is H, neither we nor anyone else has even the unexercised power to make it not-H; and if it *cannot* now be made not-H, it is now necessary (i.e. unpreventable) that it be H. The present objection notwithstanding, there really is an asymmetry between past and future possibility; for while the past is necessary both in the *de dicto* and *de re* senses, the future is necessary only in the *de dicto* sense, but not in the *de re*.

A *third* objection considers the case of Socrates' mother making a prediction about the next child to be conceived by her and suggests that, provided the prediction were sufficiently detailed, there should in principle be no difficulty in deciding that the thought was indeed about Socrates, and hence also that the mother's use of 'Socrates' did refer to Socrates. Well, let us suppose that the mother's thought was 'My first son, Socrates, will be F, G, H'. Why should it be claimed that her thought was about Socrates? Presumably, because what was predicted did turn out to be true of Socrates. Now, that is simply an invalid inference; for, from the fact that a proposition is *made true* by some thing, it cannot be inferred that it is *about* that thing. Consider, for example, the prediction that the first car to pass a certain spot in two minutes from now will be blue. The fact that it would be fulfilled (made true) by *any* blue car that was the first to pass the spot at that time shows that it could not have been about any particular car. Fulfilment by car c is only a necessary condition of the prediction's being about c: it is not a sufficient condition thereof. Likewise, the fact that the prediction 'My first son, Socrates, will be F, G, H' turns out to be *true* is only a necessary, but not a sufficient condition of its being *about* Socrates.

It might be urged, however, that if 'the individual that is F, G, H' were an *exhaustive* description of the son to be born, then that surely would ensure that the prediction was about Socrates: after all, it could hardly be about any other individual. Agreed; but the point at issue is not merely whether it is about Socrates, but whether it is about *any* individual at all; and it is hardly a denial of that particular point to observe that the prediction could be about no one *other than* Socrates. On the contrary, if the description 'the individual that is F, G, H' were to do the job proposed for it, then it would need to be able to occupy referential position even before Socrates existed. And for that to be possible, it should also be possible that a name (e.g. 'Socrates') introduced by that description should likewise be able to occupy referential position, and to refer to the future Socrates. And that, in turn, would be possible only if it were impossible that '"Socrates" refers to Socrates' ever not be true before Socrates existed. So, the objection under consideration turns out to derive its force from tacitly assuming precisely what it is supposed to prove, namely, that our conclusion is false. Such an objection can therefore be ignored.

Of course, if we deny that the prediction was about Socrates, we do owe some account of just what it was about. I suggest therefore that the prediction is to be taken as being composed not of singular term/first-level predicate ('Socrates' and '___ is F, G, H'), but rather of first-level predicable/second-level predicate, viz. 'It will be the case that (exactly one thing is a first son of mine, is called "Socrates", and is F, G, H)'. This shows that the prediction need not be about Socrates at all, as the objection required it to be, but was about what the various first-level predicables refer to, namely, the properties of being a first son of the person making the prediction, of being called 'Socrates', and of being F, G, H. What is being said about those properties is that they are co-instantiated exactly once. Although not about Socrates, the prediction may well be made true by him – but that does nothing to support the objection.

The *fourth* objection has been formulated as follows:

> Even in an indeterminate Universe God could create islands of determinism.
>
> Suppose, therefore, that God resolves irrevocably to create an individual of a certain character (i.e. conforming to an extremely specific definite description) by setting up such an island of determinism, a fragment of the Universe governed by deterministic laws which will result in a particular individual.
>
> Then, once God's irrevocable decision has been made, surely that individual could be referred to.

This is a theistic version of an objection that could equally be framed in non-theistic terms, namely, in terms of possible worlds which were either wholly deterministic or contained an island of determinism. The theistic version, however, offers the opportunity for comment on God's referring to individuals. For that reason let us continue with it.

The first thing to be said is that it is not lightly to be assumed that even God could create a deterministic Universe or one containing an island of determinism. Nor does an appeal to God's omnipotence afford us any guidance, for not only is there wide agreement that omnipotence does *not* mean that God can literally do all things, there are also notorious difficulties in determining precisely how omnipotence is to be understood.[4] Hence, although we do know that a material Universe (ours) is subject to the requirements of quantum theory and thermodynamics, it is unclear whether there could be any material universe that was *not* subject to those requirements. So, it is by no means clear that even an omnipotent God could create a determinate Universe, let alone an island of determinism in an indeterminate Universe. Nor, of course, is it at all clear that he could not do these things. I mention them merely to indicate that, even *prima facie*, the objection is far from being a knock-down one.

For the moment, however, I propose to set the objection's assumptions to one side, and to suppose that an omnipotent God really could do all that the objection assumes he can. From premiss (3.9) of my main argument it is clear that, in a *deterministic* Universe or in an island of determinism, humans could indeed refer to an individual before it existed. Whether God could do so is another question, and that is my main reason for addressing the objection. I begin with his irrevocable decision which is depicted as being to create an individual 'conforming to an extremely specific definite description'. Now, if the description were a pure one (i.e. unmixed with proper names, demonstratives, or reference to singular properties), it might be applicable to precisely one individual yet without being restricted to any precise one (e.g. Socrates). In other words, it would be applicable to any (though only one) individual that happened to satisfy it. Although Socrates may have happened to be that individual, any clone of Socrates would have satisfied it equally well. Such a description, no matter how specific, is therefore not designed to refer to Socrates.

Perhaps, however, the description was not meant to be a pure one, but was to include some singular reference, e.g. to some

---

4 Cf. T. Flint and A. Freddoso, 'Maximal Power', in A. Freddoso (ed.), *The Existence and Nature of God* (Notre Dame: Notre Dame University Press, 1983), pp.81–114. Geach prefers to speak of God as being almighty rather than omnipotent, commenting that 'no graspable sense has ever been given to this sentence ['God can do all things'] that did not lead to self-contradiction or at least to conclusions manifestly untenable from the Christian point of view' (P.T. Geach, *Providence and Evil* (Cambridge: Cambridge University Press, 1977), p.4).

parcel of matter as in 'the person who in 470 BC will stem from this parcel of matter and will be F, G, H'. Such a description might be satisfied by Socrates *alone*, though only on condition that God were able to refer to this parcel of matter before Socrates existed. Although it is true that a temporal God could certainly so refer, I am not moved by that consideration, since I should argue for the classical theistic view that God is not temporal (an admittedly disputed view that cannot be settled here). In an atemporal God, however, there is obviously no temporal priority or posteriority, and hence no question of God's being able to refer to the parcel of matter temporally prior to Socrates' existing. Recourse to the mixed description would therefore fail to do what it was supposed to do.

Still, exception might be taken to this conclusion on the grounds that, although there would be no *temporal* priority and posteriority in such a God, there would still be logical priority and posteriority. For example, God's knowledge of the object of his intention would be logically prior to the intention itself, and his forming the intention would be logically prior to his implementing it. So, in regard to an eternal (i.e., atemporal) God the question of whether he could refer to Socrates or to this parcel of matter (say, Alpha) before they existed turns out to be the question of whether they could have been the object of his creative *intention* and therefore logically prior to his creative *act*.

The answer depends on whether creation is to be regarded as an instantiation, an exemplification, or an actualization. If an instantiation, the intention would be to create something that would instantiate a number of properties, even something such as would have no properties in excess of those specified in the intention. Now, on this view the object of God's intention (the properties he intended to co-instantiate) was, obviously, *instantiable*. However, what he created (an individual) was, equally obviously, *not* instantiable. For just that reason, what God would *refer* to in his intention to create by instantiation could not have been the individual that he did create, even though that individual would certainly have *fulfilled* his intention. The ensuing individual would have been merely an *instance* of those properties that God had considered in his intention to create.

Suppose, however, that creation were not an instantiation but an exemplification. In that case, God would have in mind an exemplar and his intention would be to create something conforming to that exemplar. The exemplar in God's mind could not be even the same kind of thing as its exemplifier in our world, for the latter could exercise efficient causality whereas what was in God's mind could not. In referring to the exemplar, therefore, God could not have been referring to Socrates. Nor could he have referred to Socrates by using the description 'the individual that exemplifies this exemplar', for the exemplifier could have been merely a clone of Socrates.

Now suppose that creation were neither an instantiation, nor an exemplification, but an actualization. In that case, Socrates would be depicted as already existing in the intentional mode, and his creation would consist in his being actualized, i.e. in his transition to the actual mode.[5] And, if that were indeed the correct model for creation, there would be no denying that what God referred to in his intention would be the same as what he created, albeit in a different mode. But this model could hardly be the correct one, precisely because it presupposes that the intentional Socrates be identical with the actualized one, though admittedly in a different mode. Irrespective of how similar the non-actualized Socrates might be to the actualized Socrates, however, it could not be identical with him. The reason is the same as in the exemplar/exemplifier case, viz. that whereas the actualized Socrates could exercise efficient causality, the non-actualized Socrates could not. Whatever God might be doing in referring to a non-actualized Socrates in his intention, therefore, he could not be referring to Socrates.

What has now emerged is that, no matter how creation might be conceived, not even an omnipotent God could refer to Socrates (logically) prior to bringing him to exist.[6] This is true irrespective of whether God could or could not create a deterministic Universe or even islands of determinism in an indeterminate Universe. Neither does this mean that God could, as it were, be surprised

---

5 The terminology for the modes is of no consequence. Three options are 'subsist/exist', 'exist/be actual', 'exist intentionally/exist actually (really)'. Doubtless there could be others.

6 Of course, this would be false if the doctrine of God's Middle Knowledge were true; but, even for reasons unconnected with chapter 3, I take that doctrine to be untenable. Among my reasons are those in W. Hasker, *God, Time, and Knowledge* (Ithaca: Cornell University Press, 1989), pp.39–52, and R.M. Adams, 'Plantinga on the Problem of Evil', in J. Tomberlin and P. Van Inwagen (eds), *Alvin Plantinga* (Dordrecht: Reidel, 1985), especially pp.231–2.

to find just what had fulfilled his intention – like someone trying blindfold to draw a picture and being surprised at what he saw when the blindfold was removed. For God's knowledge is not exclusively speculative (*scientia speculativa*) but is also practical (*scientia practica*); and in the latter case he knows Socrates *in* creating him, i.e. neither logically prior nor logically posterior to the creative act.

A *fifth* objection suggests that if we can talk about fictional and mythical characters (e.g. Hamlet and Zeus respectively), we can surely talk about, and hence refer to, Socrates before he began to exist. But this misses the point; for I have not been saying that the thought had by Socrates' mother before his conception was about *nothing*, but merely that it was not about Socrates, a concrete individual who did later come to exist. No matter what the talk containing 'Hamlet' or 'Zeus' might be about, it is not about any concrete individual. Hence, it likewise fails as a counter example to the thesis for which I have been arguing.

A *sixth* objection confuses the argument in chapter 3 with the following (in which two of the technical expressions derive from Gareth Evans):[7]

> Before Socrates existed there could be no information-link between users of 'Socrates' and its bearer.
>
> But, any use of 'Socrates' as a proper name must be information based.
>
> Therefore, before Socrates existed 'Socrates' could not be used as a proper name (and hence could not refer to Socrates).

This is decidedly not my argument; for I hold not only that descriptions can be used to introduce a name, but that they can also be converted into names, e.g. by converting the description 'the mountain on the horizon' into the name 'the-mountain-on-the-horizon', in which 'mountain' and 'horizon' would have no more significance than do 'bull' and 'bush' in 'The Bull and Bush'. I also hold, and take chapter 3 to have demonstrated, that there is

---

7 G. Evans (*The Varieties of Reference* (Oxford: Oxford University Press, 1983)) distinguished proper names of two kinds, viz. 'Russellian' and 'descriptive'. The former presuppose some 'information-link' between users of the name and its bearer. The latter presuppose no such link, but are names whose reference is fixed by description, e.g. 'Let us call whoever invented the zip "Julius"'.

a limitation on the use of descriptions to introduce proper names. The limitation is that a description can be used to introduce a name of a bearer only if that bearer either does exist or has existed: it cannot be so used if the bearer has not yet existed.

Against this background it is not difficult to detect the flaw in the following objection: the Smiths have no children now. Let us assume, however, that they will have one in two years. Can we designate this child now? Yes, with the expression 'the Smiths' first child'. But what about the proper name designation? Well, why not 'Kate' (leaving issues about gender aside)? This is a proper name – a *descriptive* proper name in Evans's sense – and can be handled by a semantic theory just as ordinary proper names are.

The flaw lies in thinking that Evans's distinction can be drawn in the following way:

Information-based names *cannot* refer to individuals that have not yet existed.

Descriptive names *can* refer to individuals that have not yet existed.

The truth is that *neither* the former nor the latter can refer to individuals that have not yet existed. Of course, there is nothing against our using the expression 'the Smiths' first child' and we may, if we like, use 'Kate' as an abbreviation thereof. All that I claim to have shown is that neither the description nor its abbreviation could refer to the child before she came to exist. This is because it is *RT*-possible that there be no bearer for them in this actual world, and hence *RT*-possible also that '"Kate" refers to Kate' be false before Kate existed. Once the child has come to exist, however, the situation is radically different; for once that had happened, there immediately ceased to be any such *RT*-possibility.

Appendix to chapter 4

I FLAWS IN THE RUSSELLIAN AND QUINEAN-TYPE VIEWS

Russellian-type views

Russellian-type views on existence may be summed up as claiming:

4.11 '____ exists' is always a second-level predicate, never a first-level one.
4.12 Existence is always a property of propositional functions,[1] never a property of individuals.

General existential propositions like 'Dragons exist' would be rendered as 'the propositional function "____ is a dragon" is satisfied at least once', i.e. '$(\exists x)(x$ is a dragon)'. Singular existential propositions like 'Socrates exists' would be treated in essentially the same way. In accordance with Russell's views that ordinary proper names were really disguised descriptions, 'Socrates exists' would be transformed into some such proposition as 'The teacher of Plato exists', a form of proposition to which his theory of descriptions would then be applicable. It would thus be transformed into 'Exactly one thing is a teacher of Plato' or 'the propositional function "____ is a teacher of Plato" is satisfied exactly once', i.e. '$(\exists x)[Fx \ \& \ (y)(Fy \supset x = y)]$', where '$Fx$' abbreviates '$x$ is a teacher of Plato'. Thus, all singular existential

---

1 Russell's propositional functions are what I have been calling 'first-level predicates'.

propositions would be assimilated to general ones, and every occurrence of '____ exists' would be a second-level one. Moreover, the property of existence would cause no problems, since it would now be a property not of individuals but merely of propositional functions.

Although not implausible, Russell's approach fails as an account of singular existential propositions. It fails because its neglects to distinguish between two kinds of uniqueness.[2] One is the uniqueness of a *precise* individual, which, while achieved by *non*-fictional proper names, is unattainable by descriptions or predicates of any kind. The other is the uniqueness of *precisely one* individual, which is the most that predicates and descriptions can achieve.

Let me enlarge on this briefly with the help of the following two propositions:

4.13 The one and only individual that is F is thinking dark thoughts.
4.14 Socrates is thinking dark thoughts.

In regard to (4.14) it would make perfectly good sense to point to an individual and ask, 'Is *that* the individual that (4.14) is about?'; for the proposition can be made true only by a particular individual, Socrates. On the contrary, there is no particular individual required to make (4.13) true. It would be true if there were *any* (though, admittedly, only one) individual that is F. For that reason, although it would make sense to point to an individual that is F and ask 'Is (4.13) *satisfied* by that individual?', it would make no sense whatever to ask 'Is that the individual that (4.13) is *about*?' The individual pointed to may make (4.13) true, but it cannot be the one that (4.13) is about, since *any* individual that is F would make (4.13) true, provided it was the *only* individual to be F. Precisely one individual is required to make (4.13) true, but no precise one.

The distinction I am drawing would be of dubious value if, as Strawson once claimed, the notion of what a proposition is *about* were far from clear. However, the notion could hardly be clearer: what a proposition is about is determined by the kind of logical analysis (or analyses) to which it is amenable. The general rule to be followed is that what a proposition is about is whatever its lowest level logical part stands for. This rule applies no matter what the analysis of the proposition may be. For example, 'Socrates is thinking dark thoughts' is composed of a name ('Socrates') and a first-level predicate ('____ is thinking dark thoughts'). The proposition is *about* whatever the expression of lower-level stands for, namely, 'Socrates'. The higher level expression tells us just what is being said about Socrates, namely, that he is thinking dark thoughts.

Of course, that same proposition admits also of a different analysis, namely, '(Of Socrates it is true that)(he is thinking dark thoughts)', in which case it is taken to be composed of the first-level predicable '____ is thinking dark thoughts' and the second-level predicate '(of Socrates it is true that)(he ____)'. As so analysed, it would be about the thinking of dark thoughts: and what was being said about it would be that the thinking of dark thoughts occurs in Socrates. Exactly the same kind of analysis applies to 'The one and only individual that is F is thinking dark thoughts', for it is composed of the first-level predicable '____ is F & ____ is thinking dark thoughts' and the second-level predicate '(Exactly one thing is such that)(it ..... it .....)'. Thus, what the proposition is about is the conjunction of being F and of thinking dark thoughts; and what is being said about that conjunction is that it has exactly one instance. While this proposition admits of a first-level/second-level analysis, it differs from the previous analysis in not admitting of a name/first-level one.

So far as concerns what propositions (4.13) and (4.14) are about, there is a quite clear distinction. Proposition (4.14) admits of a name/first-level analysis as well as a first-level/second-level one, and hence can be said to be about either Socrates or about the thinking of dark thoughts, depending on its analysis. As we have seen, however, proposition (4.13) can be said to be about the thinking of dark thoughts, but not about Socrates.[3] Thus, (4.13) cannot be an adequate rendering of (4.14), for, although both may be made true by Socrates, only (4.14) can be about Socrates.

Precisely the same point can be made about the suggestion that 'Socrates exists' should be understood as 'Exactly one thing is a

3 Of course, the *speaker* may be thinking about Socrates while uttering (2), or may even intend it to be understood that it is Socrates who is thinking the dark thoughts. The point I am making, however, concerns neither what the speaker may have in mind nor intend, but what the proposition is about.

teacher of Plato, etc.' The point is that while 'Socrates exists' can be taken to be about Socrates, its proposed substitute cannot be so taken, and hence is inadequate as a reparsing of that proposition.

Quinean-type views

A flaw in the Russellian-type account that I forebore to mention, because it was unnecessary to do so, was its assumption that there could be only one individual to satisfy the predicates being employed. That assumption could well be true as a matter of fact, but it is at least arguable that it could never be true as a matter of principle. Indeed, if the Identity of Indiscernibles is false, as I think it to be, the assumption is false. One way of viewing the Quinean-type account is as an attempt to avoid that particular criticism. Speaking of the proposition 'Pegasus exists', Quine suggests:

> if the notion of Pegasus had been so obscure or so basic a one that no pat translation into a descriptive phrase had offered itself along familiar lines, we could still have availed ourselves of the following artificial and trivial-seeming device: we could have appealed to the unanalyzable, irreducible attribute of *being Pegasus*, adopting, for its expression, the verb 'is-Pegasus', or 'pegasizes'.[4]

Thus, 'Pegasus exists' would become 'Something pegasizes', i.e. '$(\exists x)(x$ pegasizes$)$'. Likewise, 'Socrates exists' would become 'Something socratizes', i.e. '$(\exists x)(x$ socratizes$)$'.[5]

It might be argued that, unlike the Russellian-type proposals, Quine's cannot be charged with not being about Socrates. After all, 'Socrates' does occur in '$(\exists x)(x = \text{Socrates})$', which therefore can quite well be viewed as composed of the name 'Socrates' and the first-level predicate '$(\exists x)(x = \underline{\quad})$', i.e. 'Something is identical with $\underline{\quad}$'. Now, although it could indeed be viewed in that way, that seems not to be how Quine intended it to be viewed, for his express aim was to eliminate proper names in favour of

4 W.V. Quine, 'On What There Is', in his *From a Logical Point of View* (New York: Harper, 1963), p.7.
5 W.V. Quine, *Word and Object* (Cambridge, MA.: Massachussetts Institute of Technology Press, 1960), p.179.

predicables, e.g. 'Socrates' was to be eliminated in favour of '____ socratizes'. Were it possible to regard that predicable as eliminating 'Socrates' rather than as simply a shorthand for '____ = Socrates', then, unlike 'Socrates exists', the proposed reparsing would not be about Socrates even though it would of course be made true or false by him.

The reparsing fails too on another score. I have noted earlier that a singular proposition '*a* is *F*' may be regarded as structured in two different ways – either as '*F(a)*' or as '(Of *a* it is the case that)(it is *F*)'. Of course, in either case '*a* is *F*' is made true if *F* is instantiated in *a*. However, if viewed as '*F(a)*', it says nothing about *F*'s being instantiated, but says merely that *a* is *F*. I do not deny that *F* is instantiated in *a*; I deny only that the '*F(a)*' schema requires *F* to be conceived of as being instantiated. Only on the second analysis is *F* actually conceived of in terms of instantiation, since, as we have seen, it is about *F*; and what it says about *F* is that it is instantiated in *a*.

Now, it is the second form of analysis (i.e. an analysis having the form first-level predicable/second-level predicate) that Quine presents not simply as an alternative to 'Exists(*a*)', but as *the* canonical form of '*a* exists'. In his attempt to eliminate proper names he therefore substitutes for '*a* exists' – in which no property has to be conceived of as instantiated – the proposition '$(\exists x)(x = a)$' in which a property *does* have to be conceived of as instantiated. However, instantiation is doubly relative: it is instantiation *of* something (a property) *in* something (an individual), as becomes abundantly clear by recalling that instantiation seems to be akin to the second-level function that Frege called the *application* of a function to an object.[6] Frege considered that if we take 'Germany' from 'the capital of Germany', we get the first-level functional expression 'the capital of ξ', and that if we remove 'the capital of' as well we get '$\phi(\xi)$',which is a second-level functional expression. The same could be done with 'the wisdom of Socrates', and the resulting second-level expression would stand for the second-level function that we call instantiation. A second-level function would be inconceivable except in relation to what are stood for by the expressions filling the gaps in '$\phi(\xi)$', viz. a first-level function and an individual respectively. Similarly, as a second-level property,

6 Cf. M. Dummett, *Frege, Philosophy of Language* (London: Duckworth, 2nd edn 1981), pp.251–3, 255.

instantiation would be inconceivable except in relation to first-level properties and individuals.

The foregoing conclusion is quite unaffected by the fact that such propositions as 'The property F is instantiated at least once' make no mention of any individual in which the instantiation might occur. The simple reason is that even that proposition contains variables which, at least in the case of objectual quantification, could have no role unless individuals were included in the universe of discourse. Thus the conclusion stands: as a second-level property, instantiation would be inconceivable except in relation to first-level properties and to individuals.

The upshot so far as concerns Quine's account of 'a exists' is this. Quine seeks to reparse 'a exists' so that, instead of its being construed as saying 'a has (the property) existence', it is construed as saying 'The property of socratizing is instantiated at least once': talk of an individual's having a property is replaced by talk of a property's being instantiated. This creates the illusion of banishing individuals from the universe of discourse. It is an illusion because the notion of instantiation of properties is unintelligible without the notion of an individual.[7] The very best that might be said for Quine's account, therefore, is that it is logically posterior to the propositions which it purports to reparse. That, however, is to say too little; for it would still be consistent with '$(\exists x)(x = a)$' being a possible alternative to analysing 'a exists' according to the '$F(a)$' schema. As we have seen, it is not a possible alternative at all.

I now mention another reason. If '$(\exists x)(x = \text{Socrates})$' were an adequate reparsing of 'Socrates exists', it should never be possible for the one to be true when the other was false. However, 'Socrates exists' once was true, but now is false. Its suggested reparsing, on the contrary, is no more false today than it was when Socrates was born. It would make no more sense to say 'Someone *was* identical with Socrates' than to say 'Socrates *was* identical with Socrates'. It would, however, make perfectly good sense to say 'Socrates exist*ed* (in the fifth century BC)'. Hence a further reason for rejecting any reparsing of singular existential propositions which would take the existential role to be played not by a first-level predicate but by a second-level one.

---

7 It might be said that the objection fails to impinge on Quine's position, since he eschews properties in favour of classes. However, the classes which replace properties are no more intelligible without the notion of an individual than are the properties they are supposed to replace.

II EXISTENCE IS IRREDUCIBLE TO OTHER PROPERTIES

Just because '____ exists' is a first-level predicate it would be premature to conclude that the property it stands for is non-formal, let alone an irreducible one. There have been suggestions that '____ exists' is merely a formal predicate, that it is an excluder, a predicate variable, or that it does duty for a disjunction of predicates. The question, therefore, is whether any of these suggestions is correct.

'____ exists' as a formal predicate?

It is worth considering whether existence might not be what Wittgenstein called a formal concept, and whether '____ exists' might not be the kind of predicate that expresses such a concept, even if only improperly. Examples of such predicates are '2 is a number', '"2" is a numeral', 'Tom is an object', '"Tom" is a name', '"The mother of Socrates" is a complex'.

What interests us about these predicates is that, although they are first-level ones, they attribute no real property to what they are said of, but simply place them in some category. The propositions in which they occur are all quite uninformative; and, although like tautologies in that particular respect, they are unlike tautologies in that their denial is not self-contradictory. 'Black stones are not black' is self-contradictory, whereas '2 is not a number' is not, even though it can never be true. These characteristics might suggest that '____ exists', too, is a formal predicate, for it is commonly claimed that 'Socrates exists' is uninformative and that 'Socrates does not exist' is not self-contradictory, although in certain circumstances it would be extremely odd to affirm it.

Now, an interesting feature of the propositions listed above is that, despite not being tautologies, each of them is necessarily true: 2 cannot cease to be a number, '2' cannot cease to be a numeral, Tom cannot cease to be an object, nor can 'Tom' cease to be a proper name, though it may well fall into disuse. It may not have been necessary that there be a 2, '2', Tom, or 'Tom'; but, given that we do have them, it can never be false to predicate the relevant formal predicates of them. It is no more true to say 'Socrates is no longer an individual' than to say '2 is no longer a number'.

It is just that characteristic of formal predicates which disqualifies '____ exists' from being one of them. If '____ is F' is a formal predicate, then, once 'Socrates is F' is true, it can never be false. On the contrary, although 'Socrates exists' was once true, it not only can be false but indeed is now false. Consequently, '____ exists' cannot be a formal predicate, attractive as it may have been to think otherwise.

'____ exists' as an excluder?

To have ruled out '____ exists' being a formal predicate is not necessarily to have ruled out all possibility of its being a first-level predicate without existence being a real property. One other possibility is that it be what Roland Hall[8] has called 'an excluder', and which he introduces as follows:

> Adjectives that . . .(1) are attributive as opposed to predicative, (2) serve to rule out something without themselves adding anything, and (3) ambiguously rule out different things according to context, I call 'excluders'.

As examples, he suggests 'ordinary', 'absolute', 'accidental', 'barbarian', 'base', 'civil', 'real', amongst many others. The one most relevant to our purposes, however, is 'real'.

According to Hall, 'real' is the kind of adjective that merely rules out something without itself adding anything. According to context, it can rule out a's being imaginary, or artificial, or counterfeit. In doing so, however, it attributes nothing positive to what it is said of: its contribution is purely negative. Moreover, what it excludes varies with context, and therein, says Hall, lies its ambiguity. Although Hall himself does not suggest that '____ exists' is an excluder, others have done so, and still others have suggested that '____ exists' means simply '____ is real'. On either suggestion existence would not be a real property, and that is why these views might commend themselves to anyone who was bothered by the apparent difficulty in allowing existence to be a property of concrete individuals.

Let us therefore consider whether '____ exists' really does have the three marks required of an excluder. Since it is not an adjective at all, it obviously cannot be an attributive one. However, that is of no account, for in his closing remarks Hall allows that excluders may be found not only among adjectives, but also among 'nouns

8 R. Hall, 'Excluders', *Analysis* 20 (1959–60), pp.1–7.

and other parts of speech'.[9] The questions we have to ask of '____ exists' therefore are:

4.15 Is it ambiguous?
4.16 Not merely *can* it be defined negatively, but *must* it be so defined?

If '____ exists' is to be an excluder, the answer has to be 'yes' not merely to one of these questions, but to both. If we allow that '____ exists' is ambiguous, then the question of its being an excluder will turn on whether it satisfies (4.16), e.g. on whether '*a exists' must* be understood simply in terms of what *a* was precluded from being. If so, then no matter how different the context, '*a* exists' could *only* be understood negatively, e.g. as '*a* is not-fictional', '*a* is not-dead', '*a* is not-illusory', '*a* is not-mythical', or '*a* is not-nonexistent'. The simplest case to consider is the last. We might envisage a seer predicting that in two years a son would be born to parents *b* and *c*, and that he would be called 'Socrates'. When the prediction was fulfilled, we might imagine the seer announcing triumphantly 'At last Socrates exists, just as I said he would'. If '____ exists' were an excluder, then the *only* way of understanding the seer would be as excluding some property from Socrates; and in this case the property excluded would be that of non-existence. As said by the seer, therefore, 'At last Socrates exists' could only mean 'At last Socrates is not-nonexistent'. If he really were to mean that, we should be entitled to ask him just when Socrates could ever have been said to have been nonexistent, i.e. never to have existed. In fact, before Socrates existed he could not even have been referred to, and hence at that time nothing at all could have been attributed to him, not even the property of being nonexistent. Thus, it would be impossible for 'At last Socrates exists' to mean 'At last Socrates is no longer nonexistent'. Consequently, '____ exists' could not be an excluder, for there was never any property for it to exclude.

Still, in other contexts 'Socrates exists' might be proposed as meaning 'Socrates is not-dead' or 'Socrates is non-fictional', and '____ exists' as excluding from Socrates the properties of being dead and being fictional respectively. The first case can scarcely be evidence for '____ exists' being an excluder, for '____ is dead' is itself to be understood as '____ is not-alive'. If it were evidence

9 ibid., p.7, where he notes: 'Examples would be *choice, intuition, luck*'.

for anything, it would be for '____ exists' as a synonym for '____ is alive', except that 'The Euston Arch no longer exists' could hardly be understood as 'The Euston Arch is no longer alive'.

As for 'Socrates is non-fictional' ('Socrates is a non-fictional character' would be better), it could support the claim that '____ exists' is an excluder only if Socrates really could have been a fictional character. That, however, could have occurred only if a fictional character could be the same person as a real-life one, something which I have argued elsewhere[10] is impossible, even though it is entirely possible that a real-life character should *satisfy the description* of a fictional one. Precisely the same point can be made about any attempt to depict '____ exists' as excluding '____ is mythical'. Since Socrates never *could* have been either a fictional or mythical character, there is nothing for '____ exists' to exclude. That is not to say that it is wrong to say 'Socrates is not fictional' or 'Socrates is not mythical', but only that it is misleading to construe those propositions as 'Socrates is not-fictional' and 'Socrates is not-mythical' rather than as 'Not(Socrates is fictional)' and 'Not(Socrates is mythical)'. From all this it is clear enough that the answer to (4.16) above is 'No, "exists" need *not* be defined or understood purely negatively'. For that reason '____ exists' cannot be an excluder.

'____ exists' as either a predicate variable or a disjunction of predicates?

Here we are offered two ways of construing '____ exists'. According to one suggestion, it is to be construed as a predicate variable, in which case 'a exists' would be rendered as 'a has some property or other' or '$(\exists P)(P$ is had by $a)$', where 'P' is a predicate variable. According to the other suggestion '____ exists' would be construed as a disjunction of predicates, in which case 'a exists' might be rendered as 'a is F or G or H', where 'F', 'G', and 'H' are first-level predicates. On either suggestion the result would be to disqualify existence from being an irreducible property of a. In the first case, although a might be allowed to have the properties referred to by whatever the predicates substituted for 'P', it would have no irreducibly existential property. Similarly in the second

---

10 'Could Any Fictional Character Ever be Actual?', *Southern Journal of Philosophy* 23 (1985), pp.325–35.

case; although *a* might have one of the properties *F*, *G*, and *H*, it would have no property of existence.

If the first suggestion were correct, 'Socrates does not exist' could be rendered as 'Socrates has no properties'. Likewise, if the second suggestion were correct, 'Socrates does not exist' could be rendered as 'Socrates has neither *F*, nor *G*, nor *H*,' i.e. 'Socrates has no properties'. In either case, therefore, 'Socrates does not exist' is to be understood as 'Socrates has no properties'. However, 'Socrates has no properties' could be true *only* if Socrates were a bare particular. 'Socrates does not exist', on the contrary, could be true *irrespective* of whether Socrates was or was not a bare particular. Yet, there should be no such difference, if 'Socrates does not exist' were to be understood as 'Socrates has no properties'. Therefore, 'Socrates exists' can be rendered neither by 'Socrates has some property or other' nor by 'Socrates is either *F* or *G* or *H*'.

Index